The Political Economy of Corruption

'Grand' corruption, generally used to define corruption amongst the top political elite, has drawn increasing attention from academics and policy-makers during recent years. Current understanding of the causes and mechanisms of this type of corruption, however, falls short of a full awareness of its importance and consequences.

In this volume, leading academics and practitioners analyse the economic and political conditions that allow 'grand' corruption to survive. Contributions include:

- Case studies of countries that have witnessed flagrant misuse of political powers.
- Theoretical papers which present models of corruption and project their possible effects.
- Empirical studies which raise research questions and test the theoretical models using insightful methodologies.

The studies in this work not only indicate the importance of the economic implications of 'grand' corruption, but also provide a framework for understanding its processes. Academics and policy-makers working in the fields of economics, political science and sociology will find this an illuminating and valuable work.

Arvind K. Jain is Associate Professor at Concordia University, Montreal. His current research focuses on corruption and on international financial crises. His past research papers have dealt with corruption, agency theory and the debt crisis, capital flight, international lending decisions of banks, oligopolistic behaviour in banking, foreign debt and foreign trade in developing countries, impact of culture on saving behaviour and commodity futures markets. He has previously written two books and edited a volume entitled *Economics of Corruption*.

Routledge Contemporary Economic Policy Issues

Series editor: Kanhaya Gupta

This series is dedicated to new works that focus directly on contemporary economic policy issues. It aims to include case studies from around the world on the most pressing questions facing economists and policy-makers at both a national and international level.

The Political Economy of Corruption

Edited by Arvind K. Jain

London and New York

First published 2001 by Routledge
11 New Fetter Lane, London EC4P 4EE

Simultaneously published in the USA and Canada
by Routledge
29 West 35th Street, New York, NY 10001

Routledge is an imprint of the Taylor & Francis Group

Typeset in Sabon by Curran Publishing Services Ltd, Norwich
Printed and bound in Great Britain by
TJ International Ltd, Padstow, Cornwall

British Library Cataloguing in Publication Data
A catalogue record for this book is available from the British Library

Library of Congress Cataloging in Publication Data
The political economy of corruption / edited by Arvind K. Jain
        p. cm. – (Routledge contemporary economic policy issues series)
    Includes bibliographical references and index.
    1. Political corruption. 2. Political corruption–Economic aspects.
    I. Jain, Arvind K., 1945– II. Series
JF1081 .P653 2001   00-065330
330.9–dc21

ISBN 0–415–23446–8

Contents

Figures

Tables

Contributors

Aftab Ahmad studied constitutional law in his native Pakistan. He currently lives in Canada and has been a consultant to the Government of Pakistan as well as some large multinationals. Since his retirement, he has devoted his time to enjoying his family and to analyzing events in Pakistan.

Wesley Cragg is the Gardiner Professor of Business Ethics at the Schulich School of Business, York University (Canada) with a cross appointment to the philosophy department. He is responsible for encouraging and coordinating research and curriculum development on the ethical dimensions of public, para-public, not-for-profit, and private sector management in the business school. He has published widely in applied ethics, philosophy of law and punishment, philosophy of education, and moral, social, political, and legal theory. His current research includes issues in business and occupational ethics, environmental ethics, and the use and effectiveness of voluntary codes in the regulation of international business transactions.

Hamid Davoodi is an Economist at the Fiscal Affairs Department of the International Monetary Fund. Prior to joining IMF, he worked at the World Bank, where he was a member of the 1997 *World Development Report* team. He was previously a research associate at the Federal Reserve Bank of San Francisco and a visiting lecturer at Georgetown University. He has written articles on decentralization, growth, and corruption published in *Journal of Urban Economics*, and *The Welfare State, Public Investment and Growth* (Shibata and Ihori, eds). Mr Davoodi holds a PhD in Economics from University of Wisconsin at Madison and a BSc in Economics from London School of Economics.

Sanjeev Gupta joined the International Monetary Fund in 1986 and is currently Chief, Expenditure Policy Division of the Fiscal Affairs Department, a position he has held for around five years. Before joining the IMF, he was Secretary of the Federation of Indian Chambers of Commerce and Industry. He has also been Lecturer at Punjab University, Fellow at the Kiel Institute of World Economics and Professor at the

Administrative Staff College of India. His more recent books are: *Social Safety Nets: Issues and Experiences*, edited together with Ke-young Chu, and *Economic Policy and Equity*, edited together with Vito Tanzi and Ke-young Chu. In addition, he has authored or co-authored over sixty papers on fiscal, international finance, and economic development issues that have been published in journals such as *Journal of Finance, Journal of Development Economics, Journal of Policy Modeling, Defence and Peace Economics, Energy Economics, Weltwirtschaftliches Archiv*, and *World Development*. Mr Gupta holds BA degrees from Delhi and Oxford; an MA from the University of New Brunswick; and a PhD in economics from Simon Fraser University.

Arvind K. Jain has been a faculty member at Concordia University in Montreal since 1990. He earned his PhD from the University of Michigan, Ann Arbor. Before joining Concordia, he had taught at Indiana University, McGill University, the University of Michigan and the University of Dar es Salaam. He has held short-term or visiting appointments at University of Otago, New Zealand, Helsinki School of Economics, Finland, International University of Japan, and Tianjin University, China. Besides teaching, he has worked in industry or in the public sector in India, the United States, Tanzania, and Mexico. His current research focuses on the impact of corruption on economic development, management of exchange risk, and capital markets. His past research papers dealing with corruption, agency theory and the debt crisis, capital flight, international lending decisions of banks, oligopolistic behavior in banking, foreign debt, and foreign trade of developing countries, impact of culture on saving behavior, and commodity futures markets have appeared in *Journal of International Business Studies, Journal of Money, Credit and Banking, Economics Letters, Journal of Economic Psychology, Journal of Economic Surveys*, and other academic journals. He has written two books: *Commodity Futures Markets and the Law of One Price* (1981) and *International Financial Markets and Institutions* (1994), and his edited volume, *Economics of Corruption*, was published by Kluwer Academics in 1998. He is on the editorial board of two journals, including the *Journal of International Business Studies*.

Michael Johnston (PhD, Yale, 1977) is Professor of Political Science at Colgate University in Hamilton, New York, USA. He has been working on corruption and reform issues since 1975, and for the last fifteen years has emphasized comparative analysis and questions of development. Recently he has been a consultant to the World Bank, the Organization for Economic Cooperation and Development, the United Nations Development Program, the US Agency for International Development, the Open Society Institute, and the Asia Foundation. He is also a member of the board of directors of Transparency International – USA.

Recent publications include *Political Corruption 2000* (co-editor Arnold J. Heidenheimer), and articles in journals such as *Revue Tiers Monde*, *European Journal of Development Research*, and the annual volume of the Shelby Cullom Davis Center for Historical Studies, Princeton University. Current projects include a comparative analysis of democratic consolidation and syndromes of corruption.

Oskar Kurer is Professor and Head of Department at the Institute of Political Economy at the University of Erlangen-Nuremberg. He received his PhD in Economics from the London School of Economics. He subsequently taught at the University of Papua New Guinea and the Queensland University of Technology in Brisbane, Australia and held visiting appointments at the University of the South Pacific. His major research interests are in the history of economic thought, particularly J. S. Mill, and the analysis of the interaction between economic development and political structures. His publications include articles in the *Journal of History of Political Thought*, *History of Political Economy*, *European History of Political Economy*, *Economic Record* and *Public Choice*. His books include *J. S. Mill: The Politics of Progress* (1991) and *The Political Foundations of Development Policies* (1997).

Susan Rose-Ackerman is Henry R. Luce Professor of Law and Political Science, Yale University, and Co director of the Law School's Center for Law, Economics, and Public Policy. She holds a PhD in Economics from Yale University and has held fellowships from the Guggenheim Foundation and the Fulbright Commission. She was a Visiting Research Fellow at the World Bank in 1995–6 where she did research on corruption and economic development. She is the author of *Corruption and Government: Causes, Consequences and Reform* (1999), *Controlling Environmental Policy: The Limits of Public Law in Germany and the United States* (1995), *Rethinking the Progressive Agenda: The Reform of the American Regulatory State* (1992), and *Corruption: A Study in Political Economy* (1978), and joint author of *The Uncertain Search for Environmental Quality* (1974) and *The Nonprofit Enterprise in Market Economies* (1986). She has also published widely in law, economics and policy journals. Her research interests include comparative regulatory law and policy, the political economy of corruption, public policy and administrative law, and law and economics.

Vito Tanzi is Senior Associate at the Carnegie Endowment for International Peace and received his PhD in Economics from Harvard University. He has published many books including *The Individual Income Tax and Economic Growth* (1969), *Inflation and the Personal Income Tax* (1980), *The Underground Economy in the United States and Abroad* (1982), *Taxation, Inflation and Interest Rates* (1984), *Public Finance in Developing Countries* (1991), *Taxation in an Integrating World* (1995),

Public Spending in the XX Century (2000), and *Policies, Institutions, and the Dark Side of Economics* (2000). He has edited several books, the most recent of which is *Income Distribution and High Quality Growth* (1998) and has written a large number of articles in leading professional journals, such as the *American Economic Review*, *Journal of Political Economy*, *Review of Economics and Statistics*, *Economic Journal*, *Journal of Public Economics*, and many others. His major interests are public finance, monetary theory, and macroeconomics. In the period 1990–4, he was President of the International Institute of Public Finance. He holds honorary degrees from the University of Cordoba (Argentina) and the University of Liège (Belgium).

Erwin Tiongson is a Senior Research Officer at the Fiscal Affairs Department of the International Monetary Fund. He was previously a research assistant at the Urban Institute, Independent Sector, and Overseas Development Council. He was also a research intern at the New York City Department of Finance and was a teaching assistant in quantitative methods at Georgetown University. His papers have been published in *Challenge*, *East European Quarterly*, and *A Pacific Peace: Issues and Responses* (M. J. Hassan, ed.). He holds a BA degree from Ateneo de Manila University and graduate degrees in Economics and Public Policy from Fordham University and Georgetown University, respectively. He is currently working toward his PhD in Economics at George Washington University.

William Woof holds a BA degree from Wilfrid Laurier University and an MA degree from the University of Waterloo. He is currently a PhD candidate in Philosophy at York University, where he is focusing his studies on Business Ethics. His other interests include the writings of Jorge Luis Borges, and his MA thesis on the relationship of Borges' works with deviant logic was published in *Variaciones Borges*, one of the major Borges journals.

Part I

Governance and corruption

The emerging challenges of development

1 Power, politics, and corruption

Arvind K. Jain

A concerted fight against corruption – in some cases defined synony-mously with bribery – seems to have broken out around the globe in many spheres of social life where it rears its head. As this volume was being written in the summer of the year 2000, a senior Chinese official was actually sentenced to death for corruption. In the political sphere, the trial of former Indonesian President Suharto on charges of corruptly acquiring $210 million of state funds was about to begin. A Brazilian senator close to the President was impeached – an act unprecedented in the country's history – when it was revealed that he had requested bribes for a corrup-tion-plagued construction project. In Mexico, public disgust with corrupt politicians had finally led the people to vote PRI (Partido Revolucionario Institucional) out of office after seventy-one years of uninterrupted rule. Five British firms and fourteen others were being prosecuted in Lesotho courts for offering $3 million in bribes to officials, and the French oil-company Elf was being implicated in corruption scandals in Angola. Accusations of match-fixing and corruption were swirling around Japan's revered national sport, sumo. In Cambodia charges of corruption had led international agencies to consider cutting funds from the organization responsible for removal of millions of life-threatening land mines.

Public awareness of, and tolerance for, corruption has seen a sea change over the past decade as information and expectations have caused people to expect more from their leaders. While much of the focus of the current struggle to reduce corruption is on making bribes more difficult to pay and accept, "corruption" involves much more than bribes. Corruption, defined more comprehensively, involves inappropriate use of political power and reflects a failure of the political institutions within a society. Corruption seems to result from an imbalance between the processes of acquisition of positions of political power in a society, the rights associated with those positions of power, and the rights of citizens to control the use of that power. Power leads to temptation for misuse of that power. When such misuse is not disciplined by the institutions that represent the rights of the citizens, corruption can follow. Therefore, the study of the politics of corruption – the intent of this volume – is a study of how the political institutions should work to strike a balance between conflicting goals that individuals might have, as well as the conflict between the goals of various individuals and groups within a society. Although corruption makes itself visible as an economic transaction, it would not exist if the political institutions were able to exert the necessary influences and controls. Since available evidence fails to find any benefit associated with corruption, it would be in the society's interest to design systems and exert pressures that would eliminate corruption. Existence of corruption, therefore, reflects a failure of the "markets" – economic as well as political. A successful fight against corruption, which is really one part of the challenge for effective governance of societies, would seem to require a thorough understanding of the link between the political institutions and corruption. This volume attempts to understand some aspects of the political environment of societies that allow corruption to exist and grow or diminish over time.

How and why we study the link between politics and corruption is intimately tied to what we mean by corruption. Contributions to this volume begin with Michael Johnston's survey of how and why the meaning of this term has changed through time. Over the ages, as the relationships between individuals and states have changed, our expectation of what "the state" or "the office bearer" or "the individual" has to do has also changed. Under a monarchy or a feudal system, the individual had few rights. The state was supposed to define individuals' rights as well as the code of behavior for everyone – citizens as well as public functionaries. Corruption in that context implied failure to behave according to this moral code. Under a modern democratic system, individuals choose their values and their rulers in conformity with those values. It is therefore understood that the rulers reflect the morality of the ruled. Definition of corruption, in this context, has come to be related to the behavior of the individual who has been chosen to rule or govern. This ruler is not expected to define morality – other than in designing the legal framework – but merely to act according to the established norms. Hence the focus of contemporary discussion on corruption is on individual behavior – that of the politicians or of the bureaucrats. Politics, however, becomes important because political values, institutions, and parties play an important role in defining the values of the society and in defining the norms that individuals in positions of power have to follow, as well as in designing the control systems that determine the limits of the behavior of the political elite.

Different definitions, and hence coverage, of what corruption means may sometimes change the focus of debate from solving problems to sorting out the relative importance of various strategic issues that must be resolved, or, in other words, what has to come first. Our interest in corruption arises from a desire to improve the quality of life of people in different societies and address questions of social inequality. Who should be responsible for a society's progress and to what extent should a society attempt to eliminate inequalities – caused either by factors outside individuals' controls or by individuals' own actions and choices?[1] It is apparent that the underlying issue here is the relationship between power and wealth. These ideas interact with each other at least at three different levels within a society. Michael Johnston discusses the importance of understanding these interactions and traces some of the changes in the relationship between these two through history.

First, and most important, ownership of wealth affects the process and outcome of discussions on what will form the moral values of society. From the ancient times to the most modern – as recently as the Seattle and Washington demonstrations – corruption has been equated with a decline in the moral values of a society. Certainly the focus of contemporary demonstrations against "globalization" is based on a perception that "wealth" has a greater influence on determining who has the power to set the rules of the society than it should.

Second, pursuit of wealth leads wealth-owners to collaborate with holders of political powers to circumvent the spirit, if not the letter, of the rules by which a society has accepted to be governed. It is often difficult to identify this type of collaboration and it is especially difficult to assess when such collaboration violates the norms of the society. Naylor (1998) provides an example of such collaboration for one industry in a situation where it is easy to conclude that such violations have taken place. It is often, however, difficult to separate where the interest of the society ends and the benefit for the "wealth" – at a cost to the society – begins. Sometimes what is in the interest of a private entity may coincide with public interest but, at other times, it may only be couched in terms of "public interest." It becomes especially difficult to establish the link when the power-holder is not compensated for its decision in any observable manner.[2]

Third, wealth and power intersect in the behavior of an individual functionary who (mis-) uses public power toward ends for which it was not intended and is compensated by the wealth-owner who benefits from the misuse. The compensation can take many forms, the most common form being bribery. This interaction comes closest to the current tendency to define corruption narrowly in terms of the use of public power in exchange for bribes.

Democratic societies give equal power to citizens to choose their representatives but we know of no democratic society that does not allow, *de facto*, disproportionate power to "wealth" to influence outcomes within a society. One of the outcomes of this unequal distribution of power is unequal distribution of income and wealth. Societies differ in the extent to which unequal distribution of income, or wealth, is accepted by the populace. Even when the unequal distribution of power results from the application of the rules of the system, the poor regard the lack of income equality resulting from the consequences of unequal distribution of power as corruption. This, as Johnston points out in the first of his two contributions in this volume, is also how corruption had been defined historically. The change in the meaning of corruption – from all encompassing values of the state to the behavior of particular individuals – may be partially justified by the change in the relationship between those who govern and those who are governed. When the rulers chose themselves (kings, dictators), then they were held responsible for what values they chose for the society and how well they implemented those values through their decisions. In a modern, democratic, system, however, people elect those who will govern. Such an election ensures, at least in theory, that those who are chosen to govern represent the values of the public at large. The issue here is the extent to which unequal distribution of power within a society results from the tension between the transparent and fair application of "the rules of the game" and behind-the-scene manipulations – accompanied invariably with payments in some forms to the holders of the powers – or corruption. Hence, our focus narrows down to the behavior of the individual politician.

This volume focuses on the last two of these three interactions between wealth and power. While there would be little doubt that the first interaction between wealth and power – interaction that defines the moral codes of the society – is probably the most influential in determining the welfare of a society, we make the assumption that in a democratic society, election of the ruling elite represents the best compromise on what should be the governing values of the society. Our objective in this volume is to address some questions about the nature and functioning of political institutions that determine how much corruption will exist in a society, given that there is an agreement on the underlying values for governance. Good governance of societies will require addressing the relationship between power and wealth at the macro level – where unequal power distribution leads eventually to unequal distribution of income and wealth – as well as at the micro level where the individual behavior of those in power leads to poor implementation of agreed upon policies. The focus of this volume is on the micro aspect of corruption – how power is misused to accumulate personal wealth.

The essence of a well-functioning political system is that it allows policy decisions and outcomes to be influenced by all interest groups. Different political systems, however, differ in the extent to which they allow this to happen. Systems differ in their design – how things are supposed to happen – and in their implementation – how things actually happen – in other words, what imperfections are allowed to exist. Some systems are more efficient at allowing an aggregation of interests from various segments of the society than others. Systems also differ in mechanisms and instruments available to various groups as a means of exerting pressure when they want their interests followed. An outcome of "inclusive policy-making" also depends upon the incentives faced by the politicians and the citizens. When a segment of the society feels its interests have not been served by the political system, it will try to circumvent the accepted political processes and explore weak points within the system that will serve its interests. One of the weak points may be the existence of corrupt decision-makers. Corruption, thus, will depend upon the combination of the rents that an interest group can see itself earning through policy changes, costs (corruption-related payments) it has to incur to change policies, and the enforcement-related costs, that is, the cost of penalties associated with being discovered.[3] Political systems may even allow some interest groups to exert influences that will transfer the costs of policy changes to groups with less political influence. Policy changes will show up either as regulations or as government expenditure policies. This leads to two areas of study that concern the link between corruption and political systems. First, we examine how the design of political systems influences corruption outcomes, and second, we study how corruption influences policy outcomes.

Susan Rose-Ackerman, in Chapter 3 of this volume, examines some characteristics of democratic systems that determine the extent to which the design of the political system affects the development of corruption in the society. Democratic systems differ in terms of how leaders are elected and which of them are elected directly by the population, and the roles that political parties play in determining who acquires the positions of power. These differences lead to different manners in which various systems incorporate interests of certain sectors within the society in the policy-making process. Individuals and sectors whose interests are ignored do not, of course, accept those outcomes passively. They use other means available to them to influence the political processes. Elected representatives have to keep those possibilities in mind while making their legislative choices. The political equilibrium, including the level of corruption within a society, thus depends upon the extent to which the design of the political system within a society conforms to the public's expectations from their politicians.

Political markets that do not function well have at least two consequences related to corruption. First, unsatisfied groups, and groups with limited access to decision-makers, have an incentive to resort to corruption or other means to achieve their goals. Second, groups that are able to exert disproportionate influence can expect to receive some benefits from their access to policy-makers. Three contributors to this volume follow these themes.

Corruption, as mentioned earlier, can be a rational response for some sectors of a society that do not believe their best interests are being served by the political system. Oskar Kurer, in Chapter 4 of this volume, examines some situations in which citizens will embrace corruption in order to further their own interests. When political markets are imperfect, voters may opt for the second best solution of a corrupt politician who serves their interest rather than an honest politician who represents others as well. Politicians, of course, may exploit voters' ignorance as well as their uncertainties. Kurer's contribution identifies situations where some segments of a society will embrace corruption as a solution to imperfections in the political system within a partial equilibrium framework.

The first two chapters in the third part of this volume examine the influence of corruption on the policy decisions of politicians. The underlying premise of these chapters is that it is legitimate for all segments of a society to attempt to influence the policy-making process in order to increase the level of rents associated with their activities and assets. Such influence, however, may be exerted either openly through public debate – as should happen in corruption-free societies, or by sharing the excess rents with policy-makers, that is, with corruption. Vito Tanzi and Hamid Davoodi review evidence on the effects of corruption on selected policy outcomes. They examine how corruption can affect budgetary decisions as well as policies that influence how rents are created for organizations of various sizes. In highlighting how firms of various sizes are affected by corruption, these authors point to the importance of process by which political decisions are made: firms that have access to the policy-makers will consistently benefit from regulation.

Sectors of society that cannot offer payments to corrupt decision-makers can often receive less than their share of the available resources than would be justified in a corruption-free society. Sectors such as education and health tend not to have private rents associated with them while also having returns that accrue over long periods of time. For these reasons, interest groups representing these sectors can find it difficult to have their interests incorporated in policy-making process within a corrupt political system. It would be easy, and costless, for politicians to ignore these sectors. In Chapter 6 of this volume, Sanjeev Gupta, Hamid Davoodi and Erwin Tiongson examine the influence of corruption in the distribution of government services on the health services. Their study points to the vicious circle that exists around corruption: corruption reduces government revenue, which even if the provision of government services is corruption free, will lower the level of services; in view of lower services, some individuals may have incentive to not use these services – in which case they will avoid paying taxes – creating an underground economy and further reducing the government revenues. This study highlights the importance of effective political institutions – a sector of the economy that does not yield rents for identifiable interest groups will otherwise receive fewer resources than is justified by its potential contribution to the economy.

In the last chapter in Part III, Aftab Ahmad highlights the importance of the history of political institutions in the growth of corruption. In what is clearly a closely observed situation by the author, the close link between corruption and the control of political institutions is established with motivation for the actions shifting from graft to political power to graft. Developments in Pakistan provide strong support for the need to focus on corruption that disguises itself in the form of public policy. Ahmad establishes quite convincingly that while motivation for political actions may have been presented as a desire to save the nation, the economics of the political actions dominated the events. The corruption in this case goes far beyond any bribes that may be paid; politicians instead derive personal economic benefits through having the power to make policy decisions that favor their own interests. Tanzi and Davoodi (1997: 7) identify another example of this type of corruption: the president of a country builds an airport in his home town even when there is no need. There was no bribe involved here, thus measures looking at bribes would have failed to identify corruption, which is taking place here in the form of a misuse of power.

Contributions in the last part of this volume attempt to address the question of what can be done about corruption. Michael Johnston's contribution raises some important questions about the measurement of corruption. While recently developed measures of corruption have had remarkable success in supporting empirical work, it must be borne in mind that these measures attempt to quantify only the activities that are easily identifiable as corruption.

Wesley Cragg and Bill Woof examine the success of the oldest antibribery legislation in modern history: the Foreign Corrupt Practices Act of 1977 in the United States. Their study may, however indirectly, provide support for the argument that acts of bribery represent only a small part of corrupt activities. In the absence of political support for fighting corruption, controlling bribery may prove to be ineffective.

While many other questions about the functioning of the political institutions and the existence of corruption can be raised, it is hoped that this volume will contribute to the understanding of the importance of politics in a study of corruption, as well as in establishing that, at least in the case of corruption, economic and political analyses are inseparable.

Notes

1 For a distinction between these concepts of equality, see Dworkin 2000.
2 Kurer, in Chapter 4 of this volume, summarizes an example of such an interaction.
3 See Jain (2001) for development of these three concepts.

Bibliography

Dworkin, R. (2000) *Sovereign Virtue: The Theory and Practice of Equality*, Cambridge, Mass.: Harvard University Press.

Jain, A. K. (2001) "Corruption: A Review," *Journal of Economic Surveys*, special volume on "Issues in New Political Economy" (February).

Naylor, R. T. (1998) "Corruption in the Modern Arms Business: Lessons from the Pentagon Scandals," in A. K. Jain (ed.), *Economics of Corruption*, Boston: Kluwer Academic.

Tanzi, V. and Davoodi, H. R. (1997) "Corruption, Public Investment and Growth," IMF Working Paper Series WP/97/139, Washington, DC: International Monetary Fund.

2 The definitions debate
Old conflicts in new guises

Michael Johnston

Introduction

The recent Seattle and Washington demonstrations against "global-ization," and against the social equity issues and international institutions for which that term has (for some) become symbolic, might seem far removed from the long-standing debate over the best definitions of corruption. Certainly, reasoned discourse was not in great abundance at those events, nor always in the commentaries that followed. But looked at another way, these controversies may be just the latest manifestations of the kinds of conflict that have shaped analytical and popular notions of corruption for centuries. These are conflicts over the acceptable links between wealth and power, and over demands for accountability. Understanding them not only places our contemporary definitions of corruption, and their origins, in a useful perspective; it may also point to ways in which those ideas are about to undergo another major shift – one that reflects the changing role of the state, and important dilemmas of governance, in the emerging global system.

Debate over definitions has long been a feature of the analysis of corruption. Classical conceptions focusing on the moral vitality of whole societies have given way to more limited modern definitions, in which specific actions are classified by a variety of standards. This modern meaning of the term "corruption" is more specific, but has by no means settled the matter: the question of definitions still derails many a promising scholarly discussion. Not only are these modern definitions matters of dispute; at another level, they have come to seem incomplete, or even irrelevant to the episodes that spark public outcry. Corruption and scandal are not synonyms (Moodie 1980) – we may find either in the absence of the other – and definitions need not suit public tastes nor serve the cause of reform. But even where legal and social conceptions of corruption are relatively settled and congruent, most analytical definitions omit a large penumbra of political actions that many perceive as corrupt, and that pose significant questions relating to fairness, justice, and the connections between wealth and power. In deeply-divided or rapidly-changing societies the ideas and distinctions underlying our definitions may be irrelevant to the realities of life (Johnston and Hao 1995). Increasingly this is the case in the global system as well: political and economic liberalization, as well as the rapid integration of world and regional economies, have far outrun efforts to enhance systems of governance. The result is an intensifying debate over the moral and ethical basis of that new system which is likely, in years to come, to change the ways we think about corruption.

No one has ever devised a universally satisfying "one-line definition" of corruption (Philp 1987: 1). No more shall I. I do, however, hope to illuminate some of the political processes, and the clashing interests, that have influenced our conceptions of corruption, and to show that such processes and interests still pay an important role in the ways we define and understand the problem. I will consider both classical and modern ways of thinking about corruption, as well as newer views that can be termed "neo-classical" because of their emphasis on the collective state of health of contemporary political systems. I will suggest that the search for definitions is a political as well as an analytical process. In societies with conceptions of corruption sufficiently settled and legitimate for the behavior–classification approach to apply, notions of corruption embody settlements of politically-contested issues, such as where distinctions between public and private roles and interests lie, or which (and whose) uses of economic and political power may justly be limited or held accountable to others. Where matters are more unsettled, many of those same issues are matters of open conflict. In both settings, political contention moulds and changes the meaning of "corruption."

Thinking about corruption: wealth, power, and accountability

"Corruption" once had a much broader meaning than it does today. Plato (1957: 421d–22b, 547a–53e), Aristotle (1962: Book 2, Ch. 7; Book 5, Ch. 2), Thucydides (see Euben 1978, and Dobel 1978), and Machiavelli (1950: Book 1, Ch. 2–7: 211–30; see also Shumer 1979) used the term to refer less to the actions of individuals than to the moral health of whole societies. This they judged in terms of *virtu* (Machiavelli 1950); or, of distributions of wealth and power, relationships between leaders and followers, the sources of power and the moral right of rulers to rule; or of a people's "love of liberty," "the quality of . . . political leadership [and] the viability of . . . political values or style" (Shumer 1979: 7, 8). Politics was seen as a social process, with corruption referring at least as much to the ends and justifications of political power as to the ways it was used and pursued. For Thucydides (1954, Book 5, Ch. 7; see also Euben 1978, and Dobel 1978), the Athenians' conquest of Melos sacrificed reason to a self-justifying claim of the necessity of conquest, and signified the thoroughgoing corruption of the state. Variations on classical themes remain with us today: Dobel, for example, has defined corruption as "the loss of a capacity for loyalty" (Dobel 1978: 960). Many critics of campaign finance practices in today's democracies regard them as comprehensively corrupting, even if donations do not buy quid pro quo benefits.

The classical conception of corruption generally fared best in small-scale societies where well-defined ruling hierarchies not only held power but enunciated society's values and goals. In such a setting the moral status of rulers, and of whole societies, were naturally closely related – linked, in many cases, by the obligation of ordinary people to accept those rulers and values, and by the absence of competing visions of the political and social good. When rulers deviated from the principles by which they claimed power and loyalty, society as a whole was indeed in a moral dilemma. In later centuries, the scope of politics broadened, but ironically, conceptions of corruption were narrowed in the process. Societies have become secularized and fragmented; many are seen more as arenas for contention among groups and interests than as embodying any overarching system of values. Ethical issues in politics revolve more around maintaining the fairness and limits of those processes than around the pursuit of fundamental moral goals. The institutions of government have become so elaborate, and social groups and their agendas so differentiated, that there now seems to be no way or reason to judge the corruptness of a whole political order. These generalizations apply unevenly to democracies, and wider variations still are found in other places. However, "corruption" is today most often seen as an attribute of specific actions by specific individuals: those holding public positions and (by some definitions) those who seek to influence them. Defining corruption has become a process of classifying behavior (Moodie 1980: 209). How did these changes come to pass?

Rules, roles, and conflict

Debates over political propriety once began and ended with "The ancient rule that 'the King can do no wrong'" (Friedrich 1974: 102). As Theobald explains, "If we go back to the pre-modern era . . . the state is not regarded as an impersonal legal entity but as the living embodiment of an inheritance which reached into the dim and distant past" – as "personal property" in the sense both of a claim to territory, and of the power to govern as private property (Theobald 1990: 19–20). An absolute autocrat cannot be corrupt, in the modern sense of the concept: what limits exist upon his power or conduct? In practice this was a question of political clout, rather than of schemes for good government. A modern notion of corruption requires the existence of countervailing or "intermediary groups" (van Klaveren 1989: 78–81), with significant political resources, who can confront those who rule. With them, the sovereign must at least take others' power into account, and might eventually be made "responsible" in a rudimentary sense (Friedrich 1974: 13). Without such contending groups – indeed, without the diffusion of political resources that created distinctions between wealth and power in the first place, and that enabled (and compelled) demands for accountability, such basic notions as the distinction between the public and the private, or personal versus official powers and benefits, meant little.

Early intermediary groups were hardly moral innovators, or even advocates of any interests beyond their own. Even when their activities were channeled into formal political institutions, they did not necessarily revolve around questions of principle. New limits upon power and procedures for accountability were more likely settlements among contesting claims and grievances than positive principles of good government. But eventually "the Parliaments of the Middle Ages, which were primarily courts, found themselves confronted with the fact that the law had increasingly to be *made* rather than discovered and declared" (ibid. 31). With this came the task of devising explicit *rules* and standards.

These too have political roots. At one time, having "a role in politics" meant being related to, or a crony of, powerful people, and having a personal share of power or favor. Public–private distinctions and notions of service or merit were nonexistent; indeed, there were few obligations to anyone other than the sovereign or one's intermediate patrons. "Politics" was the exercise and defense of personal power, its ends often little more than self-enrichment. But as the scale of society increased, and as intermediary groups developed and became more powerful, political roles began to change. Ruling elites grew beyond the size of personal retinues and extended households, and became increasingly factionalized. Wars, the acquisition of territory, and the emergence of more elaborate administrative structures and functions meant that sovereigns increasingly needed money, political support, and effective work by minions whom they could not easily oversee or coerce. Expanding regulatory activities – customs collecting, various inspection functions, and the granting of patents for the manufacture and sale of goods – reflected the growing gap between wealth and power, and created new, potentially lucrative roles useful as patronage (Peck 1990). For Theobald this phase marks the difference between patriarchalism – in which "the state is viewed as personal property," and the dominant family is the main arena of politics – and patrimonialism which, while still based upon personal power, "requires an administrative apparatus" (Theobald 1990: 19–20).

In time, extended personal networks became insufficient for the expanding scope of government. Administration became a full-time task, and functionaries had to be compensated if they were to remain loyal; as a result, various *benefices* – shares of grain, or title to the produce from a tract of land – and fees for services began to emerge (ibid.: 21). So did tax- and customs-"farming" (Peck 1990: 38–44), whereby revenue-raising functions were franchised out to entrepreneurs who recouped their investments by keeping a share of the revenues. A related practice was the outright sale of such offices, as in Stuart England (Scott 1972: Ch. 3; Peck 1990). Modern conceptions of merit (which might well have recruited many of the same people who bought their way in) played little role; citizens were still more exploited than served. But to argue that an office could be purchased was to acknowledge that at some point it had been distinct from the individual holding it, and might bear certain obligations, if only the revenue-collecting functions necessary to recoup one's investment. In France, Spain, England, and to a degree in China, feudalism gave way to an "aristocratic bureaucracy" (Scott 1972: 89–94) or an "early modern patrimonial bureaucratic state" in which networks of "freehold bureaucrats" supplied their patrons with revenue, political support, and an extended intelligence network (Peck 1990: 220–1).

Eventually, the rise of a money economy made regular taxation possible, and the growth of government made it necessary. Taxation, for Weber (in Gerth and Mills 1946: 204–9), was a "presupposition of bureaucracy" allowing regular salaries for officials and weakening the notion of personal service to patrons. These were steps toward a permanent civil service enforcing its own codes of behavior, with salaries as an important means of control (Hurstfield 1973: 158–9). Enlightenment thinkers began to view officials as parts of institutions and agendas much larger than themselves. The rise of political parties and expansion of mass electorates likewise transformed elected positions, adding new notions of accountability, such as representation and service, to the winning and holding of power, and – where competition existed – introducing the possibility of defeat because of abuse of power. As Scott notes,

> Finally, in the nineteenth century, when the more democratic form of government limited the aristocracy, and the modern idea of the State came into existence, the conception of public office as private property disappeared. The State became considered as a moral entity and the exercising of public authority as a duty.
>
> (Scott 1972: 96)

This process, however, was anything but peaceful or inevitable. New ideas about official power came into being as much through the clash of interests as through deliberate reform. Consider two cases. First, in 1583 the English essayist Phillip Stubbes, in *The Anatomie of Abuses*, described an illegitimate market in admissions to an Oxford College:

> Except one be able to give the Regent or Provost of a House a piece of money, ten pounds, twenty pounds, yea a hundred pounds, a yoke of fat oxen, a couple of fine geldings, or the like, though he be never so toward a youth, nor have ever so much need of maintenances, yet he come not there I warrant you
>
> (Wraith and Simpkins 1963: 56)

Second, in 1641, a majority of the English House of Commons voiced the then-novel argument that while the King could do no wrong, his counselors were answerable to Parliament (Roberts 1966: 83, 89–91). This principle would become a cornerstone of the constitutional monarchy.

Stubbes made his lament at a time when the colleges of Oxford and Cambridge were turning out young men of high expectations in numbers greater than could be absorbed by elite institutions (Hurstfield 1973: 155–6); long-accepted traditions of patronage and preferment came under fire from those excluded. Parliament's call for ministerial accountability surfaced in a bitter debate over its impeachment of the Earl of Strafford, who countered with an even more sweeping claim – that he enjoyed the consent of the governed, to whom he and Parliament were *both* subordinate (Roberts 1966: 89–91). This struggle, in turn, was part of Parliament's larger conflict with the King over funds, its own autonomy in the face of Crown patronage, and fears of Papist plots. The idea of ministerial accountability was not so much a reform as a political club useful for belaboring the King's inner circle. As Peck points out, an old system based upon reciprocity and royal prerogative was being challenged by new conceptions of duty and justice in a conflict between "two systems of organizing obligation"; in the process, "the language of corruption became a discourse of conflict capable of undermining governmental legitimacy, especially when it became tied to other critical issues" (Peck 1990: 170, 163).

Conflicts over corruption are thus often conflicts over other things as well – often, over self-interest narrowly defined. But these struggles can produce new notions of political propriety as well as disagreement. Indeed, it may be *especially* in the course of conflict that contending parties will invoke higher justifications for their causes, and as reasons to restrain others. The settlements that may be reached, however, are by no means permanent. Customs farming, once a welcome innovation, would today be denounced as hopelessly corrupt – unless, perhaps, it was justified as "privatization." The recent expansion of financial disclosure rules for elected and appointed officials in many nations reflects the influence of new advocacy groups and their ideas of accountability.

Contemporary definitions

These conflicts – or more specifically, the accepted standards and settlements they helped create – have led to modern conceptions of corruption based upon the idea of explicitly public *roles* endowed with limited, impersonal powers. The notion of limits implies accountability for the ways those powers are used. Among the most important limits – not the only ones, but central to most contemporary definitions – are those upon the connections between wealth and power. Defining corruption, and applying definitions to actual cases, thus becomes a matter of judging behavior against these limits. Stated thus, defining corruption would seem a simple task, but in practice there are many complications and variations.

Behavior-classifying definitions

Behavior-focused definitions generally hold that corruption is the abuse of public office, powers, or resources for private benefit. But by what standards do we identify "abuse"? Moreover, what do "public or private" mean in practice, particularly when joined with the notion of "benefit"?

Many scholars have sought objective standards, arguing that answers to these questions can be found in the law or other formal regulations, or by making reference to the public interest. Others propose subjective or cultural definitions, pointing out that "the public interest" is vague and contested while laws may enjoy little legitimacy. Public opinion or cultural standards are also promoted as one way to assess the *significance* of corruption – that is, whether and how a corrupt act matters in a given context. Not surprisingly, no universally applicable standard has been found.

While social or cultural perceptions are a frequent focus for discussion, "subjective" or explicitly cultural *definitions* are relatively uncommon. The argument from social standards more often appears as a critique of legalistic definitions. Moreover, such arguments often recognize that public opinion and cultural standards vary among segments of society. Senturia proposed that "Where the best opinion and morality of the time, examining the intent and setting of an act, judge it to represent a sacrifice of public for private benefit, then it must be held to be corrupt" (Senturia 1935: 449). Peters and Welch (1978) conducted a survey of American state legislators, deriving intriguing categories and distinctions from their judgments. Gorta and Forell's ambitious survey of civil servants in New South Wales (1995) probed the sorts of considerations these officials might take into account in deciding whether or not to report instances of corruption. Gibbons' surveys of university students (1989) similarly illustrated the subtleties of perceived corruption, while

Dolan, McKeown, and Carlson (1988) conducted a sophisticated Q-method analysis. Heidenheimer (1989a) has outlined "shades" of corruption, ranging from white through gray to black, delineated by similar or contrasting elite and mass opinion, in several kinds of societies. Still, while no one advocates ignoring cultural factors, the subjectivity that is the source of richness and subtlety in such approaches can also make it difficult to build general definitions.

Most "objective" definitions fall into Heidenheimer's enduring categories of "public-office-centered," "market-centered," and "public-interest-centered" (Heidenheimer 1989b: 8–11). Nye provides the best-known example of the first kind:

> [Corruption is] behavior which deviates from the formal duties of a public role because of private-regarding (close family, personal, private clique) pecuniary or status gains; or violates rules against the exercise of certain types of private-regarding influence.
>
> (Nye 1967: 417)

The potential advantage here is relative precision. But – leaving aside the potential problems of deciding what is a public role or a private benefit – laws can be vague or contradictory, and they do change. Scott (1972: 7–8) deals with the latter problem with the idea of "proto-corruption" – actions acceptable at one time, but later defined as corrupt – a tempting solution but one that only frames the question of how a given action comes to be officially labeled corrupt. The last point is critical: Ferdinand Marcos, for example, rewrote sections of the Philippine Constitution to legalize his looting of the nation's wealth (Carbonell-Catilo 1985: 4–7, 18–19). Corruption can also have moral significance extending well beyond the letter of the law, while some illegal actions may be morally defensible. Marcos provides an example of the former sort; as for the latter, Rose-Ackerman observes that "One does not condemn a Jew for bribing his way out of a concentration camp" (Rose-Ackerman 1978: 9). Still, Nye's has been the most widely-used definition over the years.

Heidenheimer offers van Klaveren as an example of the market-centered approach:

> A corrupt civil servant regards his public office as a business, the income of which he will . . . seek to maximize. The office then becomes a "maximizing unit." The size of his income depends . . . upon the market situation and his talents for finding the point of maximal gain on the public's demand curve.
>
> (Heidenheimer 1989b: 9)

At one level, this is less a definition than a claim regarding the calculations affecting the *amount* and stakes of corruption taking place in a given situation. It overlooks not only the intangible benefits (prestige, promises of political support) that can flow from the abuse of authority, but also varieties that are not quid pro quo exchanges, such as embezzlement. Moreover – as notions of rent-seeking suggest – where "markets" for official favors do exist they can be complex, even distorted: demand for official services may be inelastic, highly individualized (as in cases of cronyism), and far in excess of supply. Consider Klitgaard's (1988: 75) well-known "equation" holding that corruption equals *monopoly* plus *discretion*, minus *accountability*. In other cases – when, for example, several officials performing identical services agree to charge the same under-the-table fees – collusion undercuts market processes. Were these conditions not the case, many kinds of corruption would be much less common. Van Klaveren does, however, capture an important issue – that of the processes (market, or authoritative, or patrimonial) appropriate for allocating various goods. Much corruption does involve the intrusion of market incentives into authoritative (and supposedly universalistic) decision-making, or of official power into markets.

Finally, public-interest-centered definitions address both the nature of the phenomenon and its consequences. Consider Friedrich:

> The pattern of corruption can be said to exist whenever a power-holder who is charged with doing certain things, i.e., who is a responsible functionary or officeholder, is by monetary or other rewards not legally provided for, induced to take actions which favor whoever provides the rewards and thereby does damage to the public and its interests.
>
> (Friedrich 1966: 74)

To his credit, Friedrich seeks to retain an important moral aspect of corruption – harm to the public – thus offering a way to distinguish between trivial and harmful cases. But even if "the public interest" had a reasonably precise meaning, let alone one comparable from time to time and place to place, the *definition* of corruption and its *consequences* are distinct issues. Consequences of agreed-upon forms of corruption might vary considerably in differing settings. Take the point about consequences away from Friedrich's definition, and – because of his reliance upon the standards attending to public office – we are left with the essentials of Nye's.

These definitions do allow us to identify patterns of corruption, to consider institutional and political reforms, and to analyze the consequences of various corrupt actions. But relationships between wealth and power, and notions of accountability, are constantly being reinterpreted, even in relatively settled systems. Indeed, Moodie argues that

officials' need for "room to manoeuvre," the difficulties of distinguish-
ing "between a ruler's public and private personality," the conflicting
expectations that apply to any official role, and questions of motive
make it unlikely that precise behavior-based definitions will ever be
found (Moodie 1980: 213, 213 n. 14). Other problems are found at the
level of basic terms and distinctions: not only can it be difficult to agree
on the meaning of "abuse"; it may also be far from clear what constitutes a public role or resource, or a private benefit. One long-running
corruption issue in China, for example, is that of *guandao* – profiteering and cozy relationships involving officials and entrepreneurs, with
many individuals occupying *both* sorts of roles, in an economic setting
neither wholly public nor private (Johnston and Hao 1995). Even where
public-private distinctions are clear, the conduct of private parties may,
or may not, be a corruption issue: the debates over rules governing
political contributions and lobbying in many nations demonstrate the
pervasiveness of this question. Even more complex is the question of
what constitutes a "private benefit." Few would restrict the idea to cash
and gifts accruing only to a public functionary, but if an official spon-
sors legislation, or uses her discretion to make administrative decisions
popular with a segment of the public, do the popularity and political
support that may result constitute a "private benefit"? What are the
limits of acceptable constituent services a parliamentarian might perform
for a party contributor? Even where norms and roles are relatively
settled, there will be substantial gray areas in any behavior-classifying
definition.

"Neo-classical" approaches

If definitions that classify behavior are too rigid to apply to all times and
places, if adapting them to those societies is likely to yield categories
vague in content and soft at their boundaries, and if such definitions still
omit a great deal of what citizens tend to regard as corrupt, what might
be better? A more recent school of thought revives some of the themes of
the classical approach, holding that corruption is not an attribute of an
action, but rather a deeper problem with politics – a problem that resides
in the broader processes through which consent is won, and influence and
authority are used.[1] Such an approach might be termed "neo-classical"
because it seeks to link modern political roles and institutions to older
concerns about the moral health of whole societies.

A "neo-classical" approach might have it that corruption is the abuse,
according to the legal *or* social standards constituting a society's system
of public order (Rogow and Lasswell 1963), of a public role or resource
for private benefit. Like others, this notion incorporates the basic idea
of the abuse of public roles or resources for private benefit. Unlike them,
it is not intended to specify a precise category of behavior as corrupt,

but rather frames corruption as a political and moral issue. Where social and legal standards are reasonably congruent, this definition would point to a "core meaning" of corruption not greatly different from many of the behavior classifications already noted, while still making room for debate and change at the margins. Where the mass/elite or state/society gap is a wide one – see, on this point, Heidenheimer's (1989a) classic typology of "black, gray, and white corruption" – or where consensus over social standards is weak, this kind of definition directs our attention to the forces contending over the meanings of concepts such as "abuse," "public role," and "private benefit." It thus encompasses both wrongful behavior *and* the political processes that help define it as such and help shape its significance.

This approach could avoid both the charge of "Western bias" leveled at many legalistic definitions by making room for the many political forces shaping a society's system of public order, and the problems of relativism entailed by considering social norms alone. It invites us to consider not only how laws affect behavior, but also how they might come to fit established customs. It links the study of corruption to the consideration of scandal via its emphasis on social values. And, as suggested above, it does not shy away from a normative view of what does, and does not, constitute good politics, thus, reintroducing classical notions that politics is a morally-charged *social* process, and the Machiavellian view that vigorous disputation can be a sign of political integrity in its broadest sense.

We do have some examples of this approach. Weber recognized that the viability of formal rules rested in part upon "social sanctions": "relatively general and practically significant reaction[s] of disapproval" (Gerth and Mills 1946: 127–30). Berg, Hahn, and Schmidhauser defined corruption as behavior that "violates and undermines the norms of the system of public order which is deemed indispensable for the maintenance of political democracy" (Berg, Hahn, and Schmidhauser 1976). Jacek Tarkowski, in an analysis of Poland and the USSR on the verge of their political transitions, proposed that:

> Corruption . . . is any activity motivated by interest, violating the binding rules of distribution, the application of which is within one's responsibility. Rules of distribution . . . refer not only to the letter of the law, but also to norms recognized as binding by society and/or to the system's "official" norms and operational codes. Also "corrupt" are those activities regarded by society as illegitimate or seen by the power elite as contradictory to the logic of the system.
>
> (Tarkowski 1989: 53–4)

Tarkowski used this approach not primarily to classify certain kinds of behavior as corrupt, but as a guide to the interplay between official institutions and the re-emerging forces of civil society, and to the "gray areas" in which that process was taking place, at the end of the Communist era (ibid.: 55–61).

Dennis Thompson's intriguing notion of "mediated corruption" also treats corruption as a property of a whole pattern of politics (Thompson 1993, 1995).[2] He does not redefine corruption as such, but rather extends the analysis beyond "conventional corruption" – outright bribery or extortion, presumably – to include actions that are corrupt because they damage the democratic process. He calls these "mediated corruption"

> because the corrupt acts are mediated by the political process. The public official's contribution to the corruption is filtered through various practices that are otherwise legitimate and may even be duties of office. As a result, both the official and citizens are less likely to recognize that the official has done anything wrong or that any serious harm has been done.
>
> (Thompson 1993: 369)

This notion is not easy to grasp: it does not delineate sharp boundaries, either around corruption itself or between mediated and conventional corruption. The focus is not upon the status of specific actions or the specific goods being exchanged, but upon the value of democratic politics itself:

> Mediated corruption . . . includes the three main elements of the general concept of corruption: a public official gains, a private citizen receives a benefit, and the connection between the gain and the benefit is improper. But mediated corruption differs from conventional corruption with respect to each of these three elements: (1) the gain that the politician receives is political, not personal and is not illegitimate in itself, as in conventional corruption; (2) *how* the public official provides the benefit is improper, not necessarily the benefit itself, or the fact that the particular citizen receives the benefit; (3) the connection between the gain and the benefit is improper because it damages the democratic process, not because the public official provides the benefit with a corrupt motive. In each of these elements, the concept of mediated corruption links the acts of individual officials to qualities of the democratic process. In this way, the concept provides a partial synthesis of conventional corruption (familiar in contemporary political science) and systematic corruption (found in traditional political theory).
>
> (Thompson 1993: 369)

Thompson applies this concept to the Keating Five case (ibid.: 369–74), involving dealings between the chairman of a failed Savings and Loan and five United States Senators. He argues that conventional notions of corruption lead to two equally unsatisfactory judgments: either that corruption is endemic and all exchanges between citizens and politicians (in this case, campaign donations for the use of influence upon regulators) are corrupt, or that such exchanges are necessary to the vitality of politics and therefore the vast majority are to be tolerated. For Thompson, both views miss the point: corruption occurred in the Keating Five case not because exchanges took place between politicians and a citizen, and not because of what was exchanged or the motives we might attribute to the participants. "[W]hat is wrong is [not] personal gain, but a certain *kind* of personal gain; and it is wrong not because it is a *personal* gain at all but because of its effects on the system" (ibid.: 372). The transactions were corrupt because they avoided the democratic *process*, which is not simply a set of "rules of the game" but rather embodies major values, such as representation, accountability, open debate, and equality.

Thompson places the health and the core values of political systems back at the center of the corruption debate. He also connects analytical views more closely to what much of the public regards as corruption, without making the concept merely a matter of public opinion. Similarly, Philp uses a corruption case in New South Wales to illustrate the ways in which "definitional disputes about political corruption are linked directly to arguments about the nature of the healthy or normal condition of politics" (Philp 1997: 30). The definitions question, for Philp, cannot be reduced to relativism or drained of its moral content; no more can it be resolved by a mere economic accounting of "who gets what." Instead, it is a part of a much more basic, and long-standing, debate over the role political processes play in building a decent society, and over the question of what values should both govern, and be upheld by, those processes.

Many behavior-classifying definitions implicitly or explicitly treat corruption in a "value-neutral" fashion, either with respect to generalizing about its effects or to the sensitivities involved in making judgments about other societies (Friedrich's is a clear exception). The idea of mediated corruption, by contrast, is explicitly value-laden: not only is this kind of corruption a bad thing, but it is bad as judged against a definite conception of what constitutes *good* politics. As Rose-Ackerman has observed, "Normative statements about corruption . . . require a point of view, a standard of 'goodness', and a model of how corruption works in particular instances" (Rose-Ackerman 1978: 9). To be sure, we might question the precision of any list of democratic values as a standard of goodness, and ask how well the notion of mediated corruption might travel to transitional or deeply divided societies. But Chinese citizens, for example, have had little difficulty in judging *guandao* as unjust and corrupt, even though its legality and political status are in flux (Johnston and Hao 1995).

Seattle revisited: new conflicts, new definitions?

The major elements of modern, behavior-classifying definitions of corruption – limited, impersonal powers, accountability, and accepted boundaries between the legitimate domains of wealth and power – may seem natural in the context of the contemporary state. But in fact they are the political, as well as analytical, consequences of the forces and contending interests that replaced the old patriarchal state (Theobald 1990), and its system of personalized power guided by a mix of self-interest and reciprocity, with the norms and structures we know today. The result of those changes was not a single coherent model of government; modern democracies, much less the undemocratic variants on the modern state, differ in important ways. Rather, they produced a conception of *governance*, that is, accepted modes of acquiring and using power and wealth, incorporating rules and restraints upon the state as well as conferring the ability to allocate important goods. Our contemporary conceptions of corruption both help to define, and are continually being redefined within, that strategy of governance.

The broad acceptance of this conception of governance – even those societies that fall well short of it often claim to uphold it, and are certainly judged against its standards – does not mean that the outlines of the concept of corruption are settled. Far from it: new interests and conflicts, and emerging conceptions of accountability, continue to redefine our conceptions of the corrupt. In many countries, the push for disclosure and for tighter rules regulating campaign finance are examples of such changes, as are transparency requirements mandating that leaders disclose their personal finances. At a far less dignified level, the deep partisan conflicts that marked the Clinton/Lewinsky scandal in the United States may not have toppled a government, but they did shift the boundaries between the public and private aspects of top officials' lives. At the analytical level, the emergence of "neo-classical" definitions may reflect the fact that behavior-classifying approaches do not effectively address major political and moral issues.

A new corruption paradigm?

But there are reasons to think that even bigger changes in the ways we conceptualize corruption may be in the offing. Like the historical processes that brought us to our present vantage point, the forces driving these changes will have more to do with political contention than with analysts' efforts to perfect their definitions. Major political and economic changes, and policies of liberalization over the past decade, have begun to redefine the role of the state and have launched a process – loosely, perhaps misleadingly, termed "globalization" – whose full consequences can only be guessed at. As in the past, these changes, and the political contention they foster, raise new questions about the relationships between wealth and power, and about the scope and mechanisms of accountability.

What are these changes? A full description and analysis lie well beyond the scope of this discussion. But at one level – the role of the contemporary state whose evolution we discussed earlier – the scope, and the legitimate means of exercising, public *power* are being redefined and, in most cases, significantly pruned back. By political mandates in many established democracies, and through the "structural adjustment" policies (and more recent variations) of international development agencies, smaller governments (in proportion to the scale of their economies), market-oriented economic strategies, and privatization have become dominant trends. The latter in particular takes on many forms: official privatization in the sense of selling off public assets to private parties, and a more pervasive if less formal privatization that takes place as families and individuals turn to the private sector to police their neighborhoods, educate their children, obtain health care, and finance their retirements. Indeed, in many societies we are seeing the evolution of a kind of gray zone that is neither public nor private, and where the rules are very much in flux: newly-deregulated industries, or the privatization of public utilities and pension plans, are examples.

The role of the state is being called into question "from below" in many societies by issues of identity: many states face separatist movements, or (as in the case of some member states of the European Union) find that cross-border regional identities are growing in salience. Economic globalization is a parallel, and if anything even more powerful, influence from "above" or from without. Both informally, via the integration of global markets and technologies, and formally, through trade pacts such as NAFTA or MERCOSUR, and through organizations such as the European Union, World Trade Organization, and the Organization for Economic Cooperation and Development, to name just a few, states are becoming parts of economic and political systems much larger than themselves. While globalization has many policy dimensions, and its implications for electoral and representative processes are finally beginning to be addressed in such long-standing organizations as the EU, it is primarily driven by economic incentives and processes – the *wealth* side of the wealth-and-power relationship that has long stood at the core of the corruption question.

As a result, the range of acceptable connections between wealth and power, and the question of to whom, if anyone, political and economic decision-makers should be held accountable, are once again very much open to debate and contention, more so, perhaps, than at any other time in the past century. With this is coming renewed debate over the abuse of power: not just how it happens and what its consequences are, but also *what the idea means* in practice. The recent Seattle and Washington protestors had little to offer by way of analysis, but the issues of equity and justice they raised are real ones. And what makes those issues all the more pressing is that at present, we lack – or, perhaps to be more optimistic, we have yet to build – mechanisms of accountability and governance on a scale commensurate with the global forces now at play. Indeed, those we have relied upon – those of the nation-state – are being cut back.

Perhaps the closest we come to a strategy for governance in this new era is the assumption that two kinds of liberalization – democracy as a way of conferring and using power, and markets as mechanisms for creating and distributing wealth – will both sustain and restrain each other. This hope is not necessarily illusory: there is a notable (if notably imperfect) correlation between market-based affluence and democracy among the countries of the world, and in those countries orderly, well-institutionalized political and economic competition mesh well and produce major social benefits.

But it is not so obvious that political and economic liberalization will necessarily converge to create a new system of governance on a global scale. Indeed, the two are *asymmetrical* in significant ways. Democratic politics rests not only on open competition, but also on institutionalized assumptions of equality (such as "one person, one vote"). While driven by private interests, democratic competition is expected to be fair, and to *aggregate* the expressions of those interests into broadly-accepted public policies.[3] Markets, by contrast, incorporate few presumptions of equality, either in process or outcome; such procedural rights and mechanisms of accountability as exist are grounded primarily in ownership, not citizenship. Gains are presumed to be private and separable. Competition, while open to new participants, is continuous and much less structured than politics, with a wider range of uncertainty in outcomes; losers are routinely driven out of markets, and winners enjoy advantages, in ways that lack political parallels. Political regimes hold power over a limited territory and population, while markets are increasingly global.

If these asymmetries did not exist, corruption would not be a problem. More or less anything could be bought and sold, and public office could be used like any other resource in the pursuit of private gain. But they do exist – indeed, they are at the heart of the grievances raised in the streets of Seattle, and in the debate over campaign finance, to name just two examples. We will thus still require workable and accepted – if not identical – limits on both political and economic power, mechanisms of accountability, and meaningful guarantees of open participation and fair, orderly competition in both politics and the economy. In well-balanced systems there are realms where official power may not intrude, and things that may not be bought and sold. Institutions on both sides must have some degree of *autonomy*: public officials need to carry out their work in an uncompromised, authoritative way, while private property and contracts must be respected. Where such boundaries exist, free interaction within each realm is more secure: it will be more difficult for economic interests to turn politics into an auction, and for officials to plunder the economy. But legitimate paths of access between the two arenas are still needed: policies must reflect economic realities, and self-interested behavior must be subject to the rule of law. If connections between the political and economic arenas do not legitimately exist, they will be created corruptly. These needs do not vanish with globalization; if anything, they are made more pressing by the absence of workable norms and institutions of governance.

All of this has direct relevance for corruption and reform, and for the ways we understand both. In some cases the issue arises through corruption that is familiar in form, but increasingly difficult to contain: the "democracy deficit" in the European Community has only recently come in for serious debate, and its possible links to extensive corruption within the Council of Ministers, and within EU programs, have yet to be fully understood. In other cases the question is how the sorts of grievances and clashing interests that have historically shaped conceptions of corruption, and acceptable restraints upon wealth and power, can find an outlet: consider China, where extensive economic liberalization has not been matched on the political side.

The implications of these changes are visible at the levels of definitions too: consider the "Washington consensus" view of corruption (primarily as a matter of rent-seeking facilitated by incomplete economic liberalization) versus the much wilder and woolier views on display in the streets outside of those institutions. Neither approach will suffice for understanding future corruption; the former is much too narrow, while the latter indiscriminately lumps important issues of wealth, power, and accountability in with a far broader range of complaints and allegations, some real and others illusory. It is tempting to dismiss the latter viewpoint out of hand, in part because of its lack of precision and underlying analysis, but perhaps here too we see emerging interests and grievances in search of a governance process that does not yet exist. In that sense, the demonstrators' view of the abuse of power closely resembles that of China, where "corruption" has come to refer to an extremely wide range of abuses and grievances, and where the issue is not just the boundaries of official behavior, but rather the fundamental sources and limits of power in society.

Is there a forum or a means of governance – indeed, is there even a common *vocabulary* corresponding to the terms echoing through the several definitions discussed in earlier sections of this chapter – that would allow a process through which these contending views can be thrashed out? At present, the answer is no, and thus the future of the corruption issue is unclear in the extreme. Will advocates of the "Washington consensus" view do away with public corruption by privatizing it – in effect, replacing public rents with private ones, perhaps collected in new and ever-more-efficient ways under the much more lenient rules of the economic, as opposed to the political, arena? Even if this does come to pass, or if bribery is eradicated by other means, the underlying corruption issues raised (however inarticulately) in the streets – those of the relationships between wealth and power, and of accountability – will be very much with us.

Our contemporary political conceptions and analytical definitions of corruption grew out of long, and often disorderly, processes of conflict and contention; once in place, they served both analysis and governance reasonably well, while continuing to evolve at the margins. Reaching similarly useful settlements in the emerging global system will require similarly open contention and debate, often disorderly in appearance. Like the conflicts of previous eras, they may well usher in definitions and categories of corruption unfamiliar to us now, but which may ultimately come to seem natural within a new conception of governance. We have the advantage of being able to watch and analyze those processes from the beginning, but at present, it is very difficult to say where they will lead.

Conclusion

It is an irony of corruption that where it is most important it can also be most difficult to define. This discussion has in no way settled that question, particularly as regards the new definitions that may be in the offing. Perhaps the safest generalization is that in studying corruption we should remember why it is important to begin with, and be aware that our definitions may vary according to the questions we wish to ask and the settings within which we ask them. Where the major political conflicts underlying the notion of corruption have been largely settled – at least for a time – and where we wish to make comparisons that are limited in scope, a definition such as Nye's may be perfectly suitable, or awkward only at the margins. But where our comparisons are more ambitious, where agreement over the meanings of "public," "private," "abuse," and "benefit" is weak, or where fundamental shifts in governance are underway, matters are more complex. There, we may wish to think of corruption as a politically-contested or unresolved concept, study the conflicts that shape it as an issue, appreciate the significance of contention rather than attempt to resolve it through definitions, and retain a focus on the moral foundations, and state of political health, of global society.

It may well turn out that the foregoing discussion vastly overstates the significance of contemporary changes and conflicts. Certainly, the current state of the discussion does not allow much specificity as to what any new conceptions of corruption might be like – much less, as to the outlines of the systems within which they become meaningful. At the very least, however, speculating about them helps put our current definitions in a useful perspective. It suggests that the search for definitions is doomed to failure if its goal is a completely precise, universally-applicable rule for classifying behavior as corrupt. On the other hand, a view of corruption as a political as well as analytical concept – one reflecting clashing interests as much as conceptions of public morality – can yield concepts that are much less neat, but are more useful for comparative analysis and for the understanding of change.

Notes

1 I am indebted to Dennis Thompson for his comments on this point.
2 In a more recent book Thompson (1995) elaborated upon this concept, and changed the term to "institutional corruption."
3 I thank Dr. Salvador Valdes-Prieto, Centro de Estudios Publicos in Santiago, Chile, for his comments on this point.

Bibliography

Aristotle (1962 edn) *The Politics* (trans. E. Barker), New York: Oxford University Press.
Berg, L. L., Hahn, H., and Schmidhauser, J. R. (1976) *Corruption in the American Political System*, Morristown, NJ: General Learning.
Carbonell-Catilo, A. (1985) "The Dynamics of Manipulation and Violence in Philippine Elections: A Case of Political Corruption," 13th World Congress, International Political Science Association, Paris.
Dobel, J. P. (1978) "The Corruption of a State," *American Political Science Review* 72: 958–73.
Dolan, K., McKeown, B., and Carlson, J. M. (1988) "Popular Conceptions of Political Corruption: Implications for the Empirical Study of Political Ethics," *Corruption and Reform* 3: 3–24.
Euben, J. P. (1978) "On Political Corruption," *Antioch Review* 36: 103–18.
Friedrich, C. J. (1966) "Political Pathology," *Political Quarterly* 37: 70–85.
—— (1974) *Limited Government: A Comparison*, Englewood Cliffs, NJ: Prentice-Hall.
Gerth, H. H. and Mills, C. W. (1946) *From Max Weber: Essays in Sociology*, New York: Oxford University Press.
Gibbons, K. M. (1989) "Toward an Attitudinal Definition of Corruption," in A. Heidenheimer, M. Johnston, and V. LeVine, *Political Corruption: A Handbook*, New Brunswick, NJ: Transaction, 165–71.
Gorta, A. and Forell, S. (1995) "Layers of Decision: Linking Social Definitions of Corruption and Willingness to Take Action," *Crime, Law, and Social Change* 23: 315–43.
Heidenheimer, A. J. (1989a) "Perspectives on the Perception of Corruption," in A. Heidenheimer, M. Johnston, and V. LeVine, *Political Corruption: A Handbook*, New Brunswick, NJ: Transaction.

—— (1989b) "Terms, Concepts, and Definitions: An Introduction," in A. Heidenheimer, M. Johnston, and V. LeVine, *Political Corruption: A Handbook*, New Brunswick, NJ: Transaction.

Hurstfield, J. (1973) *Freedom, Corruption and Government in Elizabethan England*, Cambridge, Mass.: Harvard University Press.

Johnston, M. (1991) "Right and Wrong in British Politics: 'Fits of Morality' in Comparative Perspective," *Polity* 24: 1–25.

Johnston, M. and Hao, Y. (1995) "China's Surge of Corruption," *Journal of Democracy* 6: 80–94.

Klitgaard, R. E. (1988) *Controlling Corruption*, Berkeley, Calif.: University of California Press.

Machiavelli, N. (1950 edn) *Discourses* (trans. and ed. L. J. Walker), New Haven, Conn.: Yale University Press.

Moodie, G. C. (1980) "On Political Scandals and Corruption," *Government and Opposition* 15: 208–22.

Nye, J. S. (1967) "Corruption and Political Development: A Cost-Benefit Analysis," *American Political Science Review* 61: 417–27.

Peck, L. L. (1990) *Court Patronage and Corruption in Early Stuart England*, Boston: Unwin Hyman.

Peters, J. G. and Welch, S. (1978) "Political Corruption in America: A Search for Definitions and a Theory," *American Political Science Review* 72: 974–84.

Philp, M. (1987) "Defining Corruption: An Analysis of the Republican Tradition," International Political Science Association research roundtable on political finance and political corruption, Bellagio, Italy.

—— (1997) "Defining Political Corruption" in P. Heywood (ed.), *Political Corruption*, Oxford: Blackwell: 20–46.

Plato (1957 edn) *The Republic* (trans. A. D. Lindsay), New York: E. P. Dutton.

Roberts, C. (1966) *The Growth of Responsible Government in Stuart England*, Cambridge, UK: Cambridge University Press.

Rogow, A. and Lasswell, H. D. (1963) *Power, Corruption, and Rectitude*, Englewood Cliffs, NJ: Prentice-Hall.

Rose-Ackerman, S. (1978) *Corruption: A Study in Political Economy*, New York: Academic Press.

Scott, J. C. (1972) *Comparative Political Corruption*, Englewood Cliffs, NJ: Prentice-Hall.

Senturia, J. A. (1935) "Corruption, Political," *Encyclopedia of the Social Sciences*, vol. 4. New York: Crowell-Collier-Macmillan.

Shumer, S. M. (1979) "Machiavelli: Republican Politics and its Corruption," *Political Theory* 7: 5–34.

Stubbes, P. (1583) *The Anatomie of Abuses*, quoted in R. Wraith and E. Simpkins, *Corruption in Developing Countries*, London: Allen and Unwin.

Tarkowski, J. (1989) "Old and New Patterns of Corruption in Poland and the USSR," *Telos* 80: 51–62.

Theobald, R. (1990) *Corruption, Development, and Underdevelopment*, Durham, NC: Duke University Press.

Thompson, D. F. (1993) "Mediated Corruption: The Case of the Keating Five," *American Political Science Review* 87: 369–81.

—— (1995) *Ethics in Congress: From Individual to Institutional Corruption*, Washington, DC: Brookings.

Thucydides (1954 edn) *History of the Peloponnesian War* (trans. R. Warner), London: Penguin.

van Klaveren, J. (1989 edn) "The Concept of Corruption," in A. Heidenheimer, M. Johnston, and V. LeVine, *Political Corruption: A Handbook*, New Brunswick, NJ: Transaction.

Wraith, R. and Simpkins, E. (1963) *Corruption in Developing Countries*, London: Allen and Unwin.

Part II
Political systems and corruption

3 Political corruption and democratic structures

Susan Rose-Ackerman

Are democracies less corrupt than other forms of government? The desire for re-election constrains the greed of politicians. The protection of civil liberties and free speech, which generally accompanies democratic elections, makes open and transparent government possible. In contrast, non-democratic states are especially susceptible to corrupt incentives because their rulers have the potential to organize government with few checks and balances.

But this contrast is too sharp. One need look no further than some state and municipal governments in the United States to find a number of well-established corrupt systems that compare quite well with autocratic states.[1] Recent payoff scandals have implicated elected politicians in many countries.[2] Clearly, democratic forms do not always succeed in checking corruption and may encourage wealthy private interests to participate in political life. Thus, it is worthwhile asking which features of democratic government help limit self-dealing and which contribute to corruption and insider influence.

In analyzing the incentives for corruption in democracies, one should recognize the weaknesses of even honest democratic systems in providing broad-based public goods (Shugart 1992). Some skeptics view all legislative enactments as interest group deals and favor governments that are full of checks and balances. This seems too cynical a view, but it does highlight the fact that governments frequently provide narrowly-focused benefits even without any illegal bribery. In fact, levels of corruption may be low in just those polities where special interest legislation is pervasive, and may be high where there is no legal route for wealthy interests to influence politics. Corruption depends both on the organization of electoral and legislative processes and on the extent to which wealthy interests seek benefits from the political system. Three factors are central in determining the incidence of political corruption. They affect politicians' willingness to accept illegal payoffs, voters' toleration of such payoffs, and the willingness to pay of wealthy groups. The first dimension is the existence of narrow benefits available for distribution by politicians. The second is the ability of wealthy groups to obtain these benefits legally. Third are the constraints imposed on politicians by their desire for re-election.

This chapter develops some ideas previously presented in Chapters 8 and 11 of my book *Corruption and Government: Causes, Consequences, and Reform*. It attempts to provide a more systematic account of some of the relationships between private wealth, constitutional structure, and corruption. The first part discusses the relationship between constitutional structures and corruption. The second part examines how illegal campaign contributions are influenced by the relationship between political structure and private wealth. The chapter concludes with a discussion of the preconditions for reform in democratic systems stressing both underlying constitutional structures and more temporary conditions that can create reform opportunities in all systems.

Constitutional structures

Political systems provide various mixtures of both broad-based policies and narrowly-focused private or group benefits. Some public goods like national defense also provide firms and regions with localized benefits such as defense contracts and military bases. Incentives for quid pro quo transfers between politicians and private individuals and firms are higher if the state provides narrowly-focused benefits, but the connection between corruption and political structure is complex. My goal in this section is to suggest how this connection operates for alternative constitutional forms.

Although many factors determine the actual incidence of political corruption, the fundamental constitutional structure of the state is one variable to consider. Let us begin with some stylized political systems that differ along two dimensions. First, it is important to distinguish between presidential and parliamentary systems. A presidential system has a separately-elected chief executive who serves a fixed term. In a parliamentary system a subset of parties in the legislature forms the executive, has no fixed term in office, and can be removed by a vote of no confidence.[3] The second dimension is the method of selecting legislators, which, in my stylized framework, can be plurality voting in single-member districts or national proportional representation. Within the proportional representation (PR) category, I make a distinction between candidate-centered and party-centered systems. The most familiar example of the former is open-list PR where voters rank candidates within each party. Closed-list PR, where party leaders rank the candidates, illustrates the latter. Of course, these cases do not exhaust the possibilities. France elects both a president and a prime minister; Germany mixes proportional representation with single-member constituencies; until a recent reform, the Japanese cast a single vote in multimember districts. Proportional representation frequently operates at the regional, not the national level. Nevertheless, my stylized cases will illustrate the basic points I wish to make.[4]

There are six stylized cases. I distinguish between two types of presidential systems: those, like the United States, with plurality voting in single-member districts for the legislature (1) and those that use proportional representation, such as many Latin American democracies (2). Some PR systems are party-centered (2a), and others are candidate-centered (2b). Parliamentary systems also differ in the way the legislature is selected. Westminster systems using plurality rule are represented by the United Kingdom itself, India, and many other Commonwealth countries (3). Many continental European countries have some variant of a PR parliamentary system that is either party-centered (4a) or candidate-centered (4b). Figure 3.1 presents examples of the various possibilities of constitution structures.[5]

Countries differ in the underlying political cleavages determined by such factors as race, ethnicity, religion, or region. These cleavages may be so strong and well-entrenched that they override any of the particular features of the electoral system. Other countries, although nominally democratic in constitutional structure have long had a dominant party or political grouping that routinely wins elections. Once again the structure of the constitution may be relatively unimportant.[6] I ignore these cases here, and focus instead on clear cases where political structure matters. I thus assume that party affiliations are not immutable and that the system is genuinely competitive.[7]

Broad-based versus individualized benefits

Before considering the incentives for political corruption in each of these stylized systems, I begin with the politicians' incentives to supply legal but narrowly-focused benefits in competitive political systems. Suppose that the level of economic development is not a function of the constitutional structure and that all countries have groups that seek to benefit from favorable government actions – legal or illegal. I am not trying to explain the overall size of the government budget, but only the tendency of politicians to favor particularized interests through spending, taxation or regulatory policy.

Under those conditions, how can these systems be ranked in terms of the incentives of re-election-seeking politicians to supply broad-based public services? I follow the pioneering work of Matthew Shugart in hypothesizing that electoral systems that require winners to appeal to a broad cross-section of the population are more likely to supply broad-based public goods (Shugart and Carey 1992: 167–205; Shugart 1992). The particular ranking I present here may be controversial, but the underlying principles should be clear. The ranking is an attempt to distinguish between political systems on the basis of their propensity to

	Plurality single-member districts	Proportional representation	
		Party centered	Candidate centered
Presidential	1 US, Zambia	2a Latin America: Argentina, Bolivia	2b Latin America: Brazil
Parliamentary	3 Westminster: UK, Canada	4a Belgium, Spain	4b Italy (pre-1993), Finland

Figure 3.1 Types of constitutional structures

provide narrowly-focused benefits through legal above-board processes. In the systems shown in Figure 3.1, there are two explanatory factors.

The first is a separately elected president who must appeal to a broad constituency in order to be elected. *Ceteris paribus*, I expect presidents to have an incentive to provide national public goods. The main caveat here is the legislative process that requires the president to obtain legislative support in order to promulgate laws. If individual legislators can demand special treatment for their constituents as the price of support, this will undermine the president's ability to obtain broad-gauged legislation.[8]

The second dimension is the incentives of members of the legislature. Here the important factor is whether the electoral system does or does not encourage strong parties with diverse, national constituencies (cf. Shugart 1992). Paradoxically, the lack of a separately-elected president can mean that parliamentary systems produce governments committed to the provision of broad-based public services. In the absence of a president, the members of the legislature must form a government, and they may only be able to do this if strong party discipline is the norm. Strong political party organization solves collective action problems for politicians who must form governments.[9]

Thus two factors determine the legislature's interest in national public goods: first, the incentives produced by the electoral rules, and second, the way these rules interact with the presidential or parliamentary structure of government. Under proportional representation, party-centered and candidate-centered rules operate very differently. In the former category are closed-list systems that make everyone dependent on party leaders and tend to produce powerful parties. In contrast, open-list systems generate weak parties where candidates compete with others in their own party for voters' support (Carey and Shugart 1995: 118–19, Shugart 1992: 69–70). However, in both cases there may be a large number of parties, each with a narrow political base. In contrast and subject to a number of caveats, plurality rule systems produce two dominant parties with legislators who face dual loyalties to their party and to their geographical constituency (Cox 1997).

Parties do not form the government under a presidential system. That condition alone ought to weaken the national focus of parties under all electoral systems (Shugart 1998). The president's interest in national-level legislation may be undermined by the narrow focus of legislators. This will be a more serious problem, however, for candidate-centered PR rules than for the other systems. Plurality systems would, I hypothesize, be only marginally more effective, since although the number of parties will be small, they will also be weak. At the same time, the geographical basis of representation means that political deals between president and the legislature are likely to involve geographically-based benefits.

A party-centered PR system looks superior but can produce other problems. Party loyalty is high enabling negotiations between the president and party leaders. However, if no large party controls the legislature, there may be a number of small, well-organized parties that can use their bargaining power to extract narrow benefits. In reality, the very fact that the legislature has no responsibility for government formation, may encourage the creation of such parties designed to play a "spoiler" role. Nevertheless, I would hazard the hypothesis that, on balance, the problem of narrowly-focused parties is less serious than the problems of constituency pressure under plurality rule.[10]

Now consider parliamentary systems where the executive is organized by the members of parliament. The need to form a government ought to strengthen the hand of party leaders in Westminster systems. Constituency pressures for district-based benefits are kept in check by the party leaders' leverage over the rank and file. Unless a party's governing majority is very slim, no individual legislator can use the threat of jumping ship as a device to extort benefits, and the probable existence of two major parties will further limit the bargaining power of narrow interests. However, unless small coalition partners can extract rents under party-centered PR, I would hypothesize that such a political structure would be marginally superior to a Westminster democracy in producing broad-gauged benefits simply because politicians lack individual constituencies.[11] That ranking is to some extent an empirical claim. Countries may differ in the relative importance of constituents' demands and small parties' extortionary power. Last in line is a candidate-centered PR system. The parties, in this case, need to cooperate to form a government, but they may not be able to overcome the centrifugal pressures introduced by the electoral rules.

It remains to compare presidential and parliamentary systems (Figure 3.2).[12] On the one hand, the president, by appealing to a national constituency, has a built-in incentive to propose broad-based policies. On the other hand, parliamentary systems, lacking such a figure, may produce political parties that make national appeals to increase their chances of forming a government. Of course, coalitions of minorities can form governments. Nevertheless, I would hypothesize that party-centered PR parliamentary systems (4a) and Westminster democracies (3) will be ranked first and second in providing public goods above any of the presidential systems. The unitary nature of government in parliamentary systems and the incentive for parties to cooperate to form a viable government seem to me to dominate the value of a separately elected president. Next in line I would place two presidential systems: party-centered PR (2a) and the United States system (1). Without the responsibility of maintaining the government in power, even a party-centered PR system (2a) may produce a fragmented legislature that can demand narrow benefits for the supporters of particular parties. The incentives to provide pork barrel projects are, however, limited by the fact that legislators do not represent individual constituencies. The US system with its strong separately-elected president and plurality-rule legislature (1) comes next.[13]

At the bottom are the two candidate-centered PR systems. I rank the parliamentary system (4b) above the presidential system (2b) for the reasons outlined earlier. In the former, the legislative coalition has an incentive to stick together to maintain the government. This will check

Provision of public goods	Avoidance of corruption		
4a: Party-centered parliamentary	3: Westminster parliamentary		
3: Westminster parliamentary	4a: Party-centered parliamentary		
2a: Party-centered presidential		President	Legislature
		2a: Party-centered presidential	1: US presidential
1: US presidential		2b: Candidate-centered presidential	2b: Candidate-centered presidential
4b: Candidate-centered parliamentary		1: US presidential	2a: Party-centered presidential
2b: Candidate-centered presidential	[4b: Candidate-centered parliamentary – ?]		

Figure 3.2 Ranking of constitutional systems (best to worst)

narrow demands, but this tendency is countered by the fact that legislators must out-poll other members of their own party to win the election. To win a seat, legislators can be expected to cultivate a narrow constituency within the party, and one way to achieve this is by promising narrow benefits. Party leaders, unable to impose their own agenda, maintain power by catering to these demands. With a separately-elected president, the constraints imposed by parliamentary government are lifted, and the president can accomplish little unless he gives narrow benefits to the supporters of individual members of the legislature. Because members do not necessarily represent geographical constituencies, these benefits will not generally take the form of the pork barrel projects familiar in the American system.[14] Instead, they might be subsidies targeted to particular population or business groups spread throughout the country.

Corruption and self-dealing

Now consider illegal corruption and self-dealing. One cannot make a simple one-to-one mapping from systems that provide the most narrow, but legal, benefits to those that are the most corrupt. A system that supplies narrowly-focused benefits does not need illegal payoffs to favor groups that have political clout. A system might have little political corruption simply because groups that could organize to pay bribes find that they do not need to do so.[15]

The two aspects of this analysis are first, the level of excess rents tolerated in the system and second, the proportion of the electorate that needs to pay bribes or commit fraud in order to obtain these rents. For a given level of "slack" in the system, corruption ought to be inversely related to the ability of rent-seekers to obtain individualized, above-board benefits. However, corruption also depends on the ability of politicians to create slack. In an honest system, government may produce a very inefficient mixture of goods, services, and regulatory constraints, but still be productively efficient because no one has an interest in outright waste.[16] With endemic corruption, this is no longer true – politicians create slack and divert the benefits to themselves. In a corrupt system venal politicians and bribe-paying private individuals take the place of honest politicians who allocate benefits to their narrow constituency groups, but the level of rents available for distribution may also increase if politicians are personally corrupt.

Consider the system hypothesized to have the lowest level of narrow benefits: a parliamentary government with party-centered PR voting (4a). In coalition governments, small parties needed to form the coalition may have extortionary power. With corruption, that power can be used for the private enrichment of party leaders since the rank and file in such parties has little leverage with their leaders.[17] Corruption might replace many of the narrow constituency benefits given to voters since the negotiations over government formation occur after the popular vote. The swing party must give its constituents just enough to keep them from defecting, but this may be much less than the total benefits transferred. There may be a corrupt, clientelistic equilibrium where no party has an incentive to provide an honest alternative to the voters. This result can occur when no one party can obtain majority control. Then every party knows that it must be part of a coalition in order to govern, and no party wants to discourage potential partners by pledging not to pay them off. In short, there are two possible equilibria: one with honest parties that provide public goods, and another with corrupt parties that provide a mixture of narrow benefits to voters and corrupt gains to party leaders. Overall, I would not expect such systems to rank at the top of the honesty scale. Notice that measures of the competitiveness of the political system are unlikely to be good proxies for its honesty. Party-centered PR (4a) provides incentives for honest politicians to provide broad-based public goods, but the very lack of local accountability that produces this result can help maintain a corrupt equilibrium. If the party leadership is corrupt, it will want a closed-list system as a means of controlling members through control of positions on the list. Even if those at the top of the system are not corrupt, the leadership may protect less powerful members to preserve the party's image.[18] This case raises a fundamental tension in constitutional design. Accountability to constituents may be obtained through the route of clientelistic politics. Conversely, systems capable of producing public goods can, under other conditions, produce corrupt and autocratic party bosses.

Next consider the second-ranked system on the narrow-benefit scale – the Westminster parliamentary system (3). Plurality-rule voting will, under plausible conditions, produce two parties that alternate in power. This eliminates the need for coalition formation and thus reduces the extortionary power of third parties.[19] Also, individual corrupt politicians can be voted out of office without the party losing power. Even if the party leadership assigns candidates to districts, voters who learn of the malfeasance of an incumbent can vote against him at the same time as the party wins an election. If both major parties are corrupt, it can be in the interest of one to promise to restore honesty to government and that party can expect to attract voters opposed to corruption. Thus a case in which all parties are corrupt can shift to a case in which all are honest if one party changes strategy. The high-corruption outcome can be unstable. The bilateral nature of political competition will both minimize the share of constituency benefits that can be diverted to corruption, and limit the ability of the state to increase the level of state intervention and spending in order to increase rents for the rulers. In short, subject to the problem outlined next, I would rank Westminster democracies (3) as least corrupt, above parliamentary systems with closed-list PR (4a).

The exceptions that could place a Westminster democracy lower on the corruption scale, will be ones where a plurality rule system fails to produce two national parties (see Myerson 1993, and Cox 1997). In particular, parties with no national constituency can win at the state level. Then the formation of a national government may be similar to a PR system with no majority party. Even if there are only one or two national umbrella parties, the local branches may be strongly independent and be able to hold out for narrow constituency benefits or corrupt payoffs for regional party leaders. The key issue is whether party leaders need to negotiate with other parties or factions to create a workable government. The leaders may be unable to amass a fortune themselves, but they may organize the state to facilitate payoffs which flow to those who are needed as allies.

Behind these two systems come the presidential systems (1, 2a, 2b). The president's control over rents is important (Kunicova 2000), but the three systems differ in the executive's need to share these rents with legislative leaders to obtain other political goals. Holding other factors constant, presidential malfeasance will be deterred by the costs and risks of having to make expensive deals with the legislature that reduce the benefits of corruption and also increase the risk of scandal. Conversely, the legislature will be more corrupt the easier it is for its members to extract rents from its interactions with the president.

Of course, not all factors are held constant in practice. Many presidents have the authority to issue decrees with legal force (Carey and Shugart 1998, Shugart 1992: 63–6), and this can obviously make them the target of corrupt offers independent of legislative organization. Veto authority and the exclusive right to introduce certain kinds of laws also vary across presidential systems (Shugart 1992: 61–8). In the United States, for example, although the president has veto power over legislation, he has very limited decree authority compared with his Latin American counterparts and has no exclusive agenda-setting powers over legislation. The more independent power a president has to act unilaterally or to constrain legislative actions, the greater the temptation to substitute private self-seeking for the public good.

In ranking presidential systems, I hold this aspect of presidential power constant and instead focus on the president's need to obtain the cooperation of the legislature. A fragmented legislature is beneficial for a corrupt chief executive because he only needs to buy off a majority to leave groups of legislators without significant bargaining power (Rasmusen and Ramseyer 1994). The president is potentially most corrupt in systems where the legislative parties are weak since he can expect to retain a higher proportion of the corrupt gains. Parties are weak in two cases: a US-style system (1) and candidate-centered PR (2b).

It is difficult to rank these two systems in the abstract, but I tentatively place the PR system ahead of plurality rule simply because it implies some degree of national level party organization that can bargain with the president.[20] Least favorable to presidential corruption is a legislature elected with party-centered or closed-list PR since it will produce strong party leaders capable of striking a hard bargain to share the gains. The presence of these leaders may keep the president from even proposing corrupt deals in the first place. Thus once corruption is added to the picture, I tentatively conclude that a US-style system looks more vulnerable to self-seeking than other types of presidential systems, even candidate-centered systems such as open-list PR.

However, that is not the end of the story. We also need to know if legislators give legal or illegal benefits to supporters and if the party leaders keep funds for themselves. In a US-style system, legislators need to provide benefits to supporters and do not necessarily need to pay bribes to do this. If the legislature is elected by candidate-centered PR (2b), a similar dynamic holds although the benefits will be less geographically focused. With party-centered PR (2a), however, groups of constituents have little clout unless they are members of a small strategic party. Thus party leaders can take most of the rents for themselves. This produces an ambiguous result that depends upon whether one focuses on the president or the legislature. Party-centered PR looks good for corrupt party bosses and bad for corrupt presidents unless the two groups can combine into a single autocratic political machine. Then a system that seems ideal to those who seek to give politicians an incentive to provide public goods turns out to be a potent bribe-generating machine when controlled by corrupt leaders.

Although he does not discuss corruption, Shugart's data on electoral rules in presidential systems can help illustrate my points concerning presidential systems. He classifies electoral formulas as party-centered (closed-list PR), candidate-centered (open-list PR or single non-transferable vote), or intermediate (plurality rule in single-member districts). The main difference between his approach and my own is that I do not necessarily place plurality voting systems in the intermediate category once corruption is added to the mix. In Shugart's data there are five presidential systems with weak parties (Peru, Brazil, Colombia, Taiwan, and Uruguay); five intermediate cases (Georgia, Russia, South Korea, and Philippines), and twelve with strong parties. In the latter category it seems important to distinguish between states that he judges as having strong presidents (Argentina, Chile) and the rest (Guatemala, Bolivia, Dominican Republic, Costa Rica, El Salvador, Honduras, Mexico, Nicaragua, Paraguay, and Venezuela) (Shugart 1992: 74, 76). My argument predicts that, holding other factors constant, the most corrupt presidents will be in Shugart's "intermediate" cases, followed by the weak-party and the strong-party states. Conversely, when the parties are strong and face relatively weak presidents, party leaders can initiate corrupt deals. Thus one should look for corruption among party leaders in the seven countries in this category.

Finally, consider Argentina and Chile, the two cases with strong presidents and strong parties. Here we can imagine that the two branches are in a bargaining game. In Shugart's formulation Argentina and Chile have government structures that encourage the legislature and the president to develop divergent interests. The strength of the president, however, makes him the dominant actor especially in Argentina where he has extensive decree power. Yet the countries are far apart on widely-used measures of overall corruption. Chile ranked nineteenth, just below the United States, and Argentina ranked seventy-first out of ninety-nine in the Transparency International Corruption Perceptions Index.[21] The differences illustrate the point that strong presidential powers can either produce pressures to produce public goods or provide incentives to organize the state for private gain.

The remaining case, a parliamentary system with candidate-centered PR (4b), can have very high or very low levels of corruption depending upon the amount of "slack," or, in other words, the level of competition for political office and the tolerance of the voters for corruption. This system might be quite low in corruption if the weakness of the political coalitions means that no one is able to extract many rents. Conversely, it might be very corrupt if the system becomes a rent-seeking free-for all with politicians seeking to extract whatever private benefits they can from a system that discourages professionalism and party loyalty.

In terms of constitutional structure, I would rank Westminster democracies (3) as least corrupt, followed by parliamentary systems with party-centered PR (4a). The presidential systems come next with the president being least corrupt in party-centered PR systems (2a) followed by candidate-centered PR (2b) and plurality-rule systems (1). The ranking for the legislature is the reverse. Overall corruption will depend upon other features of the political system that determine the relative power of the president and the legislature. Type (4b), a parliamentary system with candidate-centered PR, cannot be ranked because its position on the list depends significantly on the relative importance of the available rents, and the ability of individual politicians to extract these rents. Thus, I would expect parliamentary systems with either plurality or party-centered PR voting systems to be both the least corrupt and the least focused on supplying legal but narrow benefits. The presidential systems are next on both counts, but the rankings of different kinds of presidential systems may vary.

Constitutional structure, however, is not the only variable. One also needs to acknowledge the active role of wealthy private interests. In other words, it is not just the president and party leaders who seek to create "slack" and to divert it to their own uses. Private groups also actively work to obtain benefits either legally or corruptly depending upon the nature of the political system and their own scruples. Contracts or licenses to supply public services are an obvious source of payoffs. The government program can be justified on public interest grounds, but its implementation is excessively expensive because of inflated contract prices. Those who seek corrupt influence will focus on the politicians with influence who are cheapest to purchase. Everything else being equal, these will be representatives with safe seats facing little opposition, "sure losers" facing certain electoral defeat, or those who are planning to retire either voluntarily or through the operation of term limits. Term limits spur corruption by placing politicians in an end game in which they are sure that they will not be returned to office (Rose-Ackerman 1978: 15–58). Since presidents face term limits in all functioning presidential systems, this is another reason to expect relatively high levels of corruption in presidential systems (Kunicova 2000). Some systems apply term limits to members of the legislature as well.

When wealthy organized interests exist on both sides of an issue, party leaders and agenda setters may encourage competitive bribe offers and may even threaten to introduce damaging legislation as a means of extorting payoffs (McChesney 1997, Rose-Ackerman 1978: 48–51). If a single party or a stable coalition controls the government, it may be able to extract a large share of the gains from corrupt deals especially when organized interests are in competition.

Those scholars who emphasize the rent-creating character of government, favor systems with strong separation of powers such as the United States presidential system because it makes deadlock more likely, and deadlock is seen as a valuable check on rent-seeking. The problem with such theories is that they both ignore the valuable public goods that government can provide, and, for all their cynicism, they are oddly optimistic about the problem of corruption. Divided government makes it harder for citizens to hold government accountable. Corrupt presidents can buy off those who are cheapest to purchase, and they prefer legislatures with weak parties who cannot exert much bargaining power. Parliamentary governments, especially those elected by PR, have a different problem of accountability. A voter may support a party with a clear platform only to find that it has made many compromises in order to become part of the governing coalition. If there are a number of different possible governing coalitions, however, a situation can arise in which no one coalition has enough room to organize the government to produce slack which could be converted into corrupt gains. Some groups of voters may gain more than others do, but self-dealing by politicians would seem to be more difficult. The exception in any system is a configuration of political forces that entrenches one party in power over a long period of time whether it be the Christian Democrats in Italy, the Liberal Democrats in Japan, or the Institutionalized Revolutionary Party in Mexico. The presence or absence of a strong president is likely to be relatively unimportant in such systems since the dominant party plays the role of monopolist instead of the president.

Summary

Figure 3.2 summarizes my claims. These speculations need both empirical testing and a more nuanced theoretical analysis, but I present them here in a preliminary attempt to provoke further thought. The rankings reflect a judgment about the confluence of both opportunities and incentives. The basic dimensions along which systems vary are the loci of power, the kinds of possible public programs, and the links between voters' preferences and politicians' actions. Clearly, many other factors affect the level of corruption and public good provision in the real world, but on the margin, these features of democratic governments ought to have an impact. My goal is both to emphasize the fact the democracy should not be viewed as a unified category, and to argue that the analysis of corruption and self-dealing needs a somewhat different emphasis from the analysis of government service provision. The distinctive features are the benefits of waste to the venal and the politicians' post-election efforts to form coalitions that can support honest pork barrel projects or dishonest corrupt deals. The differences in the rankings between the two columns in the figure arise from the independent role of parties in legislatures that operate through inter-party coalitions.

Buying political influence

So far I have assumed that voters are a check on political corruption. If they know about it, they will penalize corrupt incumbents. Corruption occurs after the election as politicians try to use their offices for personal gain. However, payoffs for personal enrichment are only part of the problem in democracies. In addition, corruption scandals are frequently associated with the financing of political campaigns. Elections must be financed, and wealthy interests concerned with legislative outcomes and government policy may be willing to foot the bill.

Democratic political systems must find a way to finance political campaigns without encouraging the sale of politicians to contributors. Governments have drawn the line between legal and illegal gifts in quite different ways, and legal frameworks vary greatly in the limits they place on quid pro quo deals by politicians. Once again, there is a tradeoff between legal and illegal payments. A system that has very strict rules on legal campaign contributions may simply encourage illegal payoffs that are kept secret from voters.

Like those who pay illegal bribes, those who give funds to elected officials expect help in the legislative process. They may also expect special treatment on individual problems in dealing with the bureaucracy or in seeking contracts and concessions. The electoral process can discipline politicians to represent the interests of their constituents, and voters may penalize candidates who seem too deeply beholden to special interests. But voters cannot act unless they know how their representatives behave and who has given them money. Legal gifts can have a corrupting effect if they need not be made public and if the quid pro quo is not itself obvious to voters.[22] In all democratic political systems some gifts to politicians violate domestic laws, and even when the legal restrictions on fund raising seem permissive, politicians and their wealthy patrons may prefer the anonymity of an illegal gift. Keeping a gift secret can help hide the illicit quid pro quo and will facilitate efforts to siphon off funds for personal use.

The worry about undue influence would be of little concern if campaign funds were unimportant to electoral success. Then strict legal spending limits could be enforced. However, although empirical work has not conclusively determined the impact of campaign donations on electoral success, politicians and contributors certainly act as if money matters (Snyder 1992). The link between campaign funds and influence remains a persistent concern of critics of the American political system because the high cost of congressional races must be raised from private sources (Etzioni 1988).

Constitutional structure and campaign donations

Consider the relationship between the stylized political systems discussed above and the incentives to pay and to accept legal or illegal campaign funds in return for a quid pro quo. From the point of view of those who make contributions, their willingness to pay will be a function of the tendency of the state to provide narrow benefits. Even when the state provides public goods, however, it may need to contract with particular firms to produce the public service – be it a highway, a school, or a power plant. In addition, contributors must be able to estimate who is likely to have the power to deliver benefits after the election. If a particular party seems likely to win the election, and if it has the power and the incentive to initiate pork barrel projects and to provide regulatory and tax benefits, then wealthy groups who hope for favors have an incentive to contribute. They may even end up in a destructive race with each other. If there are two parties vying for power, both are likely to receive gifts as an insurance policy. If the legislature is fragmented into a multitude of small parties, or if open-list PR undermines party strength, however, contributions to legislators may not seem worthwhile since it is unclear who will be able to deliver on his or her promises. The presidential candidates are then the only politicians likely to receive large donations unless the whole system is so fractured and the president so weak that there is little chance that the state can assert much power. Thus, the donors' interest in giving to the powerful may stimulate donations in just those political systems that otherwise predispose incumbents to provide broad-based public goods. Thus, we see again in another form a basic puzzle of democratic government. Is it better to have legislators who are responsible to narrow constituencies so voters will monitor their actions, or is it better to have national parties with broad agendas whose candidates have no ties to particular groups of voters? The risk of the former is that government will produce goods and services focused only on narrow groups and will neglect broad public concerns. The risk of the latter is that the "national" politicians will behave in unaccountable ways, becoming corrupt or, at least, beholden to wealthy donors.

The recent campaign finance scandals in Germany illustrate the way an important political grouping can use its position illegally to entrench its political power. Germany is a parliamentary system with two dominant parties, at least one of which is expected to be part of any federal or state government. Recent revelations of illegal campaign contributions to the Christian Democratic Party involved secret contributions both from industrialists with close government ties, such as military contractors, and from those with something to gain from the reunification of East and West Germany. Reunification produced a one-time push to privatize East German firms and to carry out public works projects. These policies provided benefits to the country's citizens, but they also provided profitable opportunities for many private firms. Not surprisingly, these firms competed vigorously for the privatized firms and for construction contracts. For some, this competition took the form of illegal contributions to the Christian Democrats. The CDU has admitted that it accepted secret donations at both the national and state levels, but the links between donations and government decisions are not easy to make because the identity of some donors is unknown. Nevertheless, several cases have come to light.

The first involves the sale of a chemical plant in eastern Germany to the French oil firm Elf Aquitane. Observers allege that kickbacks of 80 million DM were paid to CDU officials believed to have influence. The eventual deal was a very favorable one for Elf which received German government guarantees and a network of gasoline stations in the east. However, it is not clear how much influence those paid actually had over the outcome, and it is not known how the total was divided between the private bank accounts of the lobbyists and CDU party coffers. The second allegation involves the sale of thirty-six tanks made by the German company Thyssen to Saudi Arabia in 1990–1. The German government's decision to permit the sale was said to have been influenced by heavy secret campaign contributions to the CDU. Lending credibility to this claim is information indicating that the government tried to keep the deal hidden from the public. The third case is the sale of housing owned by Germany's railway monopoly to a consortium that included one member who made public contributions to the CDU. The winners made a bid that was one billion DM less than that of a rival Japanese company. The campaign gift thus apparently violated the law's requirement that no gifts should be made "in the obvious expectation of a certain economic and political advantage."[23] In general, the scandals give the impression of a party leadership that accumulated secret funds to advance its own political agenda and that used its power to give potential donors the impression that payoffs were necessary to achieve their goals. They illustrate how otherwise worthy projects can be misused for partisan advantage – especially if the illegal donations are kept secret.

As another example, consider Italy. The testimony of Italian political operatives in the Clean Hands investigations reveals how corrupt practices can become entrenched in nominally democratic systems (Colazingari and Rose-Ackerman 1998). Party leaders placed would-be politicians in positions where the payment of bribes was routine (della Porta 1996: 354–8). Specialized "party cashiers" managed the collection of bribes and the distribution of contracts. They collected bribes for the party coffers, but some share of the gains was also kept by individuals (ibid.: 358–60). Illegal contributors had quite specific favors they wanted from the state, and there was a large discrepancy between the amount the firms reported giving and the amount the political parties reported receiving (Colazingari and Rose-Ackerman 1998). Such examples could be drawn from any established democracy. My point is simply that the presence of national parties is no protection against illegal campaign donations. They may even facilitate such practices by permitting politicians to organize for the extortion of "gifts."

Reform

In light of the need to finance campaigns and the risks of undue influence, what policies might be effective? Disclosure is one obvious option. In a highly competitive political system with informed voters who do not expect personal favors for themselves (party-centered PR, for example), a policy of prompt and complete disclosure might be sufficient. Any politician or party that relied too heavily on special interest money and voted accordingly would be defeated. More direct restrictions are needed, however, if the system is not very competitive and if voters are poorly informed. Without spending limits, politicians have leeway to favor large contributors, and the gifts can themselves be used to mislead voters as to the candidates' positions and behavior.

A basic problem in the design of campaign finance systems is trying to avoid imposing restrictions that themselves encourage illegality. Limits on donations are justified as a way to curb corrupt influences (Connolly 1996: 496), but strict legal limits can encourage unreported illegal transfers. For example, the Japanese system in force between 1975 and 1993 encouraged illegal payoffs by limiting legal business contributions (Quinn 1996: 207–8). The recently imposed ban on corporate contributions in Japan may produce a similar result. In 1995 France outlawed contributions from companies and trade unions.[24] This law may result in an increase in secret illegal contributions that make public accountability more difficult.

Recent scandals in industrialized countries point to the importance of both clear rules governing the solicitation of private money and the provision of sufficient legal sources of funds. Furthermore, the impact of corporate gifts depends upon the ability of politicians to provide individualized favors to firms. If the political system is one that encourages the provision of narrow benefits, the difference between bribes and legal campaign contributions will be blurred and will depend, first, on reporting requirements and, second, on the reaction of voters. An entrenched system of illegal payoffs may undermine efforts to reform the funding of political campaigns. In Italy campaign finance rules seem quite permissive. Yet illegal contributions featured prominently in recent anti-corruption cases (Colazingari and Rose-Ackerman 1998). Reformers need to look beyond the details of the campaign finance law to begin to understand how the basic political structure affects the discretion of politicians to favor gift-givers.

The debate over campaign finance reform in the United States has focused mainly on the undue influence afforded to large givers (Koszcuk 1997, Tanenbaum 1995). This has led to calls for public financing and a modest attempt along these lines has been in place for presidential races since 1974 (Quinn 1996: 212–16). One solution has been publicity. Firms must form Political Action Committees in order to make donations, and all gifts must be reported. All fifty states also have legislation requiring that donations be reported, but enforcement is quite weak, and loopholes are easy to find (Alexander 1991). In many states and at the federal level, contributions to political parties are not presently restrained.[25]

Solutions can approach the problem from four dimensions. First, the costs of political campaigns could be reduced by reducing the length of time for the campaign. Parliamentary systems where the date of the next election is uncertain can enforce such constraints fairly well, but in all systems time limits are hard to make operational. Restrictions could also be imposed on the methods of campaigning in an effort to keep costs down. Second, stronger disclosure rules could be established. The United States already has quite strong disclosure requirements, but many records are not made public until well after the election has taken place (Alexander 1991: 76–8). Disclosure not only permits citizens to vote against candidates who receive too much special interest money but also makes it possible for scholars to study the impact of gifts on behavior to see how close to bribes they are. One pair of scholars, however, suggests just the opposite plan. Ian Ayres and Jeremy Bulow (1998) recommend that all donations should be anonymous so that no quid pro quo is possible. This idea invites donors to find ways to cheat, but if successful, it would probably discourage contributions from all but the most ideological donors. Thus it would need to be supplemented with a system of public financing such as those outlined below.

Third, laws in many countries and in the American states limit individual donations, and other laws limit candidates' spending. However, in the United States, the Supreme Court has struggled with the tension between the goals of campaign finance reform and the protection of speech. It has found contribution limits in the federal law consistent with the protection of free speech, but lower limits in some state laws have been struck down by the federal courts (Connolly 1996). The basic issue is important: to what extent can a democratic government interfere with its citizens' wishes to express their political interests through gifts to support political parties or individual candidates? Democracies need to find ways to limit quid pro quo deals without suppressing debate.

Fourth, alternative sources of funds can be found in the public sector. In the United States the federal government provides funds only for presidential candidates under certain conditions, and several American states provide public support for political campaigns (Tanenbaum 1995). Many other countries provide public funds for political campaigns or permit tax deductions or credits (Kaltefleiter and Naßmacher 1994, Quinn 1996). A number of proposals have been made for more extensive public funding in the United States. Those who oppose these reforms worry that public funding and spending limits will protect incumbents and unduly disadvantage non-major parties. Public funding formulas could be designed to overcome the incumbency advantage, but the design of a workable system may be difficult.[26]

Alternatively, public funds could be given to candidates who can demonstrate substantial public support. Bruce Ackerman (1993) has argued that this might be done by giving vouchers to voters to support the candidates of their choice. This plan would combine public funding with an egalitarian system for allocating funds. In promoting democratic values, this plan would reduce the influence of wealthy interests. If not well-monitored, however, it might increase illegal payments. Wealthy individuals and firms with strong interests in politics would find an important legal avenue to influence closed. The result could be more under-the-table payoffs, especially to the losers in the race for vouchers.

Campaign finance reform needs to be carefully designed if it is not to introduce new incentives for malfeasance by closing off formerly legal alternatives. The issue is closely related to the discussion of constitutional structure in the previous section. If politicians have little incentive to provide public goods or to avoid corrupt payoffs, an effective legal system of campaign finance will be difficult to create. In contrast, a more public-goods oriented system ought to be easier to reform so long as voters are themselves interested in monitoring their political leaders. Otherwise, the politicians' greater distance from their constituents' day-to-day concerns can simply lead them to act with impunity; collecting campaign funds from favor seekers during the electoral campaign and supplying favors in return for bribes once in office.

Achieving anti-corruption reform in democracies

Figure 3.2 proposed a ranking of democracies in terms of the predicted level of corruption holding other factors constant. One implication is that anti-corruption reforms may require fundamental constitutional change. That is, indeed, one issue that needs to be considered in dysfunctional systems, but I do not mean to imply either that reform is impossible in systems that rank low or that high-ranking systems need not be concerned with reform. Thus, we need to consider not only constitutional fundamentals, but also the contingent factors that can produce a political coalition that supports change.

There are two basic models of the reform process: one based on the exercise of political power and the other based on a contractual model of consensus. Those who expect to lose from reform can be outvoted and out-maneuvered, or they can be co-opted or compensated to accept change. A key strategic decision for reformers is whom to include in their coalition and whom to force to accept the costs of reform. Should one buy off corrupt officials and private persons and firms, or should one shut them out of the reformed system? How much will reform goals be undermined by the process of generating a coalition to support change?

Although I have demonstrated how corruption can coexist with electoral politics, democratic governments are sometimes able to reform. The examples of reform that have been most thoroughly studied, however, involve not outright corruption, but the webs of connections and favoritism that accompany patronage networks in government employment. Nevertheless, they provide some general lessons about when durable reform can occur. In the nineteenth century the United States, Great Britain, and many urban American governments reformed their systems of public employment and procurement. Some Latin American countries with democratic structures have also had reform periods.

Barbara Geddes' (1991, 1994) work on civil service reform in Latin

American democracies provides a useful starting point. Assume that politicians and parties want to remain in power. They may then face what Geddes calls the "politicians' dilemma" where the country as a whole would benefit from an end to patronage, but no individual politician or political party has an incentive unilaterally to institute a merit system. Anyone who did so would give up votes to the opposition with no corresponding political benefit. Geddes then postulates a case in which the public benefits of reform are recognized by voters. A politician who advocates reform gains political support that can be balanced against the losses from the reduction in patronage jobs. Obviously, a minority party, with little hope of becoming part of a future government, can support reform more easily than a majority or governing party. In fact, the minority party may face a paradox. If its reform position is popular enough to give it a real chance of winning the next election, that very fact may make it a less enthusiastic reformer. Once a party obtains power, it may violate its electoral promises with the result that voters do not believe subsequent promises, discouraging such promises in the future.

Geddes argues that politicians and political parties in Latin America recognize the dilemma of reform. In her analysis there are two situations in which reform is possible. First, a single party may have a dominant position, but government inefficiency, caused by corruption and patronage, threatens its hold on power. Then it may support reform in spite of the costs borne by public officials. Elections, even if they always return the same party to power, have a constraining effect on the ruling party. Second, if several parties are evenly matched in their access to patronage appointments, and if they will benefit symmetrically from reform, they may be able to collaborate to legislate change. Colombia, Uruguay, and Venezuela provide examples of reforms carried out during periods of balance in access to patronage. In Colombia a further factor encouraging reform was partisan violence that threatened the democratic framework. All sitting politicians had an interest in reforms that would help end this violence. This argument about political balance applies to any of the political systems discussed above although it is another vote in favor of a Westminster system since it tends to produce two major parties that may be capable of bargaining over reform.

Balanced political parties are not sufficient, however. An important deterrent to reform is the personalized nature of politics. The greater the importance of personalized circles of support, the harder it will be to carry out broad-based reforms. Supporting my earlier discussion of closed-list and open-list PR, Geddes argues that voting by closed-list proportional representation facilitated the reform effort in Colombia and Uruguay because the voting rule limited the conflicts between individual politicians and political parties. In an open-list system patronage ought to be especially difficult to eliminate because individualized benefits to voters and campaign workers loom large. In fact, the two systems that did not reform, Brazil and Chile, both had open-list systems. Coalition governments in Chile, whose members had little in common, were held together by patronage. However, the contrast between closed- and open-list proportional representation is about necessary, not sufficient conditions. Thus under a closed-list system the rank and file will not be harmed by reform, but no reform will occur if party leaders use their positions to illicitly enrich themselves or their parties.

The Latin American experience has generally been quite disheartening. Political coalitions for reform are possible, but they are often fragile. Not only do some democratic forms make reform politically difficult, but even when reform does occur, it may not last. All of Geddes' "success" stories are followed by periods of breakdown when patronage, corruption, and inefficiency reappeared. Reforms are likely to be fragile if they are the product of temporarily favorable political conditions. To be sustained, the first stage of reform ought to be implemented to produce supporters who push to maintain and extend the initial successes. This is an important factor over and above the concern with democratic structure that animates Barbara Geddes' work and that is central to the analysis in the first part of this chapter.

For additional insight on these issues consider civil service reform in the United States and Great Britain in the nineteenth century. An emphasis on the balance of political forces seems relevant in both the United States and Great Britain. When reform occurred, both used first-past-the-post voting rules that typically produced two balanced parties alternating in power. No political grouping benefited disproportionately from its access to patronage, and all shared in the benefits of reform. Britain's parliamentary system, with strong party discipline, limited the scope for individual favor seeking. Even though members represented individual districts, they had a limited ability to trade favors for votes. The increase in the size of the electorate in the nineteenth century and the elimination of many small constituencies reduced the benefits of patronage appointments (Parris 1969: 70–1).

In the United States party discipline did not prevail, a factor that discouraged reform, and, in fact, reform did come later in the United States than in Britain. The separately elected president at the head of the executive branch, however, could view the tradeoff between patronage and service efficiency from a national perspective. By the late nineteenth century, a bipartisan political coalition that included the president supported the Pendleton Act that started the federal government on the road to establishing a civil service system (Maranto and Schultz 1991: 30–6, 50–5). Both countries demonstrate the strains that arise when some constituents care about the efficiency and fairness of the services provided by the state, and others just want jobs and corrupt favors. The strains are of two kinds: giving out government jobs and contracts can become a political cost instead of a benefit, and managing the conflict between constituents who want favors and those who want efficient service can be difficult. If the quality of government services begins to loom large in voters' minds, politicians – both legislators and cabinet secretaries – may begin to doubt the political benefits of patronage. The relative political salience of particularized benefits relative to public goods can shift over time even if the underlying constitutional structure remains constant.

In the United States and Britain politicians complained about how much time and energy they spent dealing with job-seekers (Chester 1981: 155–6; Johnson and Libecap 1994; Maranto and Schultz 1991; Parris 1969: 50–79). If the number of jobs is not expanding rapidly, many applicants will be disappointed. The number of the disgruntled and their families may vastly exceed the number of satisfied patronage appointees. Dispensing patronage becomes a nuisance, not a privilege (Chester 1981: 155–6; Parris 1969: 71). Neither the United States nor Britain experienced revenue windfalls during the reform period, so that fiscal constraints made the distribution of jobs politically costly. The situation in Venezuela provides a useful contrast. There, windfall oil profits undermined reform efforts as the state went on a hiring spree (Geddes 1994). In other countries statist policies require large numbers of state sector employees to staff state firms. The very size of the state sector lowers the political costs of patronage, as it increases the economic costs.

Reform politicians in America and England mobilized powerful business support for a more efficient public service. Nineteenth-century business interests wanted a post office that delivered the mail effectively, and they wanted their merchandise to pass through customs quickly. They might be willing to bribe individual customs agents for speedy service, but they generally preferred a system that eliminated such payoffs (Johnson and Libecap 1994). Businessmen may tolerate a certain level of corruption, but begin to protest if the level of graft escalates, as it apparently did in urban America in the latter part of the nineteenth century. Urban reform in the United States was given a push when graft levels increased from 10 to 30 percent of the value of contracts and benefits (Calvert 1972). In developing and transition countries businesses have voiced similar objections in the present day. For example, in Brazil President Collor's downfall was hastened by his reputed decision to increase "commissions" from an average of 15 percent of the value of deals under the previous regime to 40 percent (Fleischer 1997: 302; Manzetti and Blake 1996: 676).

In short, even with no fundamental change in the constitutional structure, the costs of allocating jobs and contracts through patronage and payoffs may come to outweigh the benefits for political leaders. In a democracy not everyone need support reform; it can be carried out if enough voters begin to see that it will be, on balance, beneficial. Reform ought to be more likely in governments with constitutional frameworks that limit the ability of politicians to benefit from patronage and corruption, and in systems where power is balanced across political groupings. Nevertheless, the United States reformed in the nineteenth century in spite of the lack of strong parties. The existence of a separately elected president subject to powerful electoral pressures helped, but part of the explanation appears to be the growing importance to voters and business interests of competently provided public services.

Conclusion

Democratic elections are not necessarily a cure for corruption. Instead, some electoral systems are more vulnerable to special interest influence than others. If narrow groups wield power, some groups use legal means, and others are corrupt. The choice of tactics can be influenced by the nature of the political system. In all democracies competitive elections help limit corruption because opposition candidates have an incentive to expose corrupt incumbents. However, the voting rules used to select the legislature, the existence of a separately elected president, and the need to finance political campaigns introduce incentives to favor special interests that do not exist in autocratic regimes.

The tendency of political systems to provide narrowly focused goods and services instead of broad-based public goods is a familiar complaint about democracy. Constitutional structures differ in their ability to overcome the influence of narrow interests and supply broad-based public services. Past work, however, has not considered corruption as a separate category but has made too simple a contrast between public goods and narrow benefits. I have tried to show that it is valuable to distinguish between benefits that flow to a politician's constituents and those that provide personal enrichment. Structural reforms designed to limit the amount of pork barrel politics may simply lead to higher levels of illegal corruption and to the use of public money and power for the private benefit of politicians and their corrupt supporters. I have isolated some of the features of a democratic government that ought to discourage corruption, everything else being held equal.

The passage of time, however, can produce reform opportunities even in political systems that seems otherwise inhospitable to reform. Furthermore, even systems at the top of the integrity list in Figure 3.2 may suffer from entrenched corruption until a change in circumstances makes reform possible. These changes include both the growth of a private economic sector that includes firms that demand a well-functioning government and the maturation of the political system to the point where politicians see that they can win elections by appealing to voters' demands for a cleaner and more effective government. Windows of opportunity may open in individual countries that can give reformers a chance to make their case.

Although the value of clean and efficient government to the electorate and the business community will ebb and flow over time, underlying constitutional structures can help or hinder reform efforts. Sometimes the structure of government is itself so dysfunctional that it is difficult to see how anything constructive can be done without fundamental changes in the way the political demands of the electorate are translated into a representative structure. Of course, I am not recommending that every nation adopt a Westminster parliamentary system. One would need to know much more about the underlying political cleavages in the country and about the impact of structure on other aspects of government. All I mean to accomplish here is to alert government reformers to the need to design constitutional systems that give politicians an incentive to provide broad-gauged public goods, and that deter both pork barrel spending and corrupt self-dealing.

Notes

This paper builds on Rose-Ackerman (1999a, 1999b). I wish to thank Bruce Ackerman and Jana Kunicova for helpful discussions on the issues raised in this paper.

1 See, for example, "Bracing for Newest Round of Inquiry in Providence," *New York Times,* March 19 2000; "Former Louisiana Governor Guilty of Extortion on Casinos," *New York Times,* May 10 2000; "US Steps Up Probe of License Selling," *Chicago Tribune,* November 6 1999.
2 Recent German cases are discussed later. On the Italian cases see Colazingari and Rose-Ackerman (1998).
3 Shugart (1992: 57) defines a presidential system as one where (1) the head of government is popularly elected, (2) the cabinet is subordinate to the president and not the assembly, and (3) terms of office are fixed, such that neither the executive nor the legislature can shorten the term of the other for political reasons. Shugart and Carey (1992) introduce several mixed categories with shared (sometimes confused) responsibility over the cabinet and divided substantive authority. They discuss several examples.
4 Carey and Shugart (1995) present a four-fold categorization that appears to exhaust the possibilities and includes several logically possible options with no real world exemplars. Carey and Shugart include four variables: the degree of control party leaders exercise over access to the party label, the degree of vote pooling, the number and type of votes cast, and district magnitude. My goal here, however, is not to provide a comprehensive taxonomy but to contrast party-centered rules (e.g. single-member districts with party endorsement or closed-list PR) with candidate-centered rules such as open-list PR.
5 The examples are from Carey and Shugart (1995). See also Cox (1997). Finland has a president but with limited, well-defined powers in foreign policy and the formation of governments (Shugart and Carey 1992: 61–3).
6 Shugart (1992: 67, 77) points to Mexico as an example where the constitutional powers of the president are weak but where the presidency is powerful because a single party has, until recently, dominated the political landscape.
7 Thus I take the political structure as given and ask how it affects public goods

provision and corruption. Shugart and Carey (1992), in contrast, study the political conditions during the founding period to help explain the choice of constitutional forms.

8 "Legislators in a presidential system with weak parties can readily evaluate every proposal on its merits (for their constituents) rather than on the national policy grounds that inevitably come to dominate decisions to vote for or against executive proposals in parliamentary systems" (Shugart 1998: 10).

9 "In a parliamentary system . . . rank-and-file legislators are in a position neither to blame somebody else nor to hold out and demand concessions. Instead the party stands or falls as a collective unit on the basis of the decisions it takes" (Shugart 1998: 10).

10 Of course, not all presidential systems are alike in the power of the presidency relative to the legislature. Shugart (1992: 61–8) ranks presidential system in terms of the president's veto authority, decree power, and agenda setting authority for certain kinds of legislation. In his sample the strongest presidents are in Argentina and Russia and the weakest in Nicaragua, Paraguay, and Venezuela.

11 A relatively high voter threshold for membership in the parliament can dampen the impact of small parties. Most PR electoral systems set a minimum percentage of the vote that a party must obtain before it obtains a share of the seats in the parliament. A common threshold is five percent of votes cast.

12 I am assuming that both options are available to any particular polity. However, one needs to take seriously Shugart's (1992) claim that most presidential systems do not have the option of shifting to parliamentary systems. He claims that most of them are too divided and too lacking in strong political parties to be able to survive as democracies with a parliamentary structure. This raises an important issue of the direction of causation that I have not explored here.

13 This ranking is consistent with Shugart (1992: 74). He, however, includes other features of the electoral system such as the overlaps in electoral cycles and constituencies between president and legislature.

14 Carey and Shugart (1995: 419) note that the incentive to cultivate a strong personal reputation will not necessarily translate into pork barrel projects if electoral districts are large.

15 Carey and Shugart (1995: 433–4) suggest that empirical work might seek to explain policy outcomes as a function of electoral systems. They suggest that both the incidence of particularity and the levels of corruption might be studied. They recognize that the correlation might not be strong, but they focus only on the cost of political campaigns as creating corrupt incentives.

16 Compare Niskanen (1971) who posited budget-maximizing bureaucrats who make take-it-or-leave-it offers to the legislature. Under plausible conditions the budget is maximized by promising technical efficiency even as the overall level of public services is much too large in Pareto Efficiency terms.

17 Of course, if the critical party has very few seats in the legislature, individual legislators may have leverage since they can threaten to destroy the coalition by switching parties. The small party's leadership will obviously be opposed to this, but even the leaders in the dominant party may prefer to make deals with their counterparts instead of facing a string of members seeking individualized deals. With closed-list PR, the risk for the potential defector is a poor ballot position next time around whether or not he jumps ship. He has clearly identified himself as a person with no party loyalty.

18 In Germany, for example, the strength of the party system helped protect individual corrupt politicians by weakening outside monitoring of individual politicians and by rewarding those who accepted donations in return for legislative quid pro quos (Seibel 1997: 95). Nevertheless, the public outcry over recent

scandals suggests that toleration of practices that were commonplace in the past may be fading.

19 Even here, however, small parties can sometimes wield such power. Suppose that candidates benefit from appearing twice on the ballot under two party labels. Then, as the Liberal Party in New York State has found, a third party can negotiate to endorse major party candidates in return for promised benefits.

20 In these cases some of Carey and Shugart's (1995) variables, especially party control over access to the party label, should be important.

21 1999 Transparency International Corruption Perceptions Index, *TI Newsletter*, December 1999.

22 Sometimes the expectations of a quid pro quo have been quite straightforward. In North Carolina in 1997, a construction firm that did not receive the favor it expected in return for a contribution to the incumbent governor's campaign asked for its money back (K. Sack, "A Road-Building Scandal Forces a Governor's Hand," *New York Times*, January 14 1998, at A10). In the early twentieth century, Canadian firms gave kickbacks to political candidates to help finance their campaigns in return for assistance in obtaining government contracts (Quinn 1996: 197, 230). In Japan, politicians who assist local firms in obtaining contracts allegedly expect a percentage of the price in return (ibid.: 231). During the 1980s in Germany, contributions disguised as charitable contributions were given to political parties in an effort to obtain legislative quid pro quos. At the time, paying members of Parliament for favors was not a punishable offense (Seibel 1997: 94).

23 The discussion of the German case is based on Nesshöver, February 24 2000 and April 10 2000.

24 "Is Europe Corrupt?" *Economist*, January 29 2000: 57–8.

25 Koszcuk (1997); Colorado Republican Federal Campaign Committee v. Federal Election Commission, 518 US 604, 116 S. Ct. 2309 (1996).

26 For example, Minnesota awarded public funds to candidates equal to one-half of the independent expenditures made against them. See Tanenbaum 1995: 156. The provision was overturned by a federal appellate court under the free speech provisions of the United States Constitution, but the Supreme Court has not ruled on this issue (ibid.: 152). One study concluded, however, that the Minnesota law did not succeed in helping challengers. In 1992 incumbents obtained almost $2,000 more in public funds than challengers (Thompson and Moncrief 1998).

Bibliography

Ackerman, B. (1993) "Crediting the Voters: A New Beginning for Campaign Finance," *American Prospect* 13: 71–80.

Alexander, H. (1991) *Reform and Reality: The Financing of State and Local Campaigns*, New York: Twentieth Century Fund.

Ayres, I. and Bulow, J. (1998) "The Donation Booth: Mandating Donor Anonymity to Disrupt the Market for Political Influence," *Stanford Law Review* 50: 837–91.

Calvert, M. A. (1972) "The Manifest Functions of the Machine," in B. M. Stave (ed.), *Urban Bosses, Machines and Progressive Reform*, Lexington, Mass.: D. C. Heath.

Carey, J. and Shugart, M. S. (1995) "Incentives to Cultivate a Personal Vote: a Rank Ordering of Electoral Formulas," *Electoral Studies* 14(4): 417–39.

—— (eds) (1998) *Executive Decree Authority: Calling Out the Tanks or Just Filling Out the Forms?* New York: Cambridge University Press.

Chester, N. (1981) *The English Administrative System 1780–1870*, Oxford: Clarendon.

Colazingari, S. and Rose-Ackerman, S. (1998) "Corruption in Paternalistic Democracy: Lessons from Italy for Latin America," *Political Science Quarterly* 113: 447–70.

Connolly, W. J. (1996) "How Low Can You Go? State Campaign Contribution Limits and the First Amendment," *Boston University Law Review* 76: 483–536.

Cox, G. (1997) *Making Votes Count: Strategic Coordination in the World's Electoral Systems*, Cambridge, UK: Cambridge University Press.

della Porta, D. (1996) "Actors in Corruption: Business Politicians in Italy," *International Social Science Journal* 48: 349–64.

Economist (2000) "Is Europe Corrupt?" January 29: 57–8.

Etzioni, A. (1988) *Capital Corruption: The New Attack on American Democracy*, New Brunswick, NJ: Transaction.

Fleischer, D. (1997) "Political Corruption in Brazil," *Crime, Law and Social Change* 25: 297–321.

Geddes, B. (1991) "A Game-Theoretic Model of Reform in Latin American Democracies," *American Political Science Review* 85(2): 371–92.

—— (1994) *Politician's Dilemma: Building State Capacity in Latin America*, Berkeley, Calif.: University of California Press.

Johnson, R. N. and Libecap, G. D. (1994) "Patronage to Merit and Control of the Federal Labor Force," *Explorations in Economic History* 31: 91–119.

Kaltefleiter, W. and Naßmacher, K-H. (1994) "Das Parteiengesetz 1994-Reform der kleinen schritte," *Zeitschrift Für Parlamentsfragen* 25: 253–62.

Koszcuk, J. (1997) "Nonstop Pursuit of Campaign Funds Increasingly Drives the System," *Congressional Quarterly*, April 5: 770–4.

Kunicova, J. (2000) "Are Presidential Systems More Susceptible to Political Corruption?" manuscript, Department of Political Science, Yale University, New Haven, Conn.

Manzetti, L. and Blake, C. (1996) "Market Reforms and Corruption in Latin America: New Means for Old Ways," *Review of International Political Economy* 3: 662–97.

Maranto, R. and Schultz, D. (1991) *A Short History of the United States Civil Service*, Lanham, Md.: University Press of America.

McChesney, F. S. (1997) *Money for Nothing: Politicians, Rent Extraction and Political Extortion*, Cambridge, Mass.: Harvard University Press.

Myerson, R. (1993) "A Theory of Voting Equilibria," *American Political Science Review* 87: 102–14.

Nesshöver, C. "The CDU Financial Scandal: Facts, Analysis, Outlook, and Possible Consequences, An AICGS Report," www.aicgs.org/issues/CDUAffair.htm (consulted February 24 2000).

—— "The CDU Financial Scandal: An Update, An AICGS Report," www.aicgs.org/issues/CDUAffair2.htm (consulted April 10 2000).

Niskanen, W. (1971) *Bureaucracy and Representative Government*, Chicago: Aldine.

Parris, H. (1969) *Constitutional Bureaucracy: The Development of British*

Central Administration Since the Eighteenth Century, London: Allen and Unwin.

Quinn, A. R. (1996) "National Campaign Finance Laws in Canada, Japan and the United States," *Suffolk Transnational Law Journal* 20: 193–245.

Rasmusen, E. and Ramseyer, M. (1994) "Cheap Bribes and the Corruption Ban: A Coordination Game Among Rational Legislators," *Public Choice* 78: 305–27.

Rose-Ackerman, S. (1978) *Corruption: A Study in Political Economy*, New York: Academic Press.

—— (1999a) *Corruption and Government: Causes, Consequences, and Reform*, Cambridge, UK: Cambridge University Press.

—— (1999b) "Political Corruption and Democracy," *Connecticut Journal of International Law* 14: 363–78.

Seibel, W. (1997) "Corruption in the Federal Republic of Germany Before and in the Wake of Reunification," in D. della Porta and Y. Meny (eds), *Democracy and Corruption in Europe*, 85–102, London: Pinter.

Shugart, M. S. (1992) "Presidentialism, Parliamentarism and the Provision of Collective Goods in Less-Developed Countries," *Constitutional Political Economy* 10: 53–88.

—— (1998) "The Inverse Relationship Between Party Strength and Executive Strength: A Theory of Politicians' Constitutional Choices," *British Journal of Political Science* 28: 1–29.

Shugart, M. S. and Carey, J. (1992) *Presidents and Assemblies: Constitutional Design and Electoral Dynamics*, Cambridge, UK: Cambridge University Press.

Snyder, Jr., J. M. (1992) "Long-Term Investing in Politicians: Or, Give Early, Give Often," *Journal of Law and Economics* 35: 15–43.

TI Newsletter (1999) 1999 Transparency International Corruption Perceptions Index, December.

Tanenbaum, A. S. (1995) "Day vs. Holahan: Crossroads in Campaign Finance Jurisprudence," *Georgetown Law Journal* 84: 151–78.

Thompson, J. and Moncrief, G. F. (1998) *Campaign Finance in State Legislative Elections*, Washington, DC: Congressional Quarterly.

4 Why do voters support corrupt politicians?

Oskar Kurer

Why do voters support corrupt politicians? This question is of vital importance if it is believed that corrupt politicians are often widely popular and that corruption has a detrimental effect on development. The answer to the question shows that democracy is not necessarily a palliative to corruption and that reducing corruption may require political changes that go far beyond the administrative reforms of the "good governance" variety.

This is not to suggest that corruption itself is popular. Indeed, we encounter a widely observed paradox: unpopular corruption and popular corrupt politicians. Despite the apparent aversion to corruption, many voters do support Silvio Berlusconi in Italy, Chart Thai in Thailand, the PRI in Mexico and the Congress Party in India. The paradox deepens when we consider that the "game" of corruption is likely to be negative-sum, thus decreasing the overall gains potentially available to the "players." Why would a majority of voters support politicians that are likely to impoverish their community, which may often include the majority of these voters themselves?

The question is not a widely discussed one. Indeed, one not infrequent ploy is to expunge it by defining democracy in such a way that excludes corruption by definition. Nevertheless, the literature yields a number of suggestions why voters might support corrupt politicians. Much of the clientelism literature attempts to explain the support for corrupt politicians by pointing to voters' desire for particularistic benefits – politicians "helping the people." At the same time, it is acknowledged that the majority of those supposedly helped by such practices are impoverished by the corrupt practices of the same politicians. A further twist is added by the claim that patronage systems serve the interest of voters whose income is low and variable. Although plausible, this claim is empirically unsubstantiated. There is little evidence that such "subsistence insurance" influences voting behavior, since it does not seem to have much practical relevance in modern patronage politics. Cultural explanations have similar weaknesses. They are unable to explain the survival of customs that impoverish precisely those who are supposed to be helped. The cultural explanation is weakened even more if it is accepted that even in non-industrialized countries many people believe that the state ought to treat its citizens impartially. Various forms of elite theories suggest that corruption is related to norms and values of elite groups. However, the little available evidence which attempts to show that elite values and behavior are uninfluenced by societal pressure is not very persuasive. Even if it were so, political changes may still occur if elite values are not homogeneous and if some sections of the elite are willing to respond to the political opportunities generated by societal demands. Perhaps the favorite explanation of corruption relates to "weak party systems." Undoubtedly an empirical link between weak party systems and corruption can be observed, but precisely what this link is and why it exists are less clear.

This chapter proceeds by employing a Schumpeterian market for politics where competing parties offer different policy packages and voters select their preferred options. At its most general, either corruption may reflect the desires of the voters – with which politicians comply – or the voters do not desire corruption but a corruption-free policy package is "not on offer." For obvious reasons the first case – where corruption reflects the desires of the voters – will be called a "demand side," and the second – where a corruption-free policy package is not available – a "supply side" explanation. Major demand-side failures include information failures as to the level and consequences of corruption, the non-existence of alternatives, and collective action problems. On the supply side, barriers to entry seem to play a role in the explanation of democratic failures, albeit as a consequence not of democratic procedures but of their failures. Factionalism might lead to a failure of the democratic process if it results in electoral volatility.

What are the policy implications of this analysis for the debate on "governance"? Concern with "governance" became fashionable again in the late 1980s. In practice, "good governance" is equated with the efficiency of government administration: "the exercise of political power to manage a nation's affairs" (World Bank 1989: 60).[1] This approach has been criticized as being "naive and simplistic" by presenting governance "almost as if it were an autonomous administrative capacity, detached from the turbulent world of politics and the structure and purpose of the state" (Leftwich 1994: 364).[2] Moreover, it effectively excludes the possibility that the causes of corruption may conceivably be found in the (regular) electoral process itself. If this turns out in fact to be the case, reforms aiming at reducing corruption become a vastly different and much more problematic enterprise than the conventional narrowly focused anti-corruption programs. The beloved administrative reforms – reformed salary structures, administrative modes and procedures, methods of selection and training, the disentanglement of the state from society – are in many cases unlikely to yield the results promised by the designers of these anti-corruption campaigns. In fact, they may be economically deleterious by generating additional ineffective layers of bureaucracy and damaging already sclerotic decision-making processes even further.[3] Good government then hinges on the nature of political processes, and fighting corruption becomes a political task.

The paradox of corruption

This first section suggests not only that supporting corrupt politicians is not in the interest of the average voter, but that such voters do not believe it is morally justified to do so. It thus poses the paradox that corrupt politicians ought not to be popular.

Why do people generally condemn corruption? Is it because they are "natural" Weberians who believe in the principle of an efficient state administration? An answer to this question requires a definition of corruption that plausibly connects corruption to popular morality.

The task is simplified by the fact that we can concentrate on administrative corruption. The question of why voters support corrupt politicians is of interest only in a reasonably functioning democracy. A high level of political corruption, through outright electoral fraud, for example, foils the democratic process; democracy and high levels of political corruption therefore being mutually contradictory. In the main, accordingly, this chapter will focus on administrative corruption.

Why is administrative corruption unpopular? Corruption is generally thought of as breaking bureaucratic rules and regulations. It is difficult to believe that popular rejection of corruption is based on a widespread conviction that administrative rules ought not to be broken – not even in the Western world. It is more likely that people oppose corruption because they feel breaking rules is unjust as it violates fundamental rules of equity that are widely shared: the government ought to treat equally people who are equally deserving. Discrimination unrelated to merit is a matter of the private sphere; in the public realm impartiality ought to reign. Thus, administrative discrimination according to likes and dislikes, ethnic or racial criteria, or social distance, is considered unjust. Administration that is not in accordance with rules therefore conflicts with popular morality. One might argue about the morality of one rule or the other, but disregarding rules habitually and independently of their intent and consequences is not generally considered acceptable. This view of popular sentiment conflicts, as will be seen later, with some cultural views on the origin of corruption. Nevertheless, the widespread condemnation of corruption does lend *prima facie* evidence to the view that corruption does conflict with popular morality. On what grounds would people condemn it if not for its injustice?

If it is indeed true that corruption is generally considered illegitimate, support for corruption might still be forthcoming if the practice increases material welfare. How, then, does corruption affect the material welfare of the average voter?

Corruption might affect economic growth through a number of channels. Corruption tends to increase the rate of taxation. Losses of government revenue as well as inefficient expenditures tend sooner or later to force the rate of taxation above the level that would have prevailed in its absence. Higher tax levels in turn influence incentives to save, innovate and invest.[4] Simultaneously, the misallocation of government funds impacts negatively on infrastructure and the provision of public services generally. Misallocation and tax increases may be compounded by a process of increasing rent-seeking: inefficient rules and regulations accumulate in order to increase the scope for bribery, extortion or kickbacks. The level of "corruption tax" may have to be fairly significant to reduce economic growth noticeably. Thailand and Italy provide examples where high levels of corruption have gone hand in hand with rapid economic growth. The critical level has however been exceeded in many sub-Saharan African states where corruption has reduced governments' ability to maintain public infrastructure and education services, and has left them unable to pay the wages of the public service. The enormous costs to private enterprise imposed by such a "state collapse" are by themselves sufficient to impede significant economic development.

Traditionally – and probably rightly – the danger to economic growth was thought to come mainly not from allocation effects but from the high degree of uncertainty generated by corruption. Classical economists have for centuries pointed to the negative effects of uncertainty on savings and investment. To take a later example, Max Weber believed that the "unpredictability and inconsistency" of such a business environment is compatible with some kinds of capitalist enterprises such as trading firms, but that industrial capitalism requires long-term planning and commitment on account of the large quantity of sunk capital and therefore "is altogether too sensitive to all sorts of irrationalities in the administration of law and taxation" (Weber 1968: 240, 1095).[5] These theoretical conclusions are supported by recent empirical research (Mauro 1995, 1998; Keefer and Knack 1997).

If indeed corruption is deemed morally wrong and tends to decrease the average voter's welfare, why do corrupt politicians and parties remain in the business of politics?

Voting for corrupt politics: a survey of explanations

The relationship between democracy and corruption has been examined in a number of ways. First, and most easily dealt with, is the "denial theory" (the next section) which holds that democracy and corruption are incompatible by definition and so the question of why people support corrupt politicians becomes meaningless. The next four approaches, discussed in the subsequent sections, however, provide substantive hypotheses for the prevalence of corruption in a democratic environment. Corruption is desired because of the (expected) material incentives it supplies (although the average voter loses); because norms and values induce people to prefer corruption to administrative rules even if they make themselves thereby worse off (cultural explanations); because problems associated with collective action prevent socially optimal results; or because voters do not have a choice. It will be shown that all these explanations are afflicted with serious flaws.

The "denial thesis"

One way of "proving" that democracy is particularly effective in containing corruption is by way of definition. Thus it is said that

> It is probably fair to argue that democratic regimes, over the long run, engender more powerful antibodies against corruption than systems in which political liberties are stifled. A regime that has frequent elections, political competition, active and well-organized opposition forces, an independent legislature and judiciary, free media, and liberty of expression is bound to generate more limits on the scope and frequency of corruption than one that does not have them.
>
> (Elliott 1997: 11)

Defining "democracy" as an institution that is endowed with an "independent legislature and judiciary" and "well-organized opposition forces" – and therefore stable political parties – leaves very little room for the emergence or persistence of endemic corruption. But what if the judiciary and the political parties are not thus happily constituted? If we are not to deny the label "democracy" to political systems that lack some or all of these antibodies to corruption, the case for an inherent brake on the scope and frequency of corruption weakens considerably.

Another version of this democratic purity thesis eliminates corruption by assuming a particular electoral process. Girling, for example, adopts what Schumpeter called the "classical theory of democracy": there is a well-defined public good, with democratic processes ensuring its realization (Schumpeter 1976: 250). Corruption, in turn, is equated to actions subverting the public good that originate from two sources: "power corruption" or "the abuse of public power for private ends" by those in government (Girling 1997: 3) on the one hand, and on the other "political-economy corruption" or the "intrusions of economic power" (ibid.: 7). In the latter case "market values" are responsible for the fact that "even politicians of integrity find themselves obliged to compromise between the interests of the public (the common good) and the interests of the economy (basically, private appropriation by the few)" (ibid.: 9). Thus self-interest of politicians and the forces of capitalist depravity threaten to derail the success of democratic processes; that voters themselves could act in ways detrimental to the general interest is not considered.

James Mill would have heartily approved: "The Community cannot have an interest opposite to its interest. To affirm this would be a contradiction in terms" (Mill 1823: 8). Only "sinister interests" can force democracy from the path of virtue, an idea, alas, that did not survive for long. Where James Mill advocated universal suffrage, annual parliaments, pledges, and election by ballot as *guaranteeing* "good government," his son abandoned all these planks of Radicalism precisely because he feared that these instruments of popular control *threatened* "good government" (Mill 1861). The possibility of democratic failures had to be faced.

Voters desire corruption: clientelism

In this tradition of analyzing failures of democratic processes, the clientelism literature establishes a causal relation between democracy and corruption: clients and thus voters desire patronage politics because of the material extra-bureaucratic benefits it supplies. Scott, for one, thought that

> As with many "new" electorates, the desire for immediate tangible gain predominates, candidates will find it difficult to provide effective inducements without violating formal standards of public conduct. The pressures to win a majority following make it likely that, in the short run at least, a party will respond to the incentives that motivate its clientele rather than attempt to change the nature of those incentives.
>
> (Scott 1972: 93)

Clientelism and corruption are caused by "the patterns of political beliefs and loyalties that prevail among voters" (ibid.: 104). In the same vein, Riley held that

> there was, in the period [after independence], a contrast between individual expectations of the state and . . . the "Weberian inheritance". Citizens regarded the prime duty of politicians to "help their people", and they viewed the efforts of politicians primarily in instrumental rather than ideological terms.
>
> (Riley 1983: 201)

Considerable evidence supports the observation that clients desired patronage politics and thus corruption. In India, efforts by politicians to create broad organizational support have usually failed "because the ordinary voter has an extremely narrow range of public responsibility and is not willing to give time and effort without the promise of immediate material reward" (Bailey 1963: 135). Similarly, Wade finds the electorate "primarily swayed by material and particularistic inducements" (Wade 1985: 486, 479): "People vote for whom they think can give *them* the most favor, in a particularistic way" (ibid.: 487).

The Thai political system has produced the *"jao pho"* (variously translated as "person of influence" or "godfather"), a usually rural businessman engaged in legal and illegal business activities whose success strongly relies on government patronage, who at the same time enters politics either himself or by financially supporting particular candidates (Phongpaichit and Piriyarangsan 1996: 59–61). Why do people vote for the candidate of the "jao pho"? Apparently partly because of the patronage he dispenses: access to schools, health facilities, credit, donations to temples and so on. Votes might be bought outright (Maisrikrod and McCargo 1997: 139). Fraud and intimidation sometimes play their part (Phongpaichit and Piriyarangsan 1996: 94), without, however, being able to explain why the Chart Thai "was most successful in building support amongst the *jao pho*" and "has been the most successful in electoral terms since the early 1980s" (ibid.: 95).

All these accounts ultimately fail to explain why voters endorse clientelism and corruption. Being "swayed by material and particularistic inducement" (Wade 1985: 486), considering the prime duty of the politicians to "help their people," and viewing politicians' efforts "in instrumental rather than ideological terms" do not explain predatory voting patterns if these efforts reduce the clients' welfare. Undoubtedly some clients do benefit, but the mass of voters lose by these clientelistic practices. The helplessness of this position is nicely illustrated by the claim that the Christian Democratic Party of Catania is "sustained by the support it is able to purchase from its clients in exchange for its distribution of benefits to them. . . . Their [the *apparatichi*] survival as patrons, as well as the survival of the party apparatus, depends upon the votes and consensus of the clients" (Caciagli and Belloni 1981: 37). At the same time it is said that the clients' "interests are subordinate to the interests of the dominant classes" (ibid.: 54).

This fundamental contradiction can be resolved if the assumption that predatory voting patterns reduce the welfare of the clients is relaxed. In principle, clients can gain by attracting a disproportionate amount of benefits and shifting the costs of corruption to non-clients. The more localized corruption is, the more plausible this case becomes. Geographic "pockets" of clientelistic networks can benefit from corruption by establishing financially rewarding links to central government, providing vote banks to national politicians or parliamentary support to governments in return. Since the costs of corruption are borne by the nation as a whole, the members' share of the costs will be less than their gains. Perhaps the Thai case is partly of this kind: an urban Bangkok agglomeration less given to corruption in contrast with rural communities where it spreads. Those rural areas might well benefit as long as growth-retarding endemic corruption does not spread to the economically dynamic parts of the country.

The more pervasive clientelism is, however, the smaller the likelihood that supporting corrupt patrons will indeed maximize welfare. Moreover, time horizons play an important role in this argument. Not only are clientelistic redistribution games – such as in Kenya – negative-sum in the short run (Easterly and Levine 1997: 1217), they become even more difficult to understand when the time horizon is longer, and the probability of a future loss of the dominant position and of retribution is taken into account. Thus the clientelist position is plausible enough in the case of local corrupt pockets acting as free-riders, but not in what constitutes the most important and interesting case, that of pervasive support of corrupt politicians by a majority of voters.

A further attempt to salvage the clientelist position integrates risk and poverty into the argument. Senegalese, it is said, are concerned first and foremost with "day-to-day survival in an economy that is perpetually in crisis. . . . In this sense, Senegal's political economy has reinforced the country's political culture based on patrimonialism" (Beck 1999: 211). Why would the poor support a system that keeps them that way?

The most sophisticated argument couples poverty with risk aversion. The proposition sounds sensible enough: as poor people's income is close to subsistence, any decrease threatens their survival. Individuals can insure themselves against this risk by joining clientele networks; the patron provides "subsistence insurance." The cost of this insurance, the "premium," so to speak, is the diminished income that accompanies corruption.

The hypothesis is considerably shakier than it appears. Doubts about how satisfactory this state of affairs actually is begin to creep in when it emerges that in many of these networks, "membership" is by no means always voluntary – as the "older" clientelist literature more or less assumed – but that clients are often kept in line only by a considerable amount of threats and violence. Nor is it entirely clear whether clientelist subsistence insurance is the optimal means of protection compared with alternative sources such as family, social ties or cooperative ventures. This is more than a moot point, when the in-built tendency of patronage systems to hamper cooperative effort that tends to threaten the power of the patron is considered. Nor is there any sound empirical evidence establishing the importance of "subsistence insurance." Casual empiricism suggests that subsistence insurance in the form of disaster relief is today generally provided by organizations other than the patronage network. Undoubtedly *access* to disaster relief is often to be had only through patronage connections. But this throws us back to the problem that patronage systems make themselves indispensable by monopolizing access to benefits that would otherwise have been available through ordinary administrative channels. Thus, it is by no means obvious that poverty and variability of income explain the support for corrupt politicians.

Might poverty alone be sufficient to explain patronage systems? Poverty, it is said, breeds "short-termism": a handout today – at election time, for example – cannot be rejected even if it costs dearly in the future. This is plausible enough if one imagines a starving individual who is offered some sustenance. However, above such a "survival-line" there is no reason to believe that poor people have an extreme time-preference favoring the present. After all, poor peasants with access to credit do not increase indebtedness at extortionate interest rates to the maximum possible level in ordinary times. Nor is there much evidence that the handouts provided are geared mainly at poverty alleviation. What kind of anti-poverty measure is the provision of a basketball court by a Filipino politician, for example?[6] As soon as they are tested, the clientelistic solutions to the paradox of corruption falter.

Cultural explanations

The clientelist literature recognizes that corruption is popular, but fails to explain this popularity if it reduces the material welfare of average voters. Culturalist explanations take a different tack: predatory voting behavior may not maximize material benefits, but leads to the intangible gains that come with upholding deeply held norms and values. In particular, cultural explanations of corruption generally point to one pervasive fundamental traditional social norm: those socially close ought to be treated differently from those socially distant. At the same time, the equality principle that condemns this familialistic norm and distinguishes between the public and private domain has no moral force:

> In many societies no such clear distinction exists. In the private sector, gift giving is pervasive and highly valued, and it seems natural to provide jobs and contracts to one's friends and relations. No one sees any reason not to carry over such practices into the public realm. In fact, the very idea of a sharp distinction between public and private life seems alien to many people.
> (Rose-Ackerman 1999: 91)

This could lead to a voting behavior supportive of "corrupt" politics – albeit not perceived as such. But is what the proposition entails plausible? Assume that person *A* receives something from the government but person *B*, in identical circumstances, receives nothing. Person *A* has received this benefit because one of *A*'s relatives works in the government. Now consider the following transaction. Person *A* has received a gift from the private income of a relative employed in the government (say, produce from a garden planted by the relative's wife). Person *B*, socially more distant, receives nothing. It is very hard to believe that these transactions are considered equivalent by either *A* or *B*: that the fact that one transaction involves government resources and the other not has no influence in the assessment of them. Why, if people do not distinguish between private and government transactions, would they condemn corruption?

What is the empirical evidence for the culturalist thesis? It turns out invariably to be equivocal. Linda Beck's illustration of the "patrimonial nature of accountability" is a case in point. It deals with the LONASE scandal involving the skimming off of large sums of money from the Senegalese lottery:

> When I first learned of the LONASE scandal, I was in a village in the department of Mbacke, listening to the nightly legislative campaign speeches on the radio with a half dozen men and women. They were all aghast. No one was surprised that the deputy who they supported for reelection was accused of embezzlement. But how could the opposition candidate making the accusations talk about such things in public? The villagers maintained that any transgression by the deputy was justified by the jobs he provided as the director of the lottery commission.
>
> (Beck 1999: 209)

What does this story prove? The villagers were clearly upset that the dealings of their representative were made public. But is this really an instance of the "patrimonial nature of accountability"? Or are the villagers perfectly aware of the public–private distinction and is their reaction in fact caused by an awareness of their moral dereliction that has just been publicized? Both interpretations are possible.

It is tempting to construct a weaker version of the cultural approach, postulating that corruption results from the relative strength of the familialistic moral norms and the non-discrimination principle. One might argue that traditional familialistic norms have withered in industrialized nations and the non-discrimination principle has gained in relative strength. In these countries, this norm-conflict has lost its edge, whereas in more "traditional" societies it is virulent, and voting behavior reflects these values: voters are aware of the non-discrimination principle, recognize both horns of the dilemma and choose traditional behavior.

This position has its shortcomings. To act according to the familialistic norm is contrary to the interest of the great majority of the electorate.

Thus we are meant to believe that voters perceive the moral dilemma that they must violate either the equity principle or the familialistic norm, and that they choose to uphold that moral precept that is against their interest.

Collective action problems

With the rise in popularity of the public choice literature, social action dilemmas begin to be employed. "For most ordinary people in developing countries, achieving increased administrative competence and honesty is a collective action problem. Consequently, their interest in reform remains latent; it does not spontaneously develop into politically compelling demands" (Geddes 1994: 35). The experience that strongly influences Geddes' analysis is the electoral failure of the Brazilian UDN (National Democratic Union), a party unable to translate its explicit appeal to competence and honesty in government into electoral currency. On the contrary, its "refusal to make deals and trade favors placed [it] at an electoral disadvantage" (ibid.: 86).

Geddes' conclusion that administrative reform suffers from collective action problems is based on the assumption that "reform" is a collective good and thus unlikely to emerge through spontaneous social action. But why is it not in the interest of a political entrepreneur to provide a reformist program? No obvious collective action problem is involved here. Geddes now shifts to other reasons why predatory voting prevails. Policies, she argues, are often not aimed at median voters (ibid.: 39). This does not explain the emergence of corruption either if all policy packages can be offered with or without corruption and if the non-corrupt version is generally superior. Equally unsatisfactory is the notion that "many citizens, especially in developing countries where levels of education are low and few read newspapers, have almost no ability to monitor the policy-relevant activities of politicians" (ibid.). Even if it is accepted that information deficiencies exist, this is not a collective action problem and it fails to recognize that voters do generally have direct experience of one policy-relevant activity: corruption. It is by no means obvious that voters are unable to make an informed judgment about the level of corruption, particularly where low and high level corruption are strongly correlated. Last, it is said that because "citizens cannot adequately monitor politicians' policy performance, electoral machines become essential to the successful mobilization of the vote. They distribute the individual benefits and favors that affect many people's electoral decisions" (ibid.: 40). But can citizens unable to monitor politician's policy performance adequately be mobilized only by corrupt political machines? The thesis opens up more questions than it answers, although it correctly points to the crucial element of information failures.

Missing alternatives

The fourth reason why voters might support corrupt politicians is the absence of an alternative. There are three versions: elite theories, weak party systems and barriers to entry.

Elite theories are based on three assertions:

- The level of corruption is determined by the political behavior of the elite.
- The political behavior of the elite is guided by their norms and values.
- Changes in these norms and values emanate from within the elite culture.

Elite culture, then, is the fountain that nourishes changes in elite values, elite behavior, and ultimately political corruption.

Etzioni-Halevi is one of the exponents of such a view. She rejects the idea that corruption – "the giving of material inducements in return for votes" – is caused by the preferences of voters: "what counts is not so much the tendencies found in the rank-and-file public" but rather changes in norms and values of the elite (Etzioni-Halevi 1979: 10, 11). Changes in norms and values of the elite are in turn a function of previous states of the elite culture, "of growing self-restraints introduced at the level of the elite and the political-administrative establishments they head." Socio-cultural developments at the level of the public itself may have marginally contributed to these changes but were not their major initiating or driving force (ibid.: 8).

Etzioni-Halevi applies the theory to the decline of electoral corruption in Britain that occurred after "the political elite turned unequivocally against electoral manipulation." Her own evidence shows, however, that "trade unions, chapels" and "friendly societies" played a significant role in this process of value formation (ibid.: 47), and the theory only survives by unduly expanding the range of the "elite." Time and time again, Etzioni-Halevi shows that the behavior of the elite was influenced by those not belonging to it, at least not as conventionally defined. In the US "the merit system was further expanded as political appointments were adversely affected by public opinion" (ibid.: 137). In Australia, "the period in which manipulation of material inducements to individuals declined was also the time at which working-class organizations began to take an active part in politics" (ibid.: 88).

Even if the unfavorable evidence is disregarded, the question remains of how such a change of elite values would occur. At the most general, one might think of a given group of people changing their values, or alternatively, that values change because the composition of the group changes.

This latter "infiltration" hypothesis, where new members with different values enter the group, has been used to explain the rise of corruption in Italy. Corruption "develops when politics begins to attract chiefly those individuals who are able and willing to derive personal benefit from the control of public resources" (della Porta 1996: 362). The entry of a new class into Italian politics set in train a process where "a political class motivated predominantly by ideology is displaced by individuals who view politics primarily as a business" (ibid.). The argument can be reversed: free-wheeling ways might come into disrepute because of a change in elite-membership.

Apart from the problem of specifying the process of value change without a change in composition of the elite, these elite theories suffer from the problem of an excluded fourth assumption: the norms and values of the elite are homogeneous. If they are not, then a pool of potential uncorrupt political entrepreneurs may be available and in a position to satisfy the demand for non-corrupt politics. Shorn of the "homogeneity of elite culture" assumption there is little left of elite theories generally. At best, the elite theory argument can be put in this way: a strong dominance of a particular set of values might reduce the pool of potential political non-corrupt innovators and thus foster corruption.

One of the most popular explanations of corruption is linked to weak party systems. "Weak" can be distinguished from "strong" parties by their relative contribution to the electoral success of a candidate. In the case of an extremely strong party, the electoral success of a candidate is exclusively determined by party membership; personal characteristics count for nothing. On the other hand, the success of candidates of a weak party is mainly a matter of the characteristics of the candidates themselves; party allegiance is relatively irrelevant. Huntington's first phase of the "usual" process of party formation, factionalism, serves as an illustration of a "weak" party system:

> [P]olitics involves a small number of people competing with each other in a large number of weak, transitory alliances and groupings. The groupings have little durability and no structure. They are typically projections of individual ambitions in the context of personal and family rivalries and affiliations. These political groupings may be called parties, but they lack the continuing organization and social support which are the essence of the party. . . . Typically they are formed within the legislature by successful candidates after they are elected rather than in the constituency by aspiring candidates in order to get elected.
>
> (Huntington 1968: 412–14)

It is almost axiomatic that factionalist "weak" party systems contribute to corruption (ibid.: 405). The link between corruption and weak party systems, however, is not obvious. Even in a factionalist "weak party system" representatives may hold seats that are reasonably contestable and be elected by a well-informed electorate desiring non-corrupt policy packages. After all, proponents of classical parliamentarianism never imagined that such a system lent itself to large-scale corruption. It was "party" government that had acquired notoriety for corruption. "Weak" party systems undoubtedly are often corrupt, but it is not clear why this is so.

Perhaps the most widely used political explanation for corruption is barriers to entry into the political market-place. "The lower the cost, the easier it would be for a new and non-corrupt party to hold the same policy platform and steal the votes of an old and corrupt one" (Galeotti and Merlo 1994: 232). Indeed, *after* a corrupt regime has established itself, barriers to entry may help to keep it in power. Barriers to entry have, however, a different status from the political failures discussed so far. They are not a systemic element of democracy, but a distortion of democratic processes. It is not democracy that causes corruption, but its malfunctioning. Nevertheless, barriers to entry are ever-present and thus they do belong to an account of why voters support corrupt politicians in actual, observable democratic systems. This issue will be taken up in the next section.

After this survey one is forced to conclude that we know very little about why – in a well-functioning democracy – voters support corrupt politicians. A satisfactory account emerges neither from the clientelist literature, nor from culturalist explanations, elite theories, or the structure of weak party systems.

Why do voters support corruption?

The purpose of this section is to explain why benefit-maximizing voters might prefer policy packages that do include corruption, despite its drawbacks. The argument proceeds on the basis of a Schumpeterian approach that looks at politics as a market where competing politicians offer different "policy" packages. It presumes that (1) endemic corruption impoverishes the average voter; (2) the average voter dislikes corruption; (3) voters will support a party or a politician according to how well the policy package fits their preferences and how likely it is that these policies will actually be implemented; and (4) voters prefer policy packages that increase rather than decrease their material welfare and involve less rather than more corruption.

Expressed in the most general terms, this approach supposes that either corruption may reflect the desires of the voters – with which politicians comply – or the voters do not desire corruption but no non-corrupt policy package is "on offer." For obvious reasons the first case will be called a "demand side," and the second a "supply side" explanation. Both "demand" and "supply" side explanations are analyzed with the help of conventional market failure arguments where spontaneous interactions of suppliers and consumers fail to generate a socially optimal result.

Demand-side explanations

In order to be able to concentrate on demand-side failures, it is assumed that there are no supply-side problems; non-corrupt policy packages corresponding to voters' preferences being (potentially) available. Two types of cases are discussed: in the first case voters support corrupt politicians because they prefer corrupt politics; in the second case they prefer non-corrupt politics but are caught in a social action dilemma.

Ignorance

Voter ignorance has already been encountered as one of the possible reasons for the persistence of a predatory voting behavior, and has been isolated consistently as one of the central problems of democracy. Schumpeter's doubts about the "definiteness and independence of the voter's will, his powers of observation and interpretation of facts, and his ability to draw, clearly and promptly, rational inferences from both" are cases in point (Schumpeter 1976: 256). Such a dictum, however, is much too general to be useful for an analysis of information deficiencies. What need to be specified are the types of information the voter has to have in order to make an informed judgment. These relate first of all to the level and the consequences of corruption and the alternatives available.

Can voters assess the level of corruption? It has been pointed out before that the majority of voters will generally have a fairly good idea about the prevalence of low-level corruption, and if low-level corruption correlates highly with high-level corruption they can make a tolerably accurate assessment of the overall situation. Moreover, many people will have some information about the honesty of the judiciary and of local and central administrations. Empirical evidence, that compares subjective voters' assessments and objective criteria, is, however, entirely missing.

Do voters assess the effects of corruption correctly? A majority of voters might falsely believe that endemic corruption serves their material interest. Again, direct evidence is missing. However, the widespread opposition to corruption in countries where it is endemic suggests awareness of some of the social and economic problems associated with it. This does not preclude that corruption might be considered a relatively minor factor in an overall assessment of the performance of a regime. A Mexican survey does suggest information deficiencies, attitudes to corruption being highly class specific:

> 38 percent of the high-income group ranked corruption as the nation's most pressing issue compared to 31 percent of the upper-middle group, 29 percent of the lower-middle, and 24 percent of the low-income group. Similarly, 34 percent viewed corruption as the principal cause of the economic crises compared to 25 percent of the upper-middle group, 20 percent of the lower-middle group, and 10 percent of the low-income group.
>
> (Morris 1991: 108)

Similarly, "the elections of 1988 confirmed a long tradition in which the firmest base of electoral support for the PRI continued to come from rural areas, particularly from the poorest regions" (Grindle 1996: 159). Assuming that higher-income groups and urban people are better informed about the consequences of corruption and are equally affected by it, their greater awareness of its costs suggests information deficiencies among lower-income groups.

A further information problem occurs when voters are unable to conceptualize an alternative system of government and public administration where corruption is largely absent. This may not be an altogether unrealistic scenario where voters have never experienced such a system. Again, it is entirely unclear the degree to which average Mexican or Indian voters, for example, can imagine what a government and an administration free of corruption would actually entail (including the absence of exceptional treatment for themselves).

Finally, a voter must be able to distinguish between corrupt and non-corrupt policy offerings. This may not be an easy task either if there are severe signaling problems. Corrupt policies may well be couched in terms of public welfare.[7]

Corrupt politicians are likely to muddy the waters by advocating anti-corruption programs themselves. They might be able to deflect criticism by suggesting that corruption is not systemic but accidental and the regime might reform itself. This is suggested by Morris in the case of Mexico, where the regime was able to present the problem as "one of a 'few bad apples'" (Morris 1991: 36). Through frequent anti-corruption movements the government socializes the public into viewing corruption as a problem of certain officials rather than as a systemic problem (ibid.: 77–8). This process of dissimulation extends to tainting non-corrupt politicians with corruption. That manifestly corrupt politicians accuse others of corruption is an all too frequent occurrence. The strategy has a reasonable chance of success: where corruption is endemic, many non-corrupt politicians will have had some dealings with individuals who are corrupt, or have been associated with some actions involving corruption, and are therefore easily brought into disrepute. It is therefore by no means obvious that voters are able to distinguish corrupt from non-corrupt policy packages.[8]

Thus one plausible failure of the political market-place might arise if the minimal relevant knowledge about corruption is not available. Ignorance about the effects of corruption, about the alternatives available, and about the intentions of those standing for election are possible reasons for voters to support corrupt politics.

Inconsistent preferences

Following Schumpeter's cue about the "definiteness . . . of the voter's will" (Schumpeter 1976: 256), corruption might be the consequence of inconsistent preferences. The story of Odysseus and the Sirens illustrates the point. Odysseus knows that if he hears the Sirens he will want to approach the coast and will suffer shipwreck. Not desiring this course of action when not under the influence of the Sirens, he has the ears of the crew plugged and himself bound to the mast. He can now listen to the Sirens, but the crew can hear neither the Sirens nor his commands to change the course of the ship. Voters not thus happily bound can change their minds when the Sirens call, preferring non-corrupt politicians as a general rule, but calling for particularistic benefits in between when the need arises.

This scenario is not an unpopular one among third-world politicians. It suggests that voters sometimes opt for non-corrupt politicians who are prevented from following bureaucratic rules by the pressure of these very voters who, subsequent to the election, change their minds and demand particularistic benefits. The blame for corruption is thus neatly shifted from politicians to voters. The explanation is consistent in a situation immediately after democratization, but becomes inconsistent thereafter. It implies that particularistic benefits received *between* elections are not honored *at* the next election, when voters are again under the influence of the general rule that corruption is morally wrong and bad for them. Indeed, the fact that extra-bureaucratic "help" was received would bar voters from supporting their "helper."

Preferences can explain the paradox of corruption only if they are *generally* inconsistent: voters believe corruption is materially disadvantageous and morally repugnant and express their feeling in anti-corruption statements, but at the same time they believe it is advantageous and morally justified to avail themselves of the opportunity it opens. It is not unknown for people to draw on departmentalized belief systems in different circumstances. Special pleading is, after all, a universal phenomenon.

Collective action dilemma

An explanation of the paradox more in line with the conventional "rationality" assumption of human behavior is based on a collective action dilemma. In a two-party contest two policy packages are offered to which an individual or group is indifferent on ideological grounds, one with and one without corruption. All voters dislike corruption, and the best possible outcome is non-corrupt politics. The second-best outcome is the "corrupt" policy package as long as the individual voter has supported the victorious "corrupt" party. The worst outcome is to have the "corrupt" party win but not to have supported it, and thus to be shut out from the clientelistic distribution network. In such a "game," the chances that the corrupt party will indeed win the election are greatly improved.

A simple payoff matrix shown in Figure 4.1 illustrates the point. Let us assume that two parties offer, from an ideological point of view, identical policy packages. One involves corruption (C) and the other not (NC). The best possible outcome for all voters is a victory for the non-corrupt party (payoff 1 in the matrix). However, individual voters take a risk: if they support the non-corrupt party, thereby repudiating their patronage connections, and the corrupt party wins, they lose their patronage income and their payoff will be minimal (0 in their payoff matrix). They therefore have an incentive to support the corrupt party, remain part of the patronage network, and hope that the non-corrupt party wins. If the majority of the voters behave in this way, the corrupt party will be elected, and the payoff will be below the optimal rate (0.5 in the matrix).

Such a scenario is not unrealistic. Sanctions against disloyal supporters are widespread. In Israel,

> [people] who were helped by the party machine were not free to change their allegiance at will. It has even been claimed that those rebels who tried to do so (and they were not too numerous) were dismissed from their jobs or even evicted from their apartments.
>
> (Etzioni-Halevi 1979: 93)

Payoff matrix		Majority votes	
		NC	C
Individual A votes	NC	1	0
	C	1	0.5

Figure 4.1 Voting choices with corrupt parties

Of course there is always the possibility of cheating: to claim falsely that one has voted for the patronage system. Cheating may be difficult, however, in tightly knit communities. As an Indian politician put it in the 1960s: "Even the secret ballot isn't really much protection because the money lender or *zemindar* soon finds out how people voted, because often they themselves can't keep quiet about it" (Bailey 1963: 194).

Even if superior non-corrupt policy options are available, the array of factors promoting corruption in democracies is formidable: information failures as to the consequences and the levels of corruption and the policy options available, collective action failures and, perhaps, inconsistent preferences. In principle, all of these failures are observable or at least indirectly ascertainable from observed behavior.

Supply-side failures

Volitions, as Schumpeter observed, "do not as a rule assert themselves directly. Even if strong and definite they remain latent, often for decades, until they are called to life by some political leader who turns them into political factors" (Schumpeter 1976: 270). What might prevent such leadership to emerge?

Barriers to entry, as we have seen, could explain why a corrupt regime is able to hold on to power. New parties will generally suffer some disadvantages compared with established parties in most regimes that unquestionably deserve to be called democracies. In analogy to the theory of contestable markets in economics, we can define a contestable political market as one where an entrant suffers no cost disadvantage in presenting a policy package to the voter (assuming a "fair" electoral process). Preferential access to the media by incumbents is an obvious example of entry barriers, but opportunity costs play a role also. Opportunity costs can be significant and may go well beyond the lost income as a consequence of time spent on campaigning. Participating in a campaign can lead to the more or less permanent closing of job or business opportunities. Such costs are particularly significant when incumbents systematically use co-optation to neutralize opponents. Forgoing offers of co-optation can be extremely costly in terms of lost income, business opportunities, job security, status and power. Considering that the benefits from political entrepreneurship are insecure and often remote, such "informal" barriers to entry can be very effective.

Contestability may suffer from the absolute size of election expenditures too. It may be useful to draw an analogy to business practices. Imagine a market where a number of similar products compete, say different brands of chocolate bars. A particular brand is able to maintain its market share only if the consumer is continuously reminded of its great virtues. A drop in advertising expenditure much below that of competitive brands will consign it to oblivion. Conversely, a new brand can establish itself only through publicity campaigns comparable to those of its competitors. These high advertising costs required to successfully establish a product constitute an effective barrier to keep competitors out of the market. A similar mechanism plays a role in a political market. Not being able to match the outlays of opponents – and not being able to compensate for this deficiency by other means such as voluntary labor – reduces significantly the chances of success of a new party. Thus expensive electioneering serves not just to combat established opponents but to keep out new competitors. Not untypically, "[n]ational and state elections, even in India, are an expensive affair with a campaign for an average urban constituency in parliament estimated to cost around 12.5 million rupees (approx. £208,000)" (Singh 1997: 218).[9]

Nevertheless, the effectiveness of such "soft" barriers to entry is easily overestimated. Not only does misgovernment add to voters' sensitivity to the messages of new entrants, but search theory suggests they would also actively seek information on ways to remove incumbents.

Weak party systems

Why are weak factionalist systems generally corrupt? There is no a priori reason that excludes the existence of non-corrupt factionalist regimes. One could easily imagine rapidly changing governments based on unstable coalitions, pursuing their pork barreling and self-promotion in a perfectly bureaucratic manner.[10] The incentives of the representatives to engage in corruption are influenced only if factionalism affects the probability of re-election. This is likely to be the case where factionalism impairs their ability to pursue coherent policies – thus reducing the welfare of the electorate at large that is trying to rid itself of ineffectual politicians. Through such a mechanism a weak party system could lead to a high turnover of representatives who have strong incentives to engage in corruption.

The causation may, of course, work in the other direction: high "electoral volatility" – defined as low probability of re-election *independent of performance in office* – adds to the incentive of augmenting current income through corruption. If indeed electoral volatility in this specific sense causes factionalism and corruption, the question arises of what causes the electoral volatility. A partial explanation is provided by Geddes' information failure: that citizens may not be able to adequately monitor politicians' policy performance. This turns the problem into one of demand failure.

Some implications and conclusions

There are a number of reasons why voters might support corrupt politicians, even if this is against their interest and even in the absence of significant barriers to entry. By its very nature, an economic approach to the problem will invite the conclusion that in the absence of barriers to entry and thus no hindrance to political entrepreneurship there ought to be no shortage of policy packages that are optimally adapted to the preferences of the voters. Market failures are likely to emerge through coordination failures in an environment of shifting coalitions in parliament that prevent the formulation and implementation of coherent policies, lower the probability of re-election and therefore provide incentives to corruption. Most importantly, however, a Schumpeterian approach will stress demand-side failures: collective action failures, and imperfect information on the levels and consequences of corruption, on the availability of alternatives (in principle and in practice), and on the performance of the incumbents.

Political market failures are likely to mutually reinforce each other, while information failures of all kinds may lead to an underestimation of collective action problems. The greater the information failures, the less distinct preference patterns are likely to be, and the easier it is to maintain inconsistent preference patterns. Barriers to entry are more effective in the case of widespread information failures, and the opportunistic shifting coalitions of weak government will send confusing signals that contribute to these.

The question of why voters support corrupt politicians has not been a popular one. One reason for its unpopularity could be the uncomfortable implications that emerge for the "good governance" debate. It jeopardizes the comfortable assumption that corruption is unrelated to the electoral process and implies that in many cases administrative reforms, and even the reduction of entry barriers, are unlikely to yield the results promised by their designers. Fighting corruption becomes the eminently political task of transforming political culture in the widest sense.

Notes

1 For variations of this theme see Boeninger (1992: 267) and Landell-Mills and Sarageldin (1992: 304).
2 Leftwich does accept that "[t]here was some limited acknowledgement of the *political* causes and context of this crisis of governance in the report [*From Crisis to Sustainable Growth*] but in practice it said little about the state or the *politics* of development. Instead it focused single-mindedly on managerial and administrative issues, as became clear in its formal statement on *Governance and Development* . . . In this and other Bank publications . . . the Bank committed itself to the seemingly more apolitical and largely technical strategy of improving governance" (Leftwich 1994: 368).
3 As described by Anechiarico and Jacobs (1996).
4 The process of outright theft can be seen in the same way: it involves a redistribution from the state to an employee and increases the cost of administering transactions.

5 There are, of course, obvious cases where a corrupt act facilitates production or exchange. The concern here is with the effect on *aggregate* GDP.

6 An apparently not atypical sort of "benefit" according to Prof. Mark Thompson.

7 Jain (2000) provides an example of a decision of the Government of Ontario in which privatization of a road in the province was motivated more by the needs of the ruling political party than by the needs of the voters. Given the complexities of the deal and lack of information, however, the decision was justified as being in the public interest.

8 A variation of this theme is reported from Angola, where out of about 150 small opposition parties only twenty are thought to be genuine. The remainder are fronts, created and financed by the MPLA (*Economist*, May 13 2000: "Angola: A Third Force": 42).

9 The process may be even more insidious: as each party increases its election budget it may well be that the amounts required to keep up with one's competitors become so large that some corruption is necessary to accumulate the funds.

10 Such as the Japanese LDP.

Bibliography

Anechiarico, F. and Jacobs, J. B. (1996) *The Pursuit of Absolute Integrity*, Chicago: Chicago University Press.

Bailey, F. G. (1963) *Politics and Social Change: Orissa in 1959*, London: University of California Press.

Beck, L. (1999) "Senegal's Enlarged Presidential Majority: Deepening Democracy or Detour?" in R. Joseph, *State, Conflict, and Democracy in Africa*, Boulder, Colo.: Lynne Rienner: 197–215.

Boeninger, E. (1992) "Governance and Development: Issues and Constraints," in H. Lawrence and S. Shah (eds), *Proceedings of the World Bank Annual Conference on Development Economics, 1991*, supplement to the World Bank Economic Review and the World Bank Research Observer, Washington, DC: World Bank: 267–87.

Caciagli, M. and Belloni, F. P. (1981) "The 'New' Clientelism in Southern Italy: The Christian Democratic Party in Catania," in S. N. Eisenstadt and R. Lemarchand (eds), *Political Clientelism, Patronage and Development*, London: Sage: 35–56.

della Porta, D. (1996) "Actors in Corruption: Business Politicians in Italy," *International Social Science Journal* 149 (March): 349–64.

della Porta, D. and Vannucci, A. (1997) "The 'Perverse Effects' of Political Corruption," *Political Studies* 45: 516–38.

Easterly, W. and Levine, R. (1997) "Africa's Growth Tragedy: Policies and Ethnic Divisions," *Quarterly Journal of Economics* 112: 1203–50.

Economist (2000) "Angola: A Third Force," May 13: 42.

Elliott, K. A. (ed.) (1997) *Corruption and the Global Economy*: Introduction, Washington, DC: Institute for International Economics.

Etzioni-Halevi, E. (1979) *Political Manipulation and Administrative Power: A Comparative Study*, London: Routledge and Kegan Paul.

Galeotti, G. and Merlo, A. (1994) "Political Collusion and Corruption in a Representative Democracy," in W. W. Pommerehne (ed.), *Public Finance and Irregular Activities*, supplement to *Public Finance* 49: 232–43.

Geddes, B. (1994) *Politicians' Dilemma: Building State Capacity in Latin America*, Berkeley, Calif.: University of California Press.

Girling, J. (1997) *Corruption, Capitalism and Democracy*, London: Routledge.

Grindle, M. S. (1996) *Challenging the State: Crisis and Innovation in Latin America and Africa*, Cambridge, UK: Cambridge University Press.

Huntington, S. P. (1968) *Political Order in Changing Societies*, New Haven, Conn.: Yale University Press.

Jain, A. K. (2001) "Corruption: A Review," *Journal of Economic Surveys*, special volume on "Issues in New Political Economy" (February).

Kaufmann, D. (1999) "Anticorruption Strategies: Starting Afresh? Unconventional Lessons from Comparative Analysis," in R. Stapenhurst and S. J. Kpundeh (eds), *Curbing Corruption: Towards a Model for Building National Integrity*, Washington, DC: World Bank: 35–50.

Keefer, P. and Knack, S. (1997) "Why Don't Poor Countries Catch Up? A Cross-National Test of Institutional Explanation," *Economic Inquiry* 35: 590–602.

Landell-Mills, P. and Serageldin, I. (1992) "Governance and the External Factor," in L. H. Summers and S. Shah (eds), *Proceedings of the World Bank Annual Conference on Development Economics, 1991,* supplement to the *World Bank Economic Review* and the *World Bank Research Observer*, Washington, DC: World Bank: 303–20.

Leftwich, A. (1994) "Governance, the State and the Politics of Development," *Development and Change* 25: 363–86.

Mainwaring, S. (1998) "Party Systems in the Third Wave," *Journal of Democracy* 9(3): 67–81.

Maisrikrod, S. and McCargo, D. (1997) "Electoral Politics: Commercialization and Exclusion," in S. Maisrikrod and D. McCargo (eds), *Political Change in Thailand: Democracy and Participation*, London: Routledge.

Mauro, P. (1995) "Corruption and Growth," *Quarterly Journal of Economics* 110(3): 681–712.

—— (1998) "Corruption and the Composition of Government Expenditure," *Journal of Public Economics* 69: 263–79.

Mill, J. (1823) *Political Writings* (1992 edn), Cambridge, UK: Cambridge University Press.

Mill, J. S. (1861) "Considerations on Representative Government," *Utilitarianism, Liberty, Representative Government* (1910 edn), London: Everyman.

Morris, S. D. (1991) *Corruption and Politics in Contemporary Mexico*, London: University of Alabama Press.

Phongpaichit, P. and Piriyarangsan, S. (1996) *Corruption and Democracy in Thailand*, Chiang Mai: Silkworm.

Riley, S. P. (1983) "The Land of the Waving Palms," in M. Clarke (ed.), *Corruption: Causes, Consequences and Control,* London: Frances Pinter.

Rose-Ackerman, S. (1999) *Corruption and Government: Causes, Consequences and Reform*, Cambridge, UK: Cambridge University Press.

Schumpeter, J. A. (1976) *Capitalism, Socialism and Democracy*, London: Allen and Unwin.

Scott, J. C. (1972) *Comparative Political Corruption*, Englewood Cliffs, NJ: Prentice-Hall.

Singh, G. (1997) "Understanding Political Corruption in Contemporary Indian Politics," in P. Heywood, *Political Corruption*, Oxford: Blackwell: 210–22.

Wade, R. (1985) "The Market for Public Office: Why the Indian State is not Better at Development," *World Development* 13: 467–97.

Weber, M. (1968) *The Theory of Social and Economic Organization*, Oxford: Oxford University Press.

World Bank (1989) *Sub-Saharan Africa: From Crisis to Sustainable Growth*, Washington, DC: World Bank.

Part III

Policy and political outcomes

5 Corruption, growth, and public finances

Vito Tanzi and Hamid Davoodi

Introduction

In the last decade corruption has received a great deal of attention from a broad spectrum of the public. The study of corruption is no longer regarded as a subject of inquiry exclusively by students of politics and sociology. It now occupies the attention of many other fields such as political economy, public administration and law. Many international and regional organizations now regard corruption and poor governance as major obstacles to good policy-making. The current interest in corruption probably reflects an increase in the scope of corruption over the years, and is in part fueled by a better understanding of the economic costs of corruption. Thus it does not just reflect a greater awareness of an age-old problem.

Until recently segments of the economic literature had presented a romantic view of corruption. This view made corruption seem an almost virtuous activity and possibly good for growth in a world stifled by bad governments. For example, in various theoretical studies it was argued that corruption removes or relaxes government-imposed rigidities; greases the wheels of commerce; allocates investment and time to the most efficient users; keeps wages low; and may even act as a political glue that holds a country together.[1] The romantic view of corruption has been replaced, in more recent years, by a more realistic and much less favorable view. According to this new view, the payment of bribes is not a panacea for overcoming red tape and cumbersome government regulations; the highest bribes are paid by rent-seekers and not by the most efficient individuals; a comprehensive civil service reform is better at reducing corruption than simply raising wages; corruption is subject to increasing returns which perpetuate it; and corruption creates an environment that, in time, can lead to the collapse of political regimes.

This chapter elaborates on these contrasting views of corruption and, from this perspective, analyzes the conceptual and empirical links between corruption, economic growth, and public finances. There are many indirect channels through which corruption lowers growth, and recently some formal models have been developed that link corruption directly to growth. By contrast, there are papers in the public finance literature, and particularly on the tax side, which systematically investigate corruption, tax evasion and the incentive structure of tax inspectors and the public. This chapter discusses some related issues.

Corruption and growth

As a point of departure, it is important to describe two associations that have appeared prominently in the recent empirical literature on corruption. First, there is a negative association between corruption perception indexes and levels of economic development measured by real per capita GDP.[2] Figure 5.1 shows, for a sample of ninety-seven countries in 1997, that countries with higher perceived corruption tend to have lower real per capita GDP. Or, putting it differently, countries with low per capita income tend to have higher corruption. The correlation coefficient is –0.80, which is statistically significant with a t-ratio of –13.2.[3] Second, there is a negative association between corruption perception indexes and economic growth as measured by growth in real per capita GDP.

The relation shown in Figure 5.2 for the same countries as in Figure 5.1 indicates that countries with higher corruption tend to have a lower growth rate. The correlation coefficient is –0.32 which is statistically significant with a t-ratio of –3.2. Although this association is consistent with causation running in both directions, some studies have used econometric techniques, such as instrumental variable techniques (Mauro 1995), to argue that the causality is from corruption to economic growth. Nevertheless, regardless of the position taken on the direction of causality,

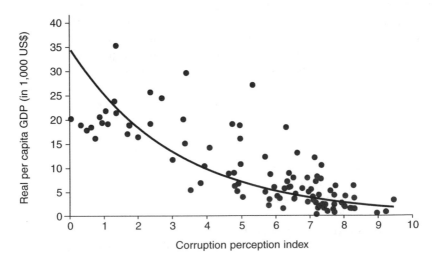

Figure 5.1 Corruption and development in ninety-seven countries

the simple negative association between corruption and growth is supported by the data. This chapter presents some arguments to explain why this relation exists. It analyzes some direct and indirect channels through which corruption may affect economic growth. No attempt is made to formalize these channels in an explicit framework. The channels analyzed are: (a) the impact of corruption on enterprises with particular attention on small enterprises and its differentiated effect between large and small enterprises; (b) the impact of corruption on investment; and (c) the impact of corruption on the allocation of talent. In the last section, we will investigate some relationships between corruption and the composition of taxes and spending.

Corruption and enterprise growth

The increase in development of enterprises as a building block of growth (at industry and national level) is an old and respected topic in economics, dating back to Adam Smith's notion of scale economies, Alfred Marshall's description of industrial evolution of small firms, and Schumpeterian forces of creative destruction and entrepreneurship. Historically, large enterprises had been viewed as the most important source of jobs, innovation and growth. However, in recent years, public policy has increasingly focused on the contributions of small and medium size enterprises (SMEs) to these objectives. Considerable empirical research conducted on OECD countries over the last decade has established a number of interesting facts which lie behind the changing perception of the role of SMEs in the economy. These are:[4]

- SMEs may comprise a smaller share of value added in the economy

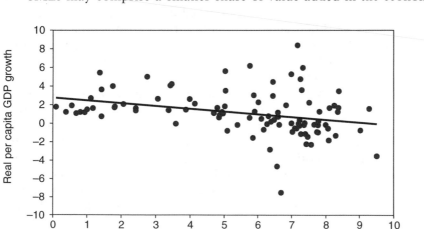

Figure 5.2 Corruption and growth in ninety-seven countries

than large enterprises, but they employ the bulk of the labor force and create most of the new jobs.

- SMEs tend to be less capital intensive, consistent with their importance in the employment share.
- SMEs tend to be product-innovative whereas large firms tend to be process-innovative.[5]
- SMEs are more financially constrained than large enterprises which have easier access to the capital market; in the United States, for example, SMEs make up half of the value added in the economy, but represent only 6 percent of total business finance.
- SMEs contribute to growth in normal as well as recession times in ways that large firms do not. In a study of twelve European countries during the first half of the 1990s, a greater increase in the smaller firm sales, compared to large firm sales, led to more growth in the national GNP in the following year.[6] During the deep recession of 1990–3 in Sweden, the SMEs' share of job gains was larger than the SMEs' share of job losses and as a result SMEs performed better than large firms.
- The survival of SMEs depends on access to finance, but also on competent entrepreneurship and talented management. It also depends on the environment that they face.

The above description of the role of SMEs is not limited to OECD countries but it covers also transition economies and developing countries. Thus, if corruption were to be more damaging to small and new enterprises than to large enterprises, it would imply that corruption would be putting breaks on the forces that promote growth. We will argue that, in fact, the effect of corruption is differentiated among the enterprises and is particularly pronounced on the small enterprises.

In a survey of 3,000 enterprises across twenty transition economies, conducted jointly for the European Bank for Reconstruction and Development (EBRD) and the World Bank – referred to as the Business Environment and Enterprise Performance Survey (BEEPS) – enterprises were asked to assess the major impediments in their business environment in terms of the extent of competition, corruption, taxes and regulations, inflation, financing and infrastructure. The results of the survey show the differential impact of corruption on firm size. Across all regions, corruption and anti-competitive practices were perceived as the most difficult obstacles by start-up firms with both barriers being ranked on average as 13 percent greater by start-ups, which tend to be largely SMEs, than by state-owned enterprises (SOEs) which tend to be older and large enterprises.[7]

A detailed breakdown of other impediments have shown that it is the access to essential business services, rather than the cost of finance per se, that is the greatest problem for start-ups. These findings seem to be consistent with other survey-based studies. For example, in a study of eighty-four wholesale trade enterprises in the city of Moscow in 1993, a dummy variable representing connection of the head of the enterprise to the relevant city government officials was a good predictor of which enterprises got soft credit. This dummy was a better predictor than the profit of the enterprise or other economic factors (Treisman 1995).

The role of connections in the allocation of credit is, of course, not unique to transition economies. In a study of Japanese firms of varying size, investment in physical capital by firms with close ties to banks was found to be much less sensitive to their liquidity than for firms raising their capital through arms' length transactions (Hoshi, Kashyap, and Scharfstein 1991). Although this finding is consistent with the role of financial intermediaries as monitoring agents that are in the business of reducing incentive problems and solving asymmetric information problems, it is also consistent with the observation that the allocation of credit based on arms' length relationships is perhaps good for growth in the long run, given the subsequent state of financial and enterprise restructuring in Japan in the 1990s and the long recession.

These findings from the experience of OECD countries and transition economies have important public policy implications. In general, the lessons are that factors that impede the growth of SMEs and stifle the entry of new firms, which tend to be small and important to a dynamic economy, will also tend to slow down the growth rate of the economy.

The conceptual link between corruption, size of enterprises and growth runs along the following lines. Large enterprises are known to find it easier to protect themselves from corrupt officials; they have specialized departments; they can use "facilitators"-individuals with skills to bypass the regulations and tax laws; their size protects them from petty bureaucrats; and they can use political power to further their rent-seeking corruption to their advantage. For large enterprises corruption is often of a cost-reducing kind as it allows them to enjoy monopoly rents and scale economies; whereas for SMEs it is often of a cost-increasing kind because they have to make payments which do not contribute to the productivity or profitability of the firm but that are necessary for their survivability. SMEs are normally preyed upon by petty bureaucrats and corrupt tax inspectors and are forced into making substantial payments and abiding by cumbersome regulations. Bribes may be required to obtain various authorizations or freedom from bureaucratic harassment. Bribe payments may amount to a substantial portion of SMEs' operating costs which can drive them out of business since they tend to operate in more competitive environments than large enterprises. In a study in Indonesia it was reported that these payments may have been as high as 20 percent of the sales of shops or small enterprises.

A growing number of surveys provides empirical support for this conceptual link:

- In a sample of 176 Ugandan firms in 1997, the median firm paid bribes equivalent to 28 percent of its investment in machinery and equipment; and there was no evidence that firms that paid higher bribes on average received more beneficial government favors (Svensson 2000). In Uganda, SMEs represent 50 percent of total employment and 96 percent of business establishments.

- Ugandan firms that are involved in exports and receive tax exemptions have a higher probability of facing corrupt bureaucrats and having to pay bribes (Svensson 2000). The implications of this finding are that (a) corruption does not grease the wheels of commerce; (b) those who can afford to pay more will be asked to pay more; and (c) trade liberalization and tax reform can reduce the opportunities for corruption. However, trade liberalization, though good for the economy as a whole, is more likely to benefit larger firms than smaller firms since traditionally the tradable sector has been dominated by large firms.

- In a survey of some 3,000 enterprises in twenty transition economies, conducted by the EBRD and the World Bank, bribes are found to act like a regressive tax (EBRD 1999); the bribes paid by smaller firms amount to about 5 percent of their annual revenue compared with 4 percent for medium-size firms, and slightly less than 3 percent for large firms.[8]

- Smaller firms pay bribes more frequently than medium size and large firms; so do the new entrants and newly privatized state enterprises (ibid.). In addition, enterprises that pay bribes more frequently also tend to pay a higher bribe per unit of revenues, in other words, a higher tax in addition to other taxes. Figure 5.3 demonstrates the relationship between frequency of bribes and their total costs to the firms.

- The evidence on the length of time spent by senior management of firms of different sizes with government bureaucrats seems to be mixed at best. This is a widely used indicator in the literature on corruption which may represent various costs of doing business with a government bureaucracy. The cost may involve forgone valuable time of a manager and may represent the time spent complying with regulations, lobbying for benefits, negotiating tax payments or bribes. The evidence based on Global Competitive Report data indicates that large firms waste less time with government bureaucrats. See Kaufmann and Wei (1999, Table 5). However, the BEEPS survey for the EBRD and the World Bank shows that senior management of state enterprises, which tend to be large, spend more time with government bureaucrats (about 12 percent of their time) than senior

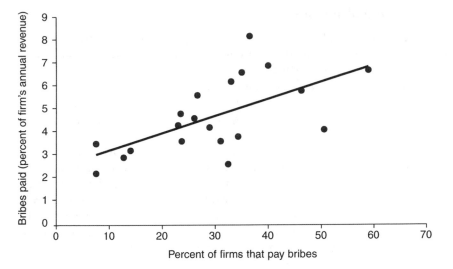

Figure 5.3 Bribes paid and their frequency in twenty transition economics

management of privatized and new entrants (10 percent each) which tend to be small firms.[9] The evidence from Ukraine is consistent with that of Kaufmann and Wei (1999, Table 5); management of new private entrants spend about 37 percent of their time with government bureaucracy, followed by 29 percent by privatized firms and 21 percent by state enterprises (Kaufmann 1997).

- Corruption can reduce the rates of return on capital of small firms by more than those of large firms. It has been estimated that public sector bureaucratic corruption in Argentina reduces the expected rates of return on invested capital by 1 to 2.5 percentage points for large firms, 2 to 2.5 percentage points for medium-sized firms and 3 to 3.6 percentage points for small enterprises (Buscaglia and Ratliff 2000). The effect is attributed by the authors to high regulatory fees and taxes. Corruption may not be expected to explain the entire difference. For example, in a different, but related study of rate of return on 1,163 World Bank-funded investment projects in sixty-one developing countries, it was found that poor quality of economic policy can reduce the rate of return by some 10 percentage points (Isham and Kaufmann 1999). However, corruption may also reduce the quality of economic policy.

In conclusion, although the evidence is often indirect and not as clear as one would wish, it is consistent with the hypothesis that corruption increases the costs of enterprises and reduces their rates of return. Furthermore, it tends to have more damaging effects on small enterprises than on large enterprises.

Corruption and investment

Most economists and much economic theory assume a positive relation-ship between investment and growth.[10] Therefore, if corruption affects investment, it must also affect growth.

Corruption may affect investment in different ways. It may affect (a) total investment, (b) the size and composition of foreign direct investment, (c) the size of public investment, and (d) the quality of the investment decisions and of investment projects.

In several papers, Paolo Mauro (1995, 1996) has shown that corrup-tion can have a significant negative impact on *the ratio of investment to GDP*. Regressing the investment ratio on a constant, the corruption index, GDP per capita in an earlier period (1960), secondary education in 1960, and population growth, he has shown that an improvement in the corruption index (i.e. a reduction in corruption) can significantly increase the investment–GDP ratio. The fall in investment–GDP ratio caused by corruption is shown to have an important effect on growth. Mauro esti-mates that a reduction in corruption equivalent to two points in the corruption index, through its positive effect on the investment–GDP ratio, could raise the growth rate by about 0.5 percent. In this relationship, the impact of corruption on the quality of investment is ignored. If the reduc-tion in investment improved the quality of investment, the positive impact on growth could be higher.

In a recent study of transition economies, Abed and Davoodi (2001) show that the impact of corruption on growth is reduced once one controls for structural reforms. These authors argue and provide evidence that structural reforms are perhaps the driving force behind the impact of corruption on growth. This interpretation and the findings have not been tested for other countries besides the transition economies and they depend on specific assessments of structural changes.

In a paper focusing on *Foreign Direct Investment* (FDI), Shang Jin Wei (1997a) has shown that while a 1 percentage point increase in the marginal tax rate on foreign direct investment (FDI) reduces incoming FDI by about 3.3 percent, an increase in the corruption index by 1 point reduces the flow of FDI into a country by about 11 percent. This would be equivalent to a 3.6 percentage points increase in the marginal tax rate. He has calculated that an increase in the corruption index, from the Singapore level to the Mexican level, would have an impact similar to that of 21–4 percentage points increase in the marginal tax rate. There is evidence in the literature that higher FDI leads to higher growth through several channels: transfer of technology, improving productivity of domestic investment and providing the necessary capital to work with complementary skilled labor (Borensztein, De Gregorio, and Lee 1998). Hence, by increasing FDI, lower corruption will lead to higher growth.

New evidence indicates that corruption also affects the composition of FDI. Using firm-level data, Smarzynska and Wei (2000) show that higher corruption in a host country shifts the composition of inward FDI towards joint ventures and away from wholly owned subsidiaries of foreign enterprises. Although the authors do not investigate the growth implications of this shift, growth is likely to be higher if such a shift re-enforces the channels identified by Borensztein, De Gregorio, and Lee (1998).

In a related work, using data from the Global Competitiveness Report, Wei (1997b) has shown that the *predictability of corruption* is also important. The less predictable the level of corruption (the higher the dispersion of individual ratings of corruption level of host countries), the greater is the impact of corruption on FDI. A higher level of dispersion makes corruption behave like an unpredictable and random tax.

> The effect of uncertainty on FDI is negative, statistically significant and . . . large. An increase in uncertainty from the level of Singapore to that of Mexico . . . is equivalent to raising the tax rate on multinational firms by 32 percentage points.
>
> (Wei 1997b)

The evidence presented by Wei (1997b) has also been corroborated using the private sector survey carried out for the World Bank's 1997 *World Development Report* (Campos, Lien, and Pradhan, 1999).

Tanzi and Davoodi (1997) have argued that corruption is likely to *increase public investment but to reduce its productivity*. They have argued that public investment is easily manipulated by powerful political or bureaucratic personalities. They have tested the hypothesis that, other things being equal, higher corruption is associated with higher public investment.

Regressing public investment (as a share of GDP) against a constant, the corruption index, real per capita GDP, and the share of government revenue in GDP, Tanzi and Davoodi show that the corruption index is highly significant (at the 1 percent level) and that the more corruption there is, the more *public* investment.

Subject to the caveat expressed earlier, the reduction in the investment-GDP ratio and in the FDI-GDP ratios can be assumed to have a clear, negative impact on growth. However, the increase in the share of public investment in GDP has a more questionable impact on growth. Some related evidence is provided by Tanzi and Davoodi (1997), Reinikka and Svensson (1999), and Ades and Di Tella (1997).

Although the difficulties in getting good data are great, Tanzi and Davoodi have presented evidence that other things being equal, (a) *high corruption is associated with low operation and maintenance expenditure*; and (b) *high corruption is associated with poor quality of infrastructure*.

Thus, while corruption is likely to increase public investment by distorting the composition of that investment and by causing a deterioration of a country's infrastructure, it is likely to reduce a country's growth prospects. Poor public infrastructure reduces private productivity or forces private investment to compensate for the poor infrastructure. In terms of statistical significance, the impact of corruption on the quality of infrastructure is strongest on the quality of roads (paved roads in good condition), on power outages, and on railway diesels in use. Most of these relationships survive when real per capita GDP is added to the equation as an independent variable. Thus: "the costs of corruption should also be measured in terms of the deterioration in the quality of the existing infrastructure. These costs can be very high in terms of their impact on growth" (Tanzi and Davoodi 1997). Studies at the micro, country level also confirm this evidence. In a study of 243 Ugandan firms observed during the period 1995–7, Reinikka and Svensson (1999) show that poor public capital, proxied by unreliable and inadequate power supply, significantly reduced productive private investment. This evidence is consistent with responses from managers of the Ugandan firms who had cited poor utility services as well as corruption as major constraints to investment; the evidence is also consistent with inefficiency in investments observed across a large cross-section of countries in Africa (Devarajan, Easterly, and Pack 1999).

Ades and Di Tella (1997) have tried to estimate the impact of industrial policies (identified with procurement preferences to "national champions" and unequal fiscal treatment to enterprises). They find that corruption is higher in countries pursuing active industrial policy. In the presence of corruption, the total effect of industrial policy on investment ranges between 84 and 56 percent of the direct effect.

In conclusion, the above evidence supports a strong presumption that the net impact of corruption on investment is to reduce its size and its quality. As a consequence, growth must also be reduced.

Corruption and the allocation of talent

Corruption and rent-seeking may have a negative impact on growth if they create incentives for highly talented individuals to go toward rent-seeking and other unproductive activities rather than toward productive activities. This connection was also seen as important in the discussion of SMEs and their growth potential. In these enterprises, managers spent a significant amount of time dealing with rent-seeking or trying to defend their enterprises from corrupt bureaucrats. This was surely an unproductive use of their time.

The hypothesis of a connection between rent-seeking and the allocation of talent was first suggested by Baumol (1990), and by Murphy, Shleifer, and Vishny (1991). Recently it has been given a more rigorous treatment by Ehrlich and Lui (1999). Unfortunately, data on use of talent and growth by firm size are not available. Therefore, only data at the aggregate level are used to investigate the issue. These data are only suggestive of a possible relationship.

We follow the approach of Murphy, Shleifer, and Vishny (1991) that one way in which rent-seeking and corruption may influence growth is by pushing able individuals toward law rather than toward more directly productive activities such as engineering. Using data from UNESCO for fifty-three countries on enrollment in law and in engineering, we found the following result:

$$Corr = 18.50 + 0.60 \text{ Laweng} - 1.64 \text{ GDP}$$
$$(5.79) \quad (3.07) \qquad\qquad (-4.47)$$

$R^2 = 0.50$, number of countries $= 53$ (numbers in parenthesis denote t-ratios).

Here Laweng is the ratio of college enrollment in law to college enroll-ment in engineering in 1980; corr refers to the corruption perception index (averaged over the period 1989–97); and GDP refers to real per capita GDP in early 1960s. The latter has been found to be a robust determinant of corruption (Treisman 2000). The regression shows that countries with high corruption tend to have a low per capita GDP and a high ratio of lawyers to engineers. *Ceteris paribus*, it would seem that a more corrupt society needs more lawyers.

Separating lawyers from engineers gives:

$$Corr = 18.00 + 0.18 \text{ Law} + 0.02 \text{ Eng} - 1.70 \text{ GDP}$$
$$(5.89) \quad (3.59) \qquad (0.82) \qquad (-5.00)$$

$R^2 = 0.56$, number of countries $= 53$.

Thus, the correlation is between corruption and the number of lawyers. The higher the index of corruption, the more individuals are attracted to degrees in law.

Furthermore, the higher the ratio of lawyers to engineers, the lower the rate of growth.

$$Growth = 21.10 - 0.36 \text{ Corr} - 0.22 \text{ Laweng} - 2.04 \text{ GDP} + 1.39 \text{ Schooling}$$
$$(4.47)(-3.00) \qquad (-1.86) \qquad\qquad (-4.06) \qquad\qquad (3.04)$$

Adjusted $R^2 = 0.39$, number of countries $= 50$.

Where,
Growth = Average real per capita GDP over the 1980–97 period (source: *World Economic Outlook*).

Corr = Index of corruption, the same as used in previous regressions.

Laweng = as defined previously.

GDP = Real per capita GDP in 1980 (source: *World Economic Outlook*).

Schooling = Mean years of secondary schooling in 1980 (source: Barro and Lee 1996).

The above regression suggests a negative impact on growth of a higher allocation of talent to law as opposed to engineering. Along with the previous regression, it shows that the allocation of talent has an indirect impact on growth and that corruption allocates talent in a growth reducing fashion. The equation suggests that growth will be lower by 0.4 percentage points as a result of the combined direct and indirect impact of allocation of talent to law.

Corruption and public finances

In the previous section, corruption and some aspects of public finance such as public investment were discussed. In the remainder of this section, additional public finance considerations which might have growth effects are taken into account, but the discussion is less directly linked to growth.

Corruption and the composition of public spending

Corruption may have additional effects beyond those identified earlier. Some of these have been identified in recent papers; and some may have an impact on growth.

Mauro (1998) has shown that corruption may have no impact on total government spending.[11] He has also shown that *corrupt countries spend less for education and health*. This result has been confirmed by Gupta, Davoodi, and Alonso-Terme (1998). Because social spending is assumed to promote growth, it must be concluded that this is another possible channel through which corruption may affect growth negatively.

Gupta, de Mello, and Sharan (2000) have shown that corruption also leads to higher military spending, expressed either as a share of GDP or of total government expenditure, given other determinants of military spending. There is also some evidence that cuts in military spending can lead to higher growth (Knight, Loayza, and Villanueva 1996). Therefore, higher corruption can reduce growth through higher military spending.

Corruption and the tax structure

The impact of corruption, and of tax evasion on tax collection is not new in the public finance literature. See Tanzi (1998b). A recent theoretical paper (Hindricks, Keen, and Muthoo 1999) has shown that in addition to loss in tax collection, the more bribes are collected, the more a tax inspector can resort to extortion in order to collect even more.[12] The existing tax system may be regressive if tax inspectors tend to go after poorer taxpayers rather than rich ones. An implication of this chapter is that collecting progressive taxes without inducing evasion or corruption may require commissions to be paid to tax inspectors when they report high revenue; and there will be a tradeoff between enhancing equity and efficiency in pursuing a progressive tax system.

Hindricks, Keen, and Muthoo (1999) do not investigate the growth implications of the tradeoff between equity and efficiency. However, the presence of such a tradeoff implies that lowering corruption through the payment of commissions to tax inspectors has an ambiguous impact on growth since enhancing equity is good for growth, as demonstrated by Persson and Tabellini (1994) and Alesina and Rodrik (1994), but efficiency losses from a progressive tax system is bad for growth. It is not clear, however, whether such a tradeoff is quantitatively important for growth.

In a series of papers, Tanzi and Davoodi (1997), Johnson, Kaufmann, and Zoido-Lobatón (1999) and Friedman, Johnson, Kaufmann, and Zoido-Lobatón (2000) have provided evidence that countries with high levels of corruption tend to have lower collection of tax revenues in relation to GDP, give other factors. This finding implies that some of the taxes paid by taxpayers are diverted toward the pockets of the tax administrators. Thus, the true burden of taxation on the taxpayers may not fall as much as the fall in the tax receipts of the government; and as a result, the tax system in practice may become less progressive.[13] Also some taxes are not collected from some taxpayers leading to less neutrality of the tax system. These arguments demonstrate that a distinction needs to be made between taxes collected by the administrators and taxes received by the treasury. Low level of taxation may lead to a suboptimal level of public spending, which may reduce its productivity and lead to higher fiscal deficits. Higher deficits may in turn lower the growth rate (Fischer 1993). Therefore, corruption may also affect growth through its effect on fiscal deficits.

Previous studies of corruption and tax collection have addressed the effect of corruption on the level of taxation and not on its composition. One may expect that different types of taxes respond differently to corruption since payment of some taxes, but not of others, may be negotiated; some taxes are self-assessed in some countries (for example, income taxes); some are assessed by tax inspectors; hence, they are subject to opportunistic behavior and extortion on the part of tax inspectors; and some are easier to administer than others (such as international trade taxes). Recent surveys eliciting respondents' views on the prevalence of corruption in different occupations often cite customs as an area rampant with corruption and kickbacks. Does corruption reduce taxes received from customs more than other types of taxes? Are weaknesses in the administration of certain taxes systematically related to corruption? Should one expect corruption to affect value added taxes (VAT) less than other taxes because VATs, in principle, require better book-keeping and tax records and because an overwhelming share of VAT revenue is collected from a few large enterprises? An understanding of the basic facts of the tax structure is needed to understand the impact of corruption on the tax structure. The analysis that follows should be seen as only suggestive.

Table 5.1 presents the average value of each tax revenue (expressed as a fraction of GDP) and the determinants of the tax structure for a sample of up to ninety countries, and two sub-samples of developing and developed countries. Developing countries tend to rely more on indirect taxes (trade taxes and taxes on domestic goods and services); they tend to have a high share of agriculture in GDP, a low tax-GDP ratio, and a high non-tax-GDP ratio. Can corruption explain any of these differences?

Table 5.1 Average of measures of tax structure and their determinants, 1980–97

Variable	World	Developed countries	Developing countries
Total revenue	26.00	33.30	24.40
Tax revenue	20.60	29.70	18.70
Income, profit, capital gains taxes	6.80	9.70	6.10
Individual	3.12	7.57	2.13
Corporate	3.38	2.36	3.61
Social security tax	3.74	7.97	2.55
Payroll tax	0.31	0.32	0.30
Property tax	0.42	0.65	0.37
Domestic taxes on goods and services	6.65	9.68	6.01
Sales, VAT, Turnover	3.97	5.77	3.57
Excise	2.07	2.97	1.86
Trade taxes	3.65	0.83	4.28
Import	3.18	0.80	3.73
Export	0.44	0.01	0.53
Non-tax revenue	5.33	3.47	5.72
Determinants of tax structure:			
Real capita GDP (PPP$)	5,120	14,100	3,780
Agriculture share of GDP	20.90	4.51	22.90
Trade share of GDP	81.20	66.10	83.50
Corruption index	4.26	1.21	4.95

Note
All variables are measured as fractions of GDP except for the corruption index. The measure of corruption is based on ICRG and BI indexes; see Tanzi and Davoodi (1997) for details. It ranges from 0 to 10 where higher values of the corruption index refer to higher values of corruption. Averages are unweighted.

Relying on the empirical models of tax structure *à la* Tanzi (1987), each type of tax revenue, expressed as a fraction of GDP, is regressed on the same set of regressors. These are: a constant, share of agriculture in GDP, real per capita GDP, share of international trade in GDP; and the corruption perception index.[14] The results are shown in Table 5.2 and can be summarized as follows.[15]

Table 5.2 Determinants of tax structure

Dependent variable	Corruption	Adjusted R-squared	Number of countries
Total revenue	−1.47*** (−1.90)	0.41	90
Tax revenue	−2.73*** (−4.05)	0.42	89
Income, profit, capital gains taxes	−0.79** (−2.25)	0.24	89
Individual	−0.63** (−2.29)	0.46	86
Corporate	−0.16 (−0.71)	0.08	86
Social security tax	−0.92*** (−3.25)	0.39	74
Payroll tax	−0.04 (−1.16)	−0.02	75
Property tax	−0.05** (−1.84)	0.37	85
Domestic taxes on goods and services	−1.08*** (−4.47)	0.29	90
Sales, VAT, turnover	−0.79*** (−4.40)	0.24	86
Excise	−0.23** (−1.98)	0.11	88
Trade taxes	−0.06 (−0.52)	0.41	90
Import	0.03 (0.23)	0.33	90
Export	−0.07* (−1.43)	0.12	89
Non–tax revenue	1.27 (1.21)	0.16	89

Notes
Regression includes an intercept, real per capita GDP, agriculture share of GDP, and trade share of GDP. It is estimated on a cross-section of countries over the period 1980–97. The corruption perception index is taken from Tanzi and Davoodi (1997) who based it on data from International Country Risk Guide and Business International. The index has been rescaled so that higher values of the index represents higher perception of corruption. Only the coefficient on the corruption perception index is shown. Numbers in parenthesis denote t-ratios based on heteroskedastic-consistent standard errors.
*** Significant at 1 percent level; ** significant at 5 percent level; and * significant at 10 percent level.

- *Level and composition effects*: A 1 point increase in the corruption index is associated with 1.5 percentage point decline in total revenue-GDP ratio, 2.7 percent decline in tax-GDP ratio, and 1.3 percentage point increase in non-tax revenue-GDP ratio.
- Higher corruption is associated with lower revenues of all types, except for non-tax revenues. The latter finding is consistent with the fact that non-tax revenues are dominated by revenues from natural resources (at least for developing countries). Some studies have shown that natural resource abundance is an important determinant of corruption (Leite and Weidmann 1999).
- Corruption has a statistically significant correlation with individual income taxes, a finding that is consistent with individuals negotiating their tax liability with corrupt tax inspectors. It is in the mutual interests of the individual taxpayer as well as the tax inspector who would conduct business as usual by living with underreporting and collecting bribes on a sustained basis. The point estimate shows that a 1 point increase in corruption is associated with a 0.63 percent of GDP decline in individual income taxes received.
- A 1 point increase in corruption reduces the ratio of direct taxes to GDP by more than the drop in the ratio of indirect taxes to GDP (1.8 percentage point vs. 1.2 percentage point, respectively).[16] Given the higher level of corruption in developing countries, corruption has therefore a larger impact on direct taxes in developing countries than in developed countries. This finding helps explain the predominance of indirect taxes in developing countries compared to developed countries. It is also consistent with the prevalence of tax evasion from income taxes in developing countries. By reducing corruption, developing countries could help correct the imbalance between direct and indirect taxes. A 4 point reduction in corruption, which is the average difference in corruption between developed and developing countries, can increase direct taxes for the developing country as a group by 7.2 percent of GDP, bringing their ratio of direct taxes to GDP within 2 percent of GDP of developed countries.
- The larger impact of corruption on direct taxes compared to indirect taxes also implies that the progressivity of the income tax system is reduced.
- Surprisingly corruption has no statistically significant correlation with trade taxes even though surveys of the public indicate the significant presence of corruption in the customs.
- Higher corruption is also associated with lower revenues collected from VAT, sales tax, and turnover tax.[17]

Many countries have adopted value added taxes to simplify their tax system and increase their revenue performance. Are corruption and VAT performance related? More specifically, is higher corruption associated with lower VAT productivity? One measure of VAT productivity is the so-called VAT efficiency ratio: the ratio of VAT revenues received to GDP divided by the standard VAT rate. This measure is bounded between 1 and 0. The higher the ratio, the more productive the VAT system. The lower the ratio, the more widespread the extent of exemptions, zero rating, tax evasion, or weak tax administration. The simple association between corruption and the VAT efficiency ratio for a sample of eighty-three countries shows that countries with high perception of corruption tend to have low VAT efficiency ratios (Figure 5.4). The correlation coefficient is −0.34 which is statistically significant at the 1 percent level. This correlation does not imply that every exemption in the VAT system is necessarily the outcome of rent-seeking activities or corruption. For example, basic food stuffs are routinely exempt from VAT in many countries; but then there are also many instances where VAT exemptions tend to grow when vested interests attempt to regain the exemptions that they used to enjoy under the previous sales taxes replaced by the VAT.

There is also some evidence to show that countries which introduced value added taxes earlier tend to have lower levels of corruption and higher VAT efficiency ratios. Specifically, the correlation coefficient for the same group of eighty-three countries, as shown in Figure 5.4, between the date of adoption of the VAT and the subsequent level of corruption is 0.23 which is statistically significant at the 5 percent level. The correlation between the date of adoption of VAT and VAT efficiency ratio is −0.2 which is statistically significantly at the 10 percent level. It should be pointed out that these correlations might be

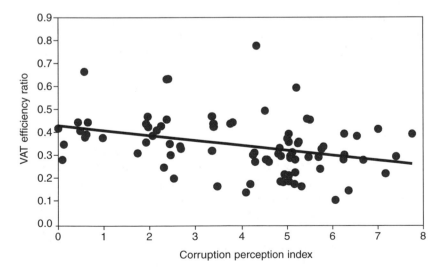

Figure 5.4 Corruption and VAT productivity in eighty-three countries

suggestive of the role that the VAT system can play in improving book-keeping records, and tax compliance, thus reducing corruption and increasing revenues.

Conclusions

This chapter has analyzed some conceptual as well as empirical direct and indirect links between corruption, growth, and public finance. Apart from reviewing the channels discussed in the literature such as the impact of corruption on investment (public and private), and its composition, the chapter has also discussed the role of small and medium-size enterprises in OECD countries, and has shown that this role is not unique to OECD countries: SMEs in many developing and transition economies are also important contributors to growth. This chapter has discussed the constraints facing SMEs and the regressive nature of bribery they encounter. It has argued that such constraints affect the allocation of time on the part of talented entrepreneurs, restrict the availability of finance to SMEs and, given their importance as engines of growth, ultimately reduce the national growth rate of the economy.

The chapter provides some evidence that there is a positive and significant association between the allocation of talent to unproductive activities and corruption. Given that corruption has a negative impact on growth, this misallocation has negative direct and indirect effects on growth of about 0.4 percentage points.

It also provides new evidence that corruption affects the structure of taxes. The evidence shows that the presence of higher corruption in developing countries may in part explain the predominant share of indirect taxes in total tax revenues. Given the spread of VATs worldwide, the chapter has also analyzed whether its adoption bears any relationship to the prevalence and awareness of corruption. Some evidence is provided that countries which adopted the VAT earlier tend to have a lower level of corruption *and* higher VAT productivity *subsequently*. However, these conclusions must be considered as highly tentative. Also the direction of causation is not obvious.

The last decade has seen a proliferation of surveys of firms and the public about costs of corruption and other obstacles to conducting business worldwide. These surveys are qualitative in nature and do not replace more objective ways of measuring such costs, but they have nevertheless provided a wealth of information consistent with objective and hard evidence provided by earlier studies conducted by researchers such as De Soto and others. In conclusion, although much of the evidence available is only suggestive, it points to a probable negative relationship between corruption and the growth rate of countries.

Notes

1 For a concise survey of this literature, see Tanzi (1998a).
2 The corruption perception index is the extended Transparency International index and is taken from Lambsdorff (1998) and real per capita GDP is in purchasing power parity US dollars and is taken from International Monetary Fund's World Economic Outlook database. The original index which ranges from 0 (highly corrupt) to 10 (highly clean) has been rescaled (i.e., adjusted index = 10–original index) so that higher values of the adjusted index represent higher perceptions of corruption.
3 Similar results are obtained using other corruption indexes. Recent studies of causes of corruption interpret this correlation as causation running from per capita GDP to corruption; see Treisman (2000).
4 See Acs, Carlsson, and Karlsson (1999) and Acs and Yeung (1999).
5 Large enterprises tend to dominate in process innovations because they have the capacity to appropriate the returns to research and development.
6 See Acs and Yeung (1999).
7 See EBRD (1999).
8 EBRD defines smaller firms as having less than forty-nine employees; medium-size firms as having between fifty and 499 employees and large firms as having more than 500 employees.
9 See Hellman, Jones, Kaufmann, and Schankerman (2000).
10 This by no means represents a unanimous view as argued in Tanzi and Davoodi (1997). See also Devarajan, Easterly, and Pack (1999), Easterly (1999), and Easterly and Levine (2000) for new international evidence in the case of Africa, and a large sample of developed and developing countries.
11 However by reducing government tax revenue, it may reduce spending or increase the fiscal deficit.
12 See also Shleifer and Vishny (1993).
13 Gupta, Davoodi, and Alonso-Terme (1998) provide evidence that corruption increases income inequality by reducing the progressivity of the tax system.
14 The corruption perception index is based on Business International data and International Country Risk Guide data, used previously by Tanzi and Davoodi (1997). A higher value of the index represents a higher perception of corruption.
15 The table represents the estimated coefficient on the corruption index only. Results for other variables included in the regression are identical to what are found in the literature. Tax revenues increase with per capita GDP, and openness, but fall with agriculture share of GDP.
16 Direct taxes are assumed to consist of four taxes in Table 5.2 (income, profit, and capital gains taxes), social security tax, payroll tax, and property tax.
17 Two caveats should be mentioned regarding the impact of corruption on VAT. First, the regression does not control for the nominal rate of the VAT; a higher rate can create greater incentives for corruption and tax evasion. Second, the available data do not allow a distinction of the revenues from VAT from those of turnover and sales taxes.

Bibliography

Abed, G. and Davoodi, H. R. (2000) "Corruption, Structural Reforms and Economic Performance in the Transition Economies," IMF Working Paper Series no. 132, Washington, DC: International Monetary Fund.
Acs, Z. J., Carlsson, B., and Karlsson, C. (eds) (1999) *Entrepreneurship, Small*

and *Medium-Sized Enterprises and the Macroeconomy*, New York: Cambridge University Press.

Acs, Z. J. and Yeung, B. (eds) (1999) *Small and Medium-Sized Enterprises in the Global Economy*, Ann Arbor, Mich.: University of Michigan Press.

Ades, A. and Di Tella, R. (1997) "National Champions and Corruption: Some Unpleasant Interventionist Arithmetic," *Economic Journal* 107 (July): 1023–42.

Alesina, A. and Rodrik, D. (1994) "Distributive Policies and Economic Growth," *Quarterly Journal of Economics* 108: 465–90.

Barro, R. J. and Lee, J. W. (1996) "International Measures of Schooling Years and Schooling Quality," *American Economic Review* 86(2): 218–33.

Baumol, W. J. (1990) "Entrepreneurship: Productive, Unproductive, and Destructive," *Journal of Political Economy* 98: 893–921.

Borensztein, E., De Gregorio, J., and Lee, J. W. (1998) "How Does Foreign Direct Investment Affect Economic Growth," *Journal of International Economics* 45 (June): 115–35.

Buscaglia, E. and Ratliff, W. (2000) *Law and Economics in Developing Countries*, Stanford: Hoover Institution.

Campos, E. E., Lien, D., and Pradhan, P. (1999) "The Impact of Corruption on Investment: Predictability Matters," *World Development* 27 (June): 1059–67.

De Soto, H. (1989) *The Other Path: The Invisible Revolution in the Third World*, New York: Harper and Row.

Devarajan, S., Easterly, W. R., and Pack, H. (1999) "Is Investment in Africa Too High or Too Low? Macro and Micro Evidence," manuscript, Washington, DC: World Bank.

Easterly, W. (1999) "The Ghost of Financing Gap: Testing the Growth Model Used in the International Financial Institutions," *Journal of Development Economics* 60: 423–38.

Easterly, W. R. and Levine, R. (2000) "It is not Factor Accumulation: Stylized Facts and Growth Models," manuscript, Washington, DC: World Bank.

Ehrlich, I. and Lui, F. T. (1999) "Bureaucratic Corruption and Endogenous Growth," *Journal of Political Economy* 107: S270–93.

European Bank for Reconstruction and Development (1999) *Ten Years of Transition*, London: European Bank for Reconstruction and Development.

Fischer, S. (1993) "Role of Macroeconomic Factors in Growth," *Journal of Monetary Economics* 32: 485–512.

Friedman, E., Johnson, S., Kaufmann, D., and Zoido-Lobatón, P. (2000) "Dodging the Grabbing Hand: The Determinants of Unofficial Activity in 69 Countries," *Journal of Public Economics* 76: 459–93.

Gupta, S., Davoodi, H. R., and Alonso-Terme, R. (1998) "Does Corruption Affect Income Inequality and Poverty?" IMF Working Paper Series WP/98/76, Washington, DC: International Monetary Fund.

Gupta, S., de Mello, L., and Sharan, R. (2000) "Corruption and Military Spending," IMF Working Paper Series WP/00/23, Washington, DC: International Monetary Fund.

Hellman, J. S., Jones, G., Kaufmann, D., and Schankerman, M. (2000) "Measuring Governance, Corruption, and State Capture: How Firms and Bureaucrats Shape the Business Environment in Transition Economies," World Bank Discussion Paper Series no. 2312, Washington, DC: World Bank.

Hindricks, J., Keen, M., and Muthoo, A. (1999) "Corruption, Extortion and Evasion," *Journal of Public Economics* 74: 395–430.

Hoshi, T., Kashyap, A., and Scharfstein, D. (1991) "Corporate Structure, Liquidity, and Investment: Evidence from Japanese Industrial Groups," *Quarterly Journal of Economics* 106(1): 33–60.

Isham, J. and Kaufmann, D. (1999) "The Forgotten Rational for Policy Reform: The Productivity of Investment Projects," *Quarterly Journal of Economics*: 149–84.

Johnson, S., Kaufmann, D., and Zoido-Lobatón, P. (1999) "Corruption, Public Finances, and the Unofficial Economy," World Bank Discussion Paper Series no. 2169, Washington, DC: World Bank.

Kaufmann, D. (1997) "The Missing Pillar of a Growth Strategy for Ukraine: Institutional and Policy Reforms for Private Sector Development," Harvard Institute for International Development Discussion Paper Series no. 603, Cambridge, Mass.: Harvard University.

Kaufmann, D. and Wei, S. (1999) "Does 'Grease Money' Speed up the Wheel of Commerce?" World Bank Discussion Paper Series no. 2254, Washington, DC: World Bank.

Knight, M., Loayza, N., and Villanueva, D. (1996) "The Peace Dividend: Military Spending Cuts and Economic Growth," IMF Staff Papers, March: 1–37.

Lambsdorff, J. G. (1998) "Corruption in Comparative Perception," in A. K. Jain (ed.), *Economics of Corruption*, Boston: Kluwer Academic.

Leite, C. and Weidmann, J. (1999) "Does Mother Nature Corrupt? Natural Resources, Corruption and Economic Growth," IMF Working Paper WP/99/85, Washington, DC: International Monetary Fund.

Mauro, P. (1995) "Corruption and Growth," *Quarterly Journal of Economics* 110 (August): 681–712.

—— (1996) "The Effects of Corruption on Growth, Investment, and Government Expenditure," IMF Working Paper WP/96/98, Washington, DC: International Monetary Fund.

—— (1998) "Corruption and the Composition of Government Expenditure," *Journal of Public Economics* 69: 263–79.

Murphy, K., Shleifer, A., and Vishny, R. (1991) "The Allocation of Talent: Implications for Growth," *Quarterly Journal of Economics* (May): 503–30.

Persson, T. and Tabellini, G. (1994) "Is Inequality Harmful for Growth?" *American Economic Review* 84: 600–22.

Reinikka, R. and Svensson, J. (1999) "How Inadequate Provision of Public Infrastructure and Services Affects Private Investment," World Bank Discussion Paper Series no. 2262, Washington, DC: World Bank.

Shleifer, A. and Vishny, R. W. (1993) "Corruption," *Quarterly Journal of Economics* 108: 599–617.

Smarzynska, B. K. and Wei, S. (2000) "Corruption and the Composition of Foreign Direct Investment: Firm-Level Evidence," World Bank Discussion Paper Series no. 2360, Washington, DC: World Bank.

Svensson. J. (2000) "Who Must Pay Bribes and How Much? Evidence from a Cross-Section of Firms," unpublished manuscript, Washington, DC: World Bank.

Tanzi, V. (1987) "Quantitative Characteristics of the Tax Systems of Developing

Countries," in D. M. G. Newbery and N. Stern (eds), *The Theory of Taxation for Developing Countries*, New York: Oxford University Press.

—— (1998a) "Corruption Around the World: Causes, Consequences, Scope, and Cures," IMF Staff Papers, December, 559–94, Washington, DC: International Monetary Fund.

—— (1998b) "Corruption and the Budget: Problems and Solutions," in A. K. Jain (ed.), *Economics of Corruption*, Boston: Kluwer Academic.

Tanzi, V. and Davoodi, H. R. (1997) "Corruption, Public Investment and Growth," IMF Working Paper Series WP/97/139, Washington, DC: International Monetary Fund.

Treisman, D. (1995) "The Politics of Soft Credit in Post-Soviet Russia," *Europe-Asia Studies* 47(6): 949–76.

—— (2000) "The Causes of Corruption: A Cross-National Study," *Journal of Public Economics* 76 (June): 399–458.

Wei, S. (1997a) "How Taxing is Corruption on International Investors?" NBER Working Paper no. 6030, Cambridge, Mass.: National Bureau of Economic Research.

—— (1997b) "Why is Corruption So Much More Taxing than Tax?" NBER Working Paper no. 2048, Cambridge, Mass.: National Bureau of Economic Research.

6 Corruption and the provision of health care and education services

Sanjeev Gupta, Hamid Davoodi, and Erwin Tiongson

Introduction

Social sectors in an economy are often characterized by market failures. To correct such failures, governments intervene through the public provision, financing, and regulation of services. There is recognition that corruption emerges as a by-product of government intervention (Acemoglu and Verdier 2000); what is not well understood, however, is that corruption can adversely affect the provision of publicly provided social services. The theoretical literature identifies three channels through which this can happen. First, corruption can drive up the price and lower the level of government output and services (Shleifer and Vishny 1993), including the provision and financing of health care and education services in many countries.[1] Second, corruption can reduce investment in human capital (Ehrlich and Lui 1999). Finally, corruption can reduce government revenue (Shleifer and Vishny 1993; Hindriks, Keen, and Muthoo 1999), which in turn can lower the quality of publicly provided services (Bearse, Glomm, and Janeba 2000).[2] The latter discourages some individuals from using these services and reduces their willingness to pay for them (through tax evasion), which shrinks the tax base and diminishes the government's ability to provide quality public services.[3] The lower quality also creates incentives for individuals to opt for privately provided services. However, in countries where private markets for health care and education services are limited, this can lead to congestion, increased delays in obtaining public services, rising opportunities for rent-seeking, and frequent use of discretionary power by government officials. Even in cases where private markets are well developed and extensive, the poor may lack the ability to pay for private services and outputs.

These predictions are consistent with a growing empirical literature on the economic consequences of corruption as well as results from surveys of users of public services. The existing empirical evidence, for example, shows that corruption reduces spending on operations and maintenance, such as medicine and textbooks (Tanzi and Davoodi 1997). Higher corruption is associated with rising military spending (Gupta, de Mello, and Sharan

2000), and lower spending on health care and education services (Mauro 1998; Gupta, Davoodi, and Alonso-Terme 1998). Corruption has also been found to lower tax revenues (Ul Haque and Sahay 1996, Tanzi and Davoodi 1997, Johnson, Kaufmann, and Zoido-Lobatón 1999a). The newly instituted surveys of users of public services further confirm the adverse impact of corruption on social services. The surveys rely on users who come in contact with officials in charge of providing social services.

Although corruption shifts the composition of public spending away from social sectors, its impact on health care and education indicators through spending may not be significant. In the empirical literature, the link between public spending and indicators of service provision, such as enrollment rate and infant mortality rates, is weak (Hanushek 1995, Jack 1999, Gupta, Verhoeven, and Tiongson 1999). The impact of corruption on indicators of provision of health care and education services can then be either direct or indirect, working through some of the channels discussed above. This chapter shows that corruption, measured by corruption perception indices, adversely affects the indicators of provision of health care and education services. Despite the overwhelming evidence from surveys of users of public services and the theoretical literature on the adverse consequences of corruption for provision of health care and education services, no systematic investigation has yet been made of the relationship between corruption and provision of health care and education services.[4]

The rest of this paper is organized as follows. The first section below illustrates how corruption can impact on the provision of social services using a theoretical model introduced by Shleifer and Vishny (1993). The subsequent section summarizes findings from national service delivery surveys to bolster the predictions from theoretical models. The data and econometric results are described in the section that follows. The last section contains the conclusions and policy implications.

Theoretical framework

Among models of corruption, the one by Shleifer and Vishny (1993) provides the simplest framework for analyzing the causes and consequences of corruption as affecting the public provision of social services. In their framework, bribes are paid by consumers to obtain government services or output. Government officials are assumed to exercise monopoly power by determining the quantity of services or output provided, either by delaying or by simply withholding them. Two cases of corruption are considered, both of which have adverse consequences for the provision of services, and are relevant in many settings.

In the first case, an official overprices by providing a service or an output at a government-established charge plus a bribe. Marginal cost to the government agent is the official price and the agent determines the quantity supplied by equating marginal revenue and marginal cost as with a typical monopolist. The bribe constitutes a tax. The official retains the bribe and transfers the official charge to the treasury. Figure 6.1a illustrates this case as "corruption without theft." The result is that the bribe drives up the price and lowers the output. Under these circumstances, some consumers will inevitably be crowded out of the market.[5] Moreover, when services affected by corruption are critical for the population, such as basic health care and education services, the full impact of government spending will not be realized. Furthermore, if teachers accept bribes for providing government-funded books or for admitting students, it will be more difficult to achieve the objective of a literate population through universal school enrollment. In fact, it has been suggested that large irregular payments required for school entrance or for passing examinations help explain low enrollment rates (Cockroft 1998). Similarly, the payment of bribes for gaining access to medical services could impact on health care indicators over time.

That government officials have the ability to limit the supply of public

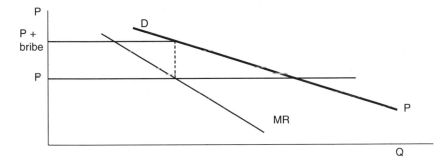

Figure 6.1a Corruption without theft

Source: Shleifer and Vishny (1993).

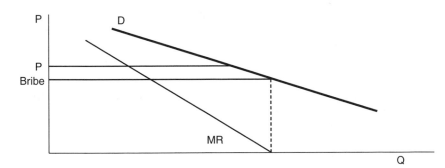

Figure 6.1b Corruption with theft

Source: Shleifer and Vishny (1993).

services has been highlighted by recent research (Kaufmann 1997, Bardhan 1997, Kaufmann and Wei 1999) – a view that was also propounded by Myrdal (1968) some thirty years ago.

In the second case, the official does not turn over to the treasury the government-imposed charge for the service or an output. This case has been referred to as "corruption with theft" (Figure 6.1b), as the government service or output is, in a way, stolen by the government official in charge of delivering it, and a bribe is collected for providing the service and output to a consumer. In this case, the official still equates marginal revenue with marginal cost, but marginal cost to the official is now zero. Thus, the bribe a consumer pays may be lower than the official price. In a sense the official "under-invoices" the cost of providing the service and output. Such a situation is attractive to the consumer and aligns his interest with that of the official, which makes corruption more difficult to detect. This creates a revenue loss for the treasury and the government official is able to exercise more discretion than in "corruption without theft." The corrupt official can choose to lower bribe level, thereby increasing the demand for a service or an output and raising revenue loss to the treasury. A smaller bribe also has the advantage of lowering the risk of detection.

The difference between the two cases is that revenue loss under the second case can be significantly higher. Although a lower bribe increases demand in the short run, it would restrict supply in the long run because of larger revenue losses.

Shleifer and Vishny's model offers policy prescriptions for anti-corruption strategies. In corruption without theft, competition in the provision of government service or output could reduce possibilities for corruption. In corruption with theft, competition complemented with enhanced monitoring of government officials and better procurement policies would help curb corruption.

Although the above model has important policy implications, it overlooks the fact that the government does not provide a single service or output. In an extension of their original model, Shleifer and Vishny (1993) present another model in which the government is still a monopolist but provides complementary services and output. The extended model recognizes that publicly provided health care and education services are complementary inputs to households' "production function" of health care and education services.[6] The government official can act as a joint monopolist and lower the bribe on a service or an output to expand demand for the complementary services and output. However, when different government agencies act as independent monopolists and do not consider the complementarity of services and outputs, the adverse impact of corruption is significant. In comparison with the joint monopolist model, a higher bribe is charged to the consumer, a lower output is supplied, and government revenue is even lower. A first-best anti-corruption solution is to allow for many producers of complementary goods and services. In comparison with joint and independent monopolist cases, this results in the lowest price, highest output, and zero bribe.

In contrast, there exists a class of models that predict exactly the opposite result. According to these models, bribes provide a mechanism for overcoming an overly centralized and overly extended government bureaucracy, red tape, and delays (Leff 1964, Lui 1985). This interpretation of bribery and corruption, sometimes referred to as the "efficient-grease" hypothesis (Kaufmann and Wei 1999), views the size of a bribe as a reflection of an individual's opportunity cost. Hence, the payment of a bribe is an efficient solution to the acquisition of a public service or output, with no adverse consequences. The next section shows that the efficient-grease hypothesis runs counter to findings of national service delivery surveys. In general, these surveys point toward the negative impact of corruption on the provision of services.[7]

National service delivery surveys

In recent years, an increasing number of public service delivery surveys have been conducted in developing and transition economies by international organizations, such as the World Bank and CIET (Community Information, Empowerment, Transparency) International, as well as by local agencies, such as the Public Affairs Center (PAC) in Bangalore, India.[8] These surveys are designed to elicit responses from users of social services, including their views on the impact of corruption on service delivery. Although most reports based on these surveys are still preliminary, they nevertheless confirm the pervasiveness of corruption and bribery in the public provision of health care and education services.

One major survey conducted worldwide by the World Bank for the 1997 *World Development Report* (WDR) examined perceptions of institutional uncertainty as viewed by the private sector.[9] This survey provides an internationally comparable dataset of indicators of perceived uncertainty about laws, policies, and regulations, the level and unpredictability of corruption, as well as the perceived quality and efficiency of government services, and the quality of health care provision. This aspect of the WDR survey provides interesting insights for this study. Figure 6.2 illustrates the relationship between an index of corruption and its unpredictability, on one hand, and government service provision, on the other, for a group of seventy-one countries.[10]

The scatterplots suggest a strong correlation between corruption and service provision; that is, countries with less corruption and higher predictability of corruption tend to have better quality of health care and more efficient provision of public services.[11] The correlation coefficients range from -0.59 to -0.66 and are significant at the 1 percent level. This high correlation further suggests that corruption and the efficient-grease hypothesis are at odds with each other.

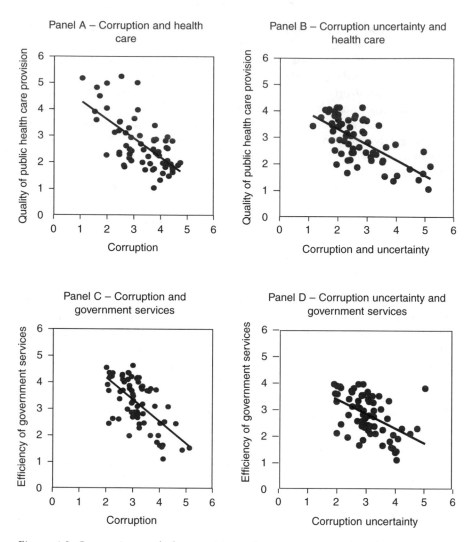

Figure 6.2 Corruption and the provision of government services in seventy-one countries

Source: World Bank (1997).

Note: The indices used in the charts correspond to the following survey questions: For corruption: Are irregular payments commonly made to officials? For corruption uncertainty: Are firms asked to pay more – in addition to irregular payments – by other officials? For quality of government services: How efficient are government services? And for quality of public health care: How is the quality of public health care provision? In the survey, these are questions 14, 16, 25, and 22d, respectively. Respondents were required to rate their responses from 1 (worst) to 6 (best). For this paper, the corruption and uncertainty indices have been rescaled from 1 (best) to 6 (worst).

The above results are reinforced by a simple regression of child mortality rate on a constant, the index of corruption, and the indicator of quality of health care provision for a group of sixty-two countries.[12] The results confirm the association between corruption and health outcomes: countries with higher corruption tend to have higher child mortality.

These results can be used to quantify the interaction between corruption and quality of health care provision and child mortality rate. Using the estimated coefficients on the explanatory variables and the mean and standard deviation of each variable in the regression, four cells are constructed, each representing a different scenario for corruption and quality of health care and the associated value for child mortality.[13] The results are shown in Figure 6.3a. The difference between the two polar cases is considerable; countries with low corruption and high quality of health care provision tend to have fifty-nine fewer child mortality per 1,000 live births than countries with high corruption and low quality of health care provision. The results are subjected to further scrutiny in the next section.

Similarly, the student dropout rate is regressed on a constant, the corruption index and the indicator of efficiency of government services for a group of fifty-three countries.[14] The results shown in Figure 6.3b are consistent with theoretical predictions. Countries with higher levels of corruption tend to have higher student dropout rates. The difference between the two polar cases is revealing: countries with low corruption and high efficiency of government services tend to have about 26 percentage points fewer student dropouts than countries with high corruption and low efficiency of government services.

Other surveys of national service delivery have solicited answers to a range of questions that were not covered in the WDR survey. The findings from these surveys can be summarized as follows.

First, *corruption can increase the cost of health care and education services*. Although primary health care and primary education are often provided by the government free of charge or at very low cost in the countries surveyed, service users often find themselves paying unofficial fees or illegal charges. The CIET social audits suggest that the percentage of students paying extra charges for education range from 10 percent to 86 percent.[15] A World Bank country study likewise finds that parents are asked to pay illegal stipends for enrolling their children in school (Langseth and Stapenhurst 1997). A PAC survey reveals that as much as 38 percent of total hospital expenses borne by households are in the form of bribes, and some 17 percent of households claim to have made unofficial payments to public hospitals (Paul 1998). One study reveals that even staff of a maternity hospital were bribed to obtain medical services (Gopakumar 1998). Another survey confirms that perception of corruption in the health sector is strongly correlated with input overpricing and unofficial payments (Gray-Molina, Perez de Rada, and Yanez 1999).

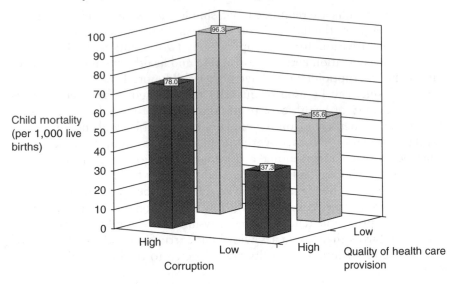

Figure 6.3a Corruption, quality of health care, and child mortality in sixty-two countries (circa 1997)

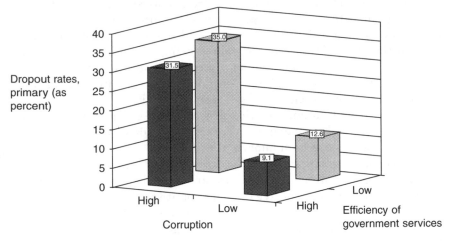

Figure 6.3b Corruption, efficiency, and dropout rates in fifty-three countries (circa 1997)

Higher user costs also create a disincentive for using government facilities. Surveys suggest that illegal payments for school entrance and other hidden costs help explain dropout rates and low school enrollment rates in developing countries (CIET 1999; Cockroft 1998).

Second, *corruption may decrease the volume of publicly provided services.* Service delivery surveys show that theft of medicines and textbooks is a common form of leakage.[16] In one country, health staff reportedly expropriated and sold drugs and medicine, depriving the poor of basic health services (Reinikka 1999). In another country, despite significant public expenditures on textbooks, only 16 percent of children have actually received them. Similarly, education supplies have been lost to payoffs, under-deliveries, and overpricing (Chua 1999).

Finally, *corruption may lower the quality of health care and education services.* In one country, bribes and payoffs in teacher recruitment and promotion have lowered the quality of public school teachers (Chua 1999); in another, inadequate treatment and lack of drugs have been attributed to corruption (CIET 1996). Officials may also create delays or bottlenecks in order to extract bribes. One survey confirms that bribes are indeed associated with slower service (Villegas, Morales, and Andersson 1998).

The next section ascertains whether these service delivery surveys are consistent with data across a range of countries.

Data and estimation

The preceding sections suggest a framework for evaluating the relationship between corruption and social indicators:

$$Y_i = \alpha + \beta X_i + \gamma Z_i + \varepsilon_i \tag{1}$$

where Y_i is a measure of aggregate education outcome or health status; X_i is an index of corruption perception in country i; and Z_i are control variables such as per capita income, public spending on health care and education services, average years of education, and other known determinants of health care and education indicators.

Although this framework addresses the adverse impact of corruption on health care and education indicators, the available data do not allow one to distinguish between the two cases of corruption discussed in the section on theoretical framework. This regression should then be seen as a reduced-form specification.

The use of aggregate data to estimate this equation has other limitations. The factors that affect health care and education indicators are often poorly captured by aggregate indicators, such as average years of education. However, there is evidence that cross-country analyses based on aggregate data are not inconsistent with findings of micro-level studies (Schultz 1993 and 1998).

The technique of Ordinary Least Squares (OLS) is used to estimate equation (1) for both cross-section and panel data covering 128 advanced and developing countries.[17] Panel data results may be less reliable because of the persistence of corruption over time in the sample countries, the limited annual data on social indicators, and the quality of reported social indicators that are often based on interpolations or estimates from demographic models. For these reasons, this chapter relies largely on cross-sectional regressions.

Semilog regressions are used to estimate various specifications of equation (1). Except for corruption, all other variables are specified in logarithmic form. This is consistent with other studies suggesting a nonlinear relationship between social indicators and their standard explanatory variables.[18]

The corruption indices were drawn from various sources. The main index is from the Political Risk Services/International Country Risk Guide (PRS/ICRG) database. This corruption index has been rescaled and ranges from 0 (least corrupt) to 10 (most corrupt).[19] Recent research by Kaufmann, Kraay, and Zoido-Lobatón (1999b) suggests the inadequacy of existing individual indices of corruption, due to high variance among the surveys that underlie these indices. These authors combine related measures of governance into aggregate indicators for what they consider to be six fundamental concepts of governance, including graft or corruption.[20] Their index of graft, with estimates ranging from about –2.5 (most corrupt) to 2.5 (least corrupt), is also used as an alternative measure of corruption. This was rescaled and ranges from –2.5 (least corrupt) to 2.5 (most corrupt). This chapter uses the PRS/ICRG index more extensively than the graft index because the graft index covers only the 1997–8 period, whereas the PRS/ICRG index covers the 1985–97 period – the same period as the health care and education indicators and the control variables.[21]

Indices of corruption constructed by Transparency International (TI), which are based on at least three surveys, are also used for testing the sensitivity of results.

At the outset, it needs to be recognized that the above indices of perception of corruption do not necessarily capture corruption in the health care and education sectors. For example, the PRS/ICRG index reflects the assessment of foreign investors about the degree of corruption in an economy. Investors are asked whether high government officials are likely to demand special payments (high-level corruption) and whether illegal payments are generally expected throughout lower levels of government especially those connected with import and export licenses, exchange controls, tax assessment, police protection, or loans (low-level corruption). However, these indices are likely to capture corruption at the service provision level to the extent they refer to corruption in the public sector as a whole.

This study uses health care and education indicators that are common to four sets of indicators endorsed at different international fora.[22] These include rates for immunization, births attended by health staff, child and infant mortality, enrollment and persistence to Grade 5, repeater, dropout, and illiteracy. Data on social indicators and the control variables are primarily drawn from the 1999 World Development Indicators, UNESCO, and Barro and Lee (1996).[23] A detailed list is provided in Tables 6.8 and 6.9 in the appendix.

OLS regressions

Table 6.1 presents baseline regressions of indicators of health care and education services on a constant and the PRS/ICRG corruption index. The results show that better health care and education indicators are positively and significantly correlated with lower corruption. When per capita GDP, considered as a major determinant of corruption (Treisman 2000), is added to the baseline regressions,[24] the corruption index remains significantly correlated with all measures of health outcomes, except for immunization rates (Table 6.2).[25] The coefficient estimates, however, are generally lower. Corruption ceases to be significantly correlated with indicators of education services when per capita income is added as a control variable, except for repeater rates and dropout rates at the primary level.

The overall results continue to hold when four other control variables are added. First, average years of education in the female population – a measure of maternal education – could have a positive impact on health outcomes (Schultz 1993, 1998) and on student performance (Barro and Lee 1997). Second, public expenditures on health care and education services are added, although evidence on their impact on social indicators is mixed.[26] Third, age-dependency ratio is meant to capture the constraints on public resources.[27] Finally, health status and education outcomes are expected to improve with increased urbanization.[28] For brevity, Table 6.3 reports the results of this exercise for child mortality alone, but this holds for infant mortality and percent of low-birthweight babies as well.[29]

Some additional controls were also tried, which did not affect the statistical significance of corruption. These were access to safe water and access to sanitation, which were both found to be statistically significant.[30] Physicians per 1,000 people, another measure of available health resources, is also significant, while adding benefit incidence as a control variable shows that corruption remains significant at the 5 percent level.[31]

As regards regressions for education indicators, corruption is consistently correlated with dropout rates at conventional levels of significance when various controls are added (Table 6.4).[32] However, this is not the case for the remaining education indicators. It is noteworthy that the presence of multicollinearity – in particular, the correlation between corruption and public spending – requires some caution in the interpretation of these results.[33]

Instrumental variable regressions

Corruption could be an endogenous variable, which would render the OLS technique inappropriate. First, both corruption and health or education indicators could be correlated with an unobserved, country-specific variable. The statistical relationship between corruption and health care or education may then be simply incidental. Second, the possibility of reverse causality cannot be ruled out as people with poor health status

Table 6.1 Baseline regressions, 1985–97: cross-sectional analysis[1]

Dependent variable	N	R^2	F statistic	Constant	Corruption
Health outcomes					
Child mortality (per 1,000 live births)	116	0.44	92.26***	5.75*** (28.01)	0.37*** (12.26)
Infant mortality (per 1,000 live births)	117	0.48	107.77***	5.37*** (30.22)	0.35*** (12.72)
Births attended by health staff (percent of total)	110	0.25	38.18***	3.42*** (22.05)	−0.13*** (−6.06)
Immunization, DPT (percent of children under 12 months)	117	0.15	21.68***	3.92*** (49.73)	−0.06*** (−5.61)
Low-birthweight babies (percent of births)	113	0.33	55.38***	3.02*** (23.34)	0.14*** (7.20)
Education outcomes					
School enrollment, primary (percent net)	111	0.05	6.24***	4.34*** (57.02)	−0.03*** (−3.30)
Repeater rates, primary (percent)	87	0.13	14.09***	3.17*** (9.51)	0.24*** (3.47)
Dropout rates, primary (percent)	88	0.32	41.30***	4.70*** (16.32)	0.36*** (7.02)
Persistence to grade 5, total (percent of cohort)	81	0.12	11.47***	4.13*** (67.58)	−0.04*** (−4.30)
Illiteracy rates (percent of population age 15 and older)	86	0.08	8.53***	4.01*** (9.09)	0.23*** (2.71)

Sources: World Bank (1999), Barro and Lee (1996), and Political Risk Services.

Note
1 Variables are means covering the period 1985–97. N denotes the number of countries. Except for corruption, all the variables are in logs. A low value of the corruption index means that a country is perceived to be less corrupt. White's heteroskedastic-consistent t-statistics are in parentheses. (***), (**), and (*) denote significance at the 1 percent, 5 percent, and 10 percent levels, respectively.

Table 6.2 Corruption, health care and education services, 1985–97: cross-sectional analysis[1]

Dependent variable	N	R^2	F statistic	Constant	Income	Corruption
Health outcomes						
Child mortality (per 1,000 live births)	116	0.82	254.42***	10.45*** (18.07)	−0.73*** (−9.11)	0.13*** (4.30)
Infant mortality (per 1,000 live births)	117	0.81	255.43***	9.35*** (19.22)	−0.62*** (−9.17)	0.14*** (5.14)
Births attended by health staff (percent of total)	110	0.48	50.52***	1.79*** (4.88)	0.25*** (5.12)	−0.05** (−2.01)
Immunization, DPT (percent of children under 12 months)	117	0.31	27.06***	3.07*** (12.31)	0.13*** (4.10)	−0.02 (−1.40)
Low-birthweight babies (percent of births)	113	0.55	68.13***	4.55*** (17.93)	−0.24*** (−7.63)	0.06*** (2.87)
Education outcomes						
School enrollment, primary (percent net)	111	0.24	18.01***	3.52*** (12.75)	0.13*** (3.51)	0.01 (0.82)
Repeater rates, primary (percent)	87	0.22	12.98***	5.63*** (6.87)	−0.36*** (−3.49)	0.15** (2.16)
Dropout rates, primary (percent)	88	0.44	35.78***	7.89*** (11.88)	−0.50*** (−5.15)	0.20*** (3.39)
Persistence to grade 5, total (percent of cohort)	81	0.43	31.71***	3.14*** (14.97)	0.15*** (4.78)	−0.00 (−0.30)
Illiteracy rates (percent of population age 15 and older)	86	0.26	16.14***	7.46*** (8.46)	−0.50*** (−4.27)	0.11 (1.34)

Sources: World Bank (1999), Barro and Lee (1996), and Political Risk Services.

Note

1 Variables are means covering the period 1985–97. N denotes the number of countries. Except for corruption, all the variables are in logs. A low value of the corruption index means that a country is perceived to be less corrupt. White's heteroskedastic-consistent t-statistics are in parentheses. (***), (**), and (*) denote significance at the 1 percent, 5 percent, and 10 percent levels, respectively.

Table 6.3 Child mortality and corruption, 1985–97: cross-sectional analysis[1]

	OLS							2SLS
	(1)	(2)	(3)	(4)	(5)	(6)	(7)	(8)
Constant	5.75***	10.45***	10.42***	10.21***	9.37***	9.31***	8.65***	8.97***
	(28.01)	(18.07)	(17.90)	(21.55)	(24.46)	(22.71)	(16.69)	(21.00)
Corruption (PRS/ICRG)	0.37***	0.13***	0.12***	0.08***	0.07***	0.07***		0.10**
	(12.26)	(4.30)	(4.28)	(3.44)	(2.70)	(2.59)		(2.03)
Corruption (graft)							0.20***	
							(3.95)	
Per capita income		-0.73***	-0.73***	-0.67***	-0.55***	-0.58***	-0.53***	-0.49***
		(-9.11)	(-8.98)	(-9.22)	(-9.75)	(-8.08)	(-6.24)	(-5.04)
Public health spending			-0.01	0.04	0.04	0.04	0.03	0.05
			(-0.30)	(0.87)	(0.90)	(0.86)	(0.80)	(0.95)
Average years of education, females, age 15 and older				-0.36***	-0.22***	-0.23***	-0.26***	-0.31**
				(-3.96)	(-2.84)	(-2.76)	(3.18)	(-1.96)
Dependency ratio					1.16***	1.13***	1.00***	0.98***
					(5.58)	(5.48)	(4.73)	(3.52)
Urbanization						0.07	0.04	0.04
						(0.15)	(0.30)	(0.28)
F statistic	92.26***	254.42***	168.27***	184.43***	195.54***	161.76***	169.36***	
Adjusted R-squared	0.44	0.82	0.81	0.89	0.91	0.91	0.92	
N	116	116	116	89	89	89	89	73
First-stage R-squared								0.69
Sargan's p-value								0.77

Sources: World Bank (1999), Barro and Lee (1996), Political Risk Services, Kaufmann *et al.* (1999b), and Treisman (2000).

Note
1 Variables are means covering the period 1985–97. N denotes the number of countries. Except for corruption, all the variables are in logs. A low value of the corruption index means that a country is perceived to be less corrupt. White's heteroskedastic-consistent t-statistics are in parentheses. (***), (**), and (*) denote significance at the 1 percent, 5 percent, and 10 percent levels, respectively. The instruments used were (log of) 1985 per capita income, democracy index, and percent Protestants. See text.

Table 6.4 Dropout rates and corruption, 1985–97: cross-sectional analysis[1]

	OLS							2SLS
	(1)	(2)	(3)	(4)	(5)	(6)	(7)	(8)
Constant	4.70***	7.89***	8.06***	6.64***	5.16***	4.73***	3.25**	3.83**
	(16.32)	(11.88)	(11.32)	(4.97)	(3.98)	(3.44)	(1.99)	(2.52)
Corruption (PRS/ICRG)	0.36***	0.20***	0.18***	0.20***	0.14**	0.13**		0.36**
	(7.02)	(3.39)	(3.08)	(2.74)	(2.12)	(2.00)		(2.51)
Corruption (graft)							0.50***	
							(2.72)	
Per capita income		-0.50***	-0.52***	-0.29***	-0.08***	-0.28	-0.15	-0.00
		(-5.15)	(-5.16)	(-1.42)	(-0.46)	(-1.28)	(-0.65)	(-0.02)
Public education spending			-0.07	-0.13	-0.23	-0.24	-0.31*	-0.08
			(-0.36)	(-0.66)	(-1.20)	(-1.20)	(1.65)	(-0.34)
Average years of education, females, age 15 and older				-0.17	0.17	0.05	0.00	0.17
				(-0.65)	(0.66)	(0.17)	(0.00)	(0.35)
Dependency ratio					2.50***	2.29***	1.95**	1.76*
					(3.49)	(3.07)	(2.53)	(1.92)
Urbanization						0.55	0.47	0.37
						(1.39)	(1.30)	(0.89)
F statistic	41.30***	35.78***	22.69***	10.95***	12.63***	11.16***	12.76***	
Adjusted R-squared	0.32	0.44	0.43	0.35	0.45	0.46	0.49	
N	88	88	36	72	72	72	72	59
First-stage R-squared								0.69
Sargan's p-value								0.17

Sources: World Bank (1999), Barro and Lee (1996), Political Risk Services, Kaufmann *et al.* (1999b), and Treisman (2000).

Note

1/ Variables are means covering the period 1985–97. N denotes the number of countries. Except for corruption, all the variables are in logs. A low value of the corruption index means that a country is perceived to be less corrupt. White's heteroskedastic-consistent t-statistics are in parentheses. (***), (**), and (*) denote significance at the 1 percent, 5 percent, and 10 percent levels, respectively. The instruments used were (log of) 1985 per capita income, democracy index, and percent Protestants. See text.

may be more willing to pay bribes to obtain services that otherwise would not be available; or poor levels of education could create an environment conducive to corruption. The instrumental variable technique addresses both possibilities. The difficulty lies in finding appropriate instruments for corruption.

For this study, the variables identified by Treisman (2000) are used as instruments. He finds that countries with lower corruption tend to be largely Protestant, former British colonies, have high per capita income, a high ratio of imports to GDP, long exposure to democracy, and a unitary form of government.[34] These variables can be taken as potential instruments for the corruption index. In the current sample, corruption is found to be highly correlated with the share of Protestants in the population, per capita income, and exposure to democracy.[35]

The results of 2SLS regressions are presented in Tables 6.3 and 6.4 (columns 8). The instruments used are the (log of) the initial value of per capita income, the share of Protestants in the population, and exposure to democracy.[36] The specification test indicates that the instruments are correctly specified and the first-stage adjusted R-squared is generally high – about 0.69 for both regressions.

In general, the results in Tables 6.3 and 6.4 indicate a statistically significant relationship between corruption and both child mortality rates and dropout rates. The 2SLS regressions of infant mortality rates and percent of low-birthweight babies are not shown but the results hold for these regressions as well. Sargan's specification test also indicates that the instruments are correctly specified for all 2SLS regressions. A partial scatterplot of the 2SLS regression in Table 6.3, column 8, is displayed in Figure 6.4.[37]

The results suggest that when corruption is reduced, the social gains, as

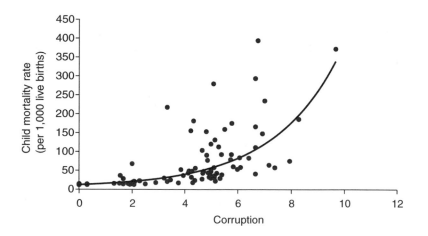

Figure 6.4 Corruption and child mortality

Source: See Table 6.3.

measured by improvement in health care and education indicators, are immense. Figure 6.5 illustrates these gains, using the estimated coefficients and the mean of each variable in the 2SLS regressions.[38] The polar cases of corruption are based on its standard deviation. Although the gains are not quite as dramatic as those suggested by the simple regression in the previous section, they remain considerable. Infant mortality rates in countries with high corruption, for example, could be almost twice as high as in countries with low corruption, holding other factors constant; dropout rates could be five times as high.

Further robustness test

Estimating OLS regressions using the aggregate governance indicator for graft produced by Kaufmann, Kraay, and Zoido-Lobatón (1999b) yields similar results (Tables 6.3 and 6.4, columns 7).[39] The adjusted R-squared is somewhat higher at 0.79 but the basic results hold.

In addition, two other indices of corruption, the 1995–8 TI index and the expanded 1997 corruption perception index constructed by Lambsdorff (1998) are also significantly correlated with child and infant mortality rates, percent of low-birthweight babies, and dropout rates.[40] These results hold when income per capita, public spending on health or education, average years of education in the female population, dependency ratio, and

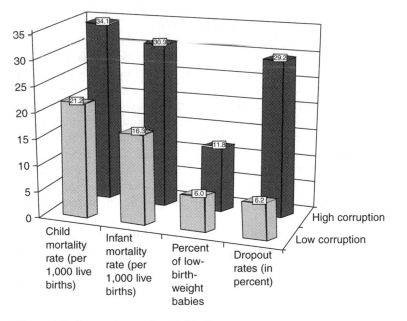

Figure 6.5 Corruption and social indicators

Source: See Tables 6.3 and 6.4.

urbanization are employed as control variables.[41] The coefficient estimates are broadly similar to those in regressions based on the PRS/ICRG index.

Previous regressions treated corruption as a continuous variable. Kaufmann, Kraay, and Zoido-Lobatón (1999b) note the imprecision of existing continuous measures of corruption. Given this uncertainty, the findings of these authors imply that corruption indices should be used to classify countries into three groups: the most corrupt, the least corrupt, and those in-between.

Table 6.5 reports the results of regressions with a two-way (high and low) and a three-way (high, medium, and low) classification of corruption scores. Dummy variables are used to define each classification.[42] For brevity, the table omits the coefficient estimates of the control variables in the regression model. In general, the results suggest that relative to countries with low corruption, countries with high and medium corruption have worse health care and education outcomes. The difference between high and medium corruption, however, is generally not significant, suggesting that a two-way classification may better characterize the data.[43]

Alternatively, the importance of corruption could also be ascertained by splitting the countries into categories of high and low corruption. Table 6.6 reports the results that use the graft index to group countries into these categories.[44] In general, the impact of health or education spending on social indicators remains insignificant. There is some evidence that corruption reduces the effectiveness of public education spending, as such spending is significant in reducing dropout rates in countries with low corruption but not in countries with high corruption. Meanwhile, the income elasticity of child mortality, infant mortality, and percent of low-birthweight babies in countries with low corruption is about twice the elasticity in high-corruption countries, suggesting that income is more effective in improving social indicators in countries with low corruption. Dependency ratios, however, pose a greater resource constraint in countries with low corruption, whereas female education is a bigger factor in reducing child and infant mortality in countries with high corruption. The finding on dependency ratios imply that as more resources are allocated toward old-age rather than younger populations, social indicators for the latter worsen. The finding on female education is equally important because it shows that social gains from increasing females' access to education can be significant, particularly in countries with high corruption.

To further address the problem of imprecision in existing corruption indices, it has been argued that weighting an index by the inverse of its standard deviation could give more accurate results (Treisman 2000). This gives more weight to corruption rankings in which there is less uncertainty or more agreement among the different surveys on which they are based. Table 6.7 presents the results of regressions of social indicators on the graft index divided by its standard deviation, along with the same control variables as in Tables 6.5 and 6.6. The results indicate that

Table 6.5 Cross-sectional analysis with dummy variables, 1985–97[1]

Corruption classification	Dependent variable				Dependent variable			
	Child mortality	Infant mortality	Low birthweight	Dropout	Child mortality	Infant mortality	Low birthweight	Dropout
	(Coefficient estimates)				Graft index			
	PRS/ICRG corruption index							
Two-way								
High (mean)	0.25** (2.54)	0.29*** (2.99)	0.25*** (3.57)	3.08 (0.33)	0.42*** (3.19)	0.48*** (3.71)	0.26*** (2.82)	0.93*** (2.83)
High (median)	0.30*** (3.31)	0.30*** (3.37)	0.29*** (4.16)	0.49** (2.13)	0.24** (2.12)	0.25** (2.30)	0.08` (1.03)	0.56* (1.90)
Three-way								
High	0.34** (1.96)	0.43*** (2.62)	0.35** (2.34)	0.81* (1.81)	0.33*** (2.39)	0.46*** (3.31)	0.33** (2.59)	1.04* (1.81)
Medium	0.33*** (3.17)	0.41*** (3.75)	0.29*** (3.31)	0.52 (1.37)	0.38*** (3.81)	0.49*** (4.63)	0.30*** (3.25)	1.02** (2.26)
N	89	89	87	72	89	89	87	72

Sources: Political Risk Services and Kaufmann et al. (1999b).

Note
1 These regressions, following previous regressions, control for log of income, sectoral spending, average years of female schooling, dependency ratio, urbanization. White's heteroskedastic-consistent t-statistics are in parentheses. (***), (**), and (*) denote significance at the 1 percent, 5 percent, and 10 percent levels, respectively. See text for classification of corruption dummies.

Table 6.6 Social indicators and low and high graft, 1985–97: cross-sectional analysis[1]

	Child mortality		Infant mortality		Low birthweight		Dropout	
	Low graft	High graft	Low graft	High graft	Low graft	High graft	Low graft	High graft
Constant	9.98***	8.23***	9.98***	6.95***	5.96***	3.65***	2.91	4.74**
	(8.91)	(16.69)	(8.91)	(16.35)	(9.42)	(5.35)	(1.56)	(2.40)
Per capita income	−0.70***	−0.41***	−0.70***	−0.29***	−0.35***	0.14	−0.19	−0.13
	(−4.38)	(−4.36)	(−4.38)	(−3.62)	(−3.87)	(1.22)	(−0.53)	(−0.40)
Public health or education spending	0.04	−0.01	0.04	−0.02	0.02	0.03	−0.40*	−0.31
	(0.73)	(−0.09)	(0.73)	(−0.39)	(0.42)	(0.47)	(−1.79)	(−1.10)
Average years of education, females, age 15 and older	−0.28	−0.25**	−0.28	−0.21**	0.09	−0.08	−0.68	0.42
	(−1.62)	(−2.56)	(−1.62)	(−2.67)	(0.73)	(−0.90)	(−1.42)	(1.14)
Dependency ratio	1.15***	0.91***	1.15***	0.66**	−0.13	0.37	2.29*	1.96**
	(3.01)	(3.35)	(3.01)	(2.61)	(−0.39)	(1.10)	(2.06)	(2.46)
Urbanization	0.07	−0.06	0.07	−0.09	−0.24	−0.57***	0.89	−0.03
	(0.22)	(−0.51)	(0.22)	(−0.84)	(−1.31)	(−2.81)	(0.98)	(−0.08)
Adjusted R-squared	0.87	0.84	0.87	0.81	0.61	0.35	0.37	0.14
F statistic	60.65***	46.48***	60.65***	37.34***	14.64***	5.57***	4.54***	2.32*
N	45	44	45	44	44	43	31	41

Sources: World Bank (1999), Barro and Lee (1996), Political Risk Services, and Kaufmann et al. (1999b).

Note
1 Variables are means covering the period 1985–97. N denotes the number of countries. Except for corruption, all the variables are in logs. A low value of the corruption index means that a country is perceived to be less corrupt. White's heteroskedastic-consistent t-statistics are in parentheses. (***), (**), and (*) denote significance at the 1 percent, 5 percent, and 10 percent levels, respectively.

Table 6.7 Social indicators and variance-weighted corruption, 1985–97: cross-sectional analysis[1]

	Child mortality	Infant mortality	Low birthweight	Dropout
Constant	8.56***	7.46***	4.23***	2.94*
	(16.47)	(15.28)	(7.94)	(1.85)
Graft/standard deviation of graft	0.05***	0.06***	0.03***	0.12***
	(4.28)	(5.67)	(2.72)	(3.30)
Per capita income	−0.52***	−0.43***	−0.03	−0.09
	(−6.16)	(−5.35)	(−0.37)	(−0.41)
Public health or education spending	0.04	0.04	0.03	−0.35**
	(0.80)	(0.92)	(0.70)	(−2.06)
Average years of education, females, age 15 and older	−0.30***	−0.26***	−0.06	−0.08
	(−3.51)	(−3.14)	(−0.85)	(−0.25)
Dependency ratio	0.96***	0.74***	0.12	1.92**
	(4.37)	(3.58)	(0.50)	(2.51)
Urbanization	0.05	0.04	−0.41***	0.47
	(0.37)	(0.35)	(−2.90)	(1.34)
Adjusted R-squared	0.93	0.92	0.62	0.56
F statistic	176.49***	157.06***	21.79***	13.86***
N	89	89	87	72

Sources: World Bank (1999), Barro and Lee (1996), Political Risk Services, and Kaufmann *et al.* (1999b).

Note

1 Variables are means covering the period 1985–97. N denotes the number of countries. Except for corruption, all the variables are in logs. A low value of the graft index means that a country is perceived to be less corrupt. White's heteroskedastic-consistent t-statistics are in parentheses. (***), (**), and (*) denote significance at the 1 percent, 5 percent, and 10 percent levels, respectively.

variance-weighted corruption is significantly related to child mortality, infant mortality, percent of low-birthweight babies, and dropout rates.

Panel data regressions

Panel data regressions generally yield weaker results. Controlling for per capita income, public spending on health, dependency ratio, and urbanization rate, corruption remains significantly correlated with child mortality rates in both fixed effects and random effects regressions, and with percent of low-birthweight babies in the random effects regression.[45]

Data limitations preclude the application of panel data techniques to education outcomes. For instance, there are relatively few observations for dropout rates for the 1985–97 period. In addition, the baseline regressions are not significant for either fixed effects or random effects.

Conclusions and policy implications

This chapter provides a cross-country analysis of the relationship between corruption perception indices and indicators of provision of health care and education services. The empirical analysis shows that a high level of corruption has adverse consequences for a country's child and infant mortality rates, percent of low-birthweight babies in total births, and dropout rates in primary schools. In particular, child mortality rates in countries with high corruption are about one-third higher than in countries with low corruption; infant mortality rates and percent of low-birthweight babies are almost twice as high, and dropout rates are five times as high. The results are consistent with predictions stemming from theoretical models and service delivery surveys.

The results have four important policy implications in light of the dominant role played by governments in the provision of health care and education services. First, improvements in indicators of health care and education services do not necessarily require higher public spending. It is equally, if not more, important to institute transparent procurement procedures and to enhance financial accountability of public spending. Second, it is likely that a reduced level of corruption in the provision of services would help improve their quality. This, in turn, would induce individuals to use these services more intensely and pay official charges for their provision.[46] Third, conditions that facilitate private sector entry into the provision of public services would help curb the monopoly power of government service providers and limit their ability to charge bribes. Finally, participation of the poor in the decisions that influence the allocation of public resources would mitigate corruption possibilities.[47] Empowerment of the poor would thus limit the monopoly power exercised by the government officials responsible for the provision of public services and outputs.

Notes

The views expressed in this chapter are those of the authors and do not necessarily represent those of the IMF or IMF policy. The authors wish to thank Emanuele Baldacci, Luiz De Mello, Gabriela Inchauste, Arvind K. Jain, and Luc Leruth for their comments. The usual disclaimer applies.

1 Governments provide a wide range of services in social sectors, as measured by intermediate health care and education indicators (e.g. immunization and school enrollment) and outcomes (e.g. literacy and mortality).
2 Government revenues are lower according to these two models because different government agencies act as independent rent-seeking, monopolist providers of complementary goods and services or because of corrupt and extortionist tax inspectors.
3 Alesina (1999) discusses this "vicious cycle" in developing countries and contrasts it with a "virtuous cycle" in developed countries.
4 Kaufmann, Kraay, and Zoido-Lobatón (1999a) test a simple association between two social indicators and various measures of governance.
5 This is similar to Alam's (1989, 1990) model, where managers increase their illicit revenues by reducing output. The result is also consistent with studies of benefit incidence of public social spending, which point to significant leakages. Benefits from public spending disproportionately accrue to the rich; the poor simply do not utilize public services as intensively as the rich, despite the fact that the poor tend to have lower levels of health care and education achievements (Castro-Leal *et al.* 1999, Davoodi and Sachjapinan 2001). Corruption, of course, is not the only reason for this leakage.
6 See, for example, Hanushek (1995) and Filmer, Hammer, and Pritchett (1998).
7 Kaufmann and Wei (1999) also report that the efficient-grease hypothesis is not supported by data.
8 The CIET social audits are available via the Internet: www.ciet.org.
9 Available via the Internet: www.unibas.ch/wwz/wifor/staff/bw/survey/index.html.
10 In the survey, corruption was defined as irregular payments made to officials, and corruption uncertainty as firms asked to pay more, in addition to irregular payments. Respondents were required to rate their responses from 1 (worst) to 6 (best). Respondents were also asked to rate the quality of health care services and efficiency of government services provided in their country, following the same scale. For ease of interpretation, this paper rescales the corruption and uncertainty indices from 1 (best) to 6 (worst), with higher values of each index representing higher corruption and higher uncertainty.
11 See Campos, Lien, and Pradhan (1999) and Wei (1997) for the concepts of corruption unpredictability and corruption uncertainty, both of which are found to have adverse impact on development.
12 The regression produces an adjusted R-squared of 0.13, with variations explained mostly by corruption and not by the quality of health care provision:

$$\text{Child mortality} = 178.8 + 22.9^* \text{ (Corruption)} -9.1^* \text{ (Quality)},$$
$$(5.50) \quad (1.75) \quad\quad\quad (-0.78)$$

where t–statistics are in parentheses. The regression does not control for other determinants of child mortality, hence the low R-squared, and does not address the endogeneity of corruption or reverse causality. These issues are discussed in section four of this chapter.
13 Each cell is calculated as one standard deviation around the mean; the results are the same when two standard deviations are used. Child mortality rates refer to under-age-five mortality rates.

14 The survey does not provide data on the quality of education service provision; the indicator of the efficiency of government services is used instead. The regression produces an adjusted R-squared of 0.29:

$$\text{Dropout rate} = 78.05 + 12.3^* \text{ (Corruption)} -2.32^* \text{ (Efficiency)},$$
$$(8.39)(3.90)(-0.52)$$

where t-statistics are in parentheses. Like the previous regression, the variation in the dependent variable is accounted for by variation in corruption rather than efficiency of government services, with the latter being statistically insignificant. Statistical inadequacy of this regression, as in the previous one, is addressed in section four of this chapter.

15 Not all informal charges are necessarily bribe payments.

16 *The Economist* (1994) reports on the theft of medical supplies.

17 Cross-sectional data are averages of each variable by country over the 1985–97 period. The actual number of observations varies depending on specifications. Descriptive statistics are provided in the appendix.

18 See, for example, Pritchett and Summers (1996) on the nonlinear relationship between income and health.

19 This procedure has been used by Tanzi and Davoodi (1997), and Gupta, Davoodi, and Alonso-Terme (1998).

20 The methodology is described in detail in Kaufmann, Kraay, and Zoido-Lobatón (1999b).

21 As noted later in the robustness tests, however, using the graft index in place of the PRS/ICRG index yields the same overall results.

22 The indicators have been endorsed by the OECD, the World Bank, and the UN; the Common Country Assessment (CCA) of the UN Development Assistance Framework; the UN/CCA Task Force on Basic Social Services; and by the UN Statistical Commission under the Minimum National Social Data Set (MNSDS).

23 Other data are taken from Davoodi and Sachjapinan (2001), and International Monetary Fund, *World Economic Outlook* (1999).

24 The link between income and social indicators is well documented. See, for example, Jack (1999) for a brief survey of the relevant health literature.

25 In general, the estimated coefficient of per capita income in the mortality regressions is consistent with previous cross-country estimates. Wang *et al.* (1999), for example, suggest that income elasticity for child mortality in 1990 was –0.71 in low-income and middle-income countries, which is close to the estimate of –0.73 obtained in this chapter.

26 See, for example, Filmer and Pritchett (1999), Gupta, Verhoeven, and Tiongson (1999) and Jack (1999) for health care, and Anand and Ravallion (1993), Noss (1991), Mingat and Tan (1998) for education.

27 Dependency ratios have been used in regressions of education outcomes. See, for example, Tan and Mingat (1992). Behrman, Duryea, and Szekely (1999) suggest that dependency ratios change the relative share of public resources available for school-age children. This effect may hold for health as well.

28 According to Schultz's (1993) survey of the literature, studies suggest that mortality is higher for rural, low-income households. Plank (1987) finds that access to education is typically better in urban areas.

29 For lack of annual data from 1985–97, 1990 data on average years of education of adult females are used. The regressions also hold when 1990 data on average years of education of all adults are used.

30 Shi (2000) finds that access to potable water and sewerage connection have a significant impact on child mortality.

31 This follows Davoodi and Sachjapinan (2001). To keep the sample size as large as possible, this chapter restricts the controls to the strongest and consistent determinants of health outcomes, limiting the sample to thirty-one countries.

32 These results also hold when pupil–teacher ratio is added as well.

33 Corruption, for example, is correlated with public spending on education and health. The health regression results generally hold even when per capita health expenditures, including private spending, is used in place of public health spending.

34 La Porta, Lopez-de-Silanes, Shleifer, and Vishny (1999) also find that countries that are less developed have higher Catholic and Muslim populations, and countries with French or socialist laws tend to have inferior measures of government performance, including higher corruption.

35 Further difficulties arise if per capita income is regarded as endogenous to health care and education indicators. Good health or better education could raise living standards, thus implying reverse causality. To address this concern, the initial value of per capita income (1985) is used as an instrument for per capita income averaged over the 1985–97 period.

36 The other control variables are assumed to act as their own instruments.

37 Removal of apparent outliers in Figure 6.4, for example, those associated with child mortality rates well above 200, in fact strengthens the relationship.

38 The relative rankings based on the OLS regression (columns 6 in Tables 6.3 and 6.4) are the same as the 2SLS regression.

39 This is not surprising, considering the high degree of correlation between the PRS/ICRG index and the graft indicator.

40 These indices are both scaled from 0 (most corrupt) to 10 (least corrupt).

41 The TI corruption index is also significantly correlated with immunization and persistence rates, controlling for all these variables. These results are available from authors upon request.

42 In the two-way classification case, the high corruption dummy takes a value of 1 when corruption scores are above the mean (or median) and 0 otherwise. In the three-way classification case, a high corruption dummy takes a value of 1 when corruption scores are greater than one standard deviation above the mean and 0 otherwise. The medium corruption is defined as 1 when corruption scores lie within one standard deviation around the mean and 0 otherwise. The low corruption dummy takes a value of 1 when corruption scores are less than one standard deviation below the mean.

43 When high corruption is used as benchmark, the dummy for low corruption is significant but medium corruption is not.

44 A country is classified under high corruption if its corruption score is higher than the median graft score; otherwise, it is classified under low corruption. The results hold when the mean is used in place of the median.

45 Average years of education in the female population was dropped as a control variable, due to lack of annual data. These results are in Appendix Table 6.8. These results hold when the regressions also control for physicians per 1,000 and, for a much smaller sample, safe water and sanitation.

46 It is, however, possible that the supply of basic public services is constrained in some countries, and would need to be expanded.

47 This participatory principle underlies the preparation of recently introduced poverty reduction strategy papers for the Highly Indebted Poor Countries (HIPCs). It is envisioned that all stakeholders in the economy will participate in the process leading to the preparation of anti-poverty programs, including for health and education, that are consistent with the overall macroeconomic framework.

Appendix

Appendix Table 6.8 Descriptive statistics: country averages, 1985–97[1]

Variable	Data source	Mean	Std Dev.	Minimum	Maximum	Observations
PRS/ICRG corruption index [1]	PRS/ICRG database	5.7	2.0	0.3	10.0	128
Graft governance indicators [1]	Kaufmann, Kraay, Lobatón, 1999	0.1	0.9	-1.6	2.1	128
Mortality rate, under 5 (per 1,000 live births)	WDI database, 1999	66.5	70.1	5.5	320.0	116
Mortality rate, infant (per 1,000 live births)	WDI database, 1999	46.0	40.6	4.5	183.5	117
Births attended by health staff (percent of total)	WDI database, 1999	72.2	27.6	7.7	100.0	110
Immunization, DPT (percent of children under 12 months)	WDI database, 1999	74.4	18.6	18.3	99.5	117
Low-birthweight babies (percent of births)	WDI database, 1999	10.6	6.2	3.2	46.0	113
School enrollment, primary (percent gross)	WDI database, 1999	95.6	20.4	27.8	133.8	111
Repeater rate, primary (percent)	UNESCO database, 1998	9.6	9.6	0.0	41.4	97
Dropout rate, primary (percent)	Barro and Lee, 1996	22.4	23.7	0.0	92.0	105
Persistence to grade 5, total (percent of cohort)	WDI database, 1999	82.0	17.3	32.9	100.0	81
Illiteracy rate, total (15 yrs old+)	WDI database, 1999	26.7	22.5	0.4	87.8	86
Per capita income (PPP)	WEO database, 1999	7,212.6	6,804.5	141.4	28,212.5	118
Public spending on health (percent of GDP)	National authorities; IMF staff estimates	2.3	1.8	0.1	8.4	117
Public spending on education (percent of GDP)	National authorities; IMF staff estimates	3.5	1.7	0.2	8.7	116
Average years of education, female (15 yrs old+)	Barro and Lee, 1996	5.3	2.8	0.5	11.5	91
Average years of education, all (15 yrs old+)	Barro and Lee, 1996	5.8	2.7	0.7	11.7	91
Health expenditure per capita, PPP (current international $)	WDI database, 1999	583.8	671.0	11.3	3,462.9	93
Age dependency ratio (dependents to working-age population)	WDI database, 1999	0.7	0.2	0.4	1.1	117
Urban population (percent of total)	WDI database, 1999	55.0	24.1	11.5	100.0	117
Democracy dummy	Treisman, 2000	0.2	0.4	0.0	1.0	89
Protestants (percent of population)	Treisman, 2000	15.4	24.2	0.0	97.8	89
Benefit incidence (ratio of q1 to q5)	Davoodi and Sachjapinan, 2000	1.5	1.9	0.1	9.6	31
Pupil–teacher ratio, primary	WDI database, 1999	28.4	12.5	6.1	66.0	110
Physicians per 1,000 people	WDI database, 1999	1.2	1.1	0.0	3.9	115

Note: 1 The corruption indices retain their original scaling from worst to best.

Appendix Table 6.9 Health indicators and corruption, 1985–97: panel data analysis[1]

Dependent variable	Child mortality		Infant mortality		Low-birthweight babies	
	Fixed effects	Random effects	Fixed effects	Random effects	Fixed effects	Random effects
Corruption (PRS/ICRG)	0.02**	0.04***	-0.00	0.00	0.03	0.07***
	(2.08)	(4.63)	(-1.10)	(0.70)	(0.94)	(4.91)
Per capita income	-0.58***	-0.56***	-0.70***	-0.64***	-0.14	-0.02
	(-7.14)	(-12.13)	(-14.47)	(-20.57)	(-0.95)	(-0.43)
Public health spending	-0.26	-0.03	-0.02	-0.03*	-0.06	-0.02
	(-0.79)	(-1.46)	(-0.98)	(-1.80)	(-0.47)	(0.76)
Dependency ratio	0.16	0.95***	0.05	0.67***	0.67	0.22
	(0.59)	(6.35)	(0.34)	(5.58)	(0.64)	(1.47)
Urbanization	0.04	-0.10	0.31*	0.06	-0.01	-0.41
	(0.18)	(-1.01)	(1.83)	(0.84)	(-0.04)	(-4.54)
Adjusted R-squared	0.99	0.68	0.99	0.78	0.65	0.13
N	204	204	463	468	229	229

Sources: World Bank (1999), Barro and Lee (1996), and Political Risk Services.

Note

1 Except for corruption, all the variables are in logs. A low value of the corruption index means that a country is perceived to be less corrupt. White's heteroskedastic-consistent t-statistics are in parentheses. (***), (**), and (*) denote significance at the 1 percent, 5 percent, and 10 percent levels, respectively.

Bibliography

Acemoglu, D. and Verdier, T. (2000) "The Choice Between Market Failures and Corruption," *American Economic Review* 90 (March): 194–211.

Alam, M. S. (1989) "Anatomy of Corruption: An Approach to the Political Economy of Underdevelopment," *American Journal of Economics and Sociology* 48 (October): 441–56.

—— (1990) "Some Economic Costs of Corruption in LDCs," *Journal of Development Studies* 27 (October): 89–97.

Alesina, A. (1999) "Too Small and Too Large Governments," in V. Tanzi, K. Chu, and S. Gupta (eds), *Equity and Economic Policy*, Washington, DC: International Monetary Fund.

Anand, S., and Ravallion, M. (1993) "Human Development in Poor Countries: On the Role of Private Incomes and Public Services," *Journal of Economic Perspectives* 7 (Winter): 133–50.

Anderson, J. (1998) "Corruption in Latvia: Survey Evidence," Washington, DC: World Bank Institute.

Bardhan, P. (1997) "Corruption and Development: A Review of Issues," *Journal of Economic Literature* 35 (September): 1320–46.

Barro, R. and Lee, J. (1996) "International Measures of Schooling Years and Schooling Quality," *American Economic Review* 86 (May): 218–23.

—— (1997) "Schooling Quality in a Cross Section of Countries," NBER Working Paper no. 6198, Cambridge, Mass.: National Bureau of Economic Research.

Bearse, P., Glomm, G., and Janeba, E. (2000) "Why Poor Countries Rely Mostly On Redistribution In-Kind," *Journal of Public Economics* 75 (March): 463–81.

Behrman, J. R., Duryea, S., and Szekely, M. (1999) "Aging and Economic Opportunities: Major World Regions Around the Turn of the Century," Office of the Chief Economist Working Paper no. 405, Washington, DC: Inter-American Development Bank.

Campos, J. E., Lien, D., and Pradhan, S. (1999) "The Impact of Corruption on Investment: Predictability Matters," *World Development* 27 (June): 1059–67.

Castro-Leal, F., Dayton, J., Demery, L., and Mehra, K. (1999) "Public Social Spending in Africa: Do the Poor Benefit?" *World Bank Research Observer* 14 (February): 49–72.

Chua, Y. T. (1999) *Robbed: An Investigation of Corruption in Philippine Education*, Quezon City: Philippine Center for Investigative Journalism.

CIET (1996) "Final report: Baseline Service Delivery Survey in Support of Results Oriented Management in the Uganda Institutional Capacity Building Project," New York: CIET International.

—— (1999) "Corruption: The Invisible Price Tag on Education," CIET media release, October 12, New York: CIET International.

Cockroft, L. (1998) "Corruption and Human Rights: A Crucial Link," TI Working Paper, Berlin: Transparency International.

Davoodi, H. and Sachjapinan, S. (2001), "How Useful are Benefit Incidence Studies?" IMF Working Paper, Washington, DC: International Monetary Fund.

Economist (1994) "Sick Ukrainians," October 8: 56.

Ehrlich, I. and Lui, F. T. (1999) "Bureaucratic Corruption and Endogenous Growth," *Journal of Political Economy* 107 (December): S270–93.

Filmer, D., Hammer, J., and Pritchett, L. (1998) "Health Policy in Poor Countries: Weak Links in the Chain," World Bank Policy Research Working Paper no. 1874, Washington, DC: World Bank.

Filmer, D. and Pritchett, L. (1999) "The Impact of Public Spending on Health: Does Money Matter?" *Social Science and Medicine* 49: 1309–23.

Gopakumar, K. (1998) "Citizen Feedback Surveys to Highlight Corruption in Public Services: The Experience of Public Affairs Center, Bangalore," TI Working Paper, Berlin: Transparency International.

Gray-Molina, G., Perez de Rada, E. P., and Yanez, E. (1999) "Transparency and Accountability in Bolivia: Does Voice Matter?" OCE Working Paper no. R-381, Washington, DC: Inter-American Development Bank.

Gupta, S., Davoodi, H., and Alonso-Terme, R. (1998) "Does Corruption Affect Income Inequality and Poverty?" IMF Working Paper 98/76, Washington, DC: International Monetary Fund.

Gupta, S., de Mello, L., and Sharan, R. (2000) "Corruption and Military Spending," IMF Working Paper 00/23, Washington, DC: International Monetary Fund.

Gupta, S., Verhoeven, M., and Tiongson, E. (1999) "Does Higher Government Spending Buy Better Results in Education and Health Care?" IMF Working Paper 99/21, Washington, DC: International Monetary Fund.

Hanushek, E. E. (1995) "Interpreting Recent Research on Schooling in Developing Countries," *World Bank Research Observer* 10 (August): 227–46.

Hindriks, J., Keen, M., and Muthoo, A. (1999) "Corruption, Extortion, and Evasion," *Journal of Public Economics* 74 (December): 395–430.

International Monetary Fund (1999) *World Economic Outlook*, available via Internet: www.imf.org/external/pubs/ft/weo/1999/01/data/index.htm, Washington, DC: International Monetary Fund.

Jack, W. (1999) *Principles of Health Economics for Developing Countries*, Washington, DC: World Bank Institute.

Johnson, S., Kaufmann, D., and Zoido-Lobatón, P. (1999) "Corruption, Public Finances and the Unofficial Economy," World Bank Policy Research Paper no. 2169, Washington, DC: World Bank.

Kaufmann, D. (1997) "Corruption: The Facts," *Foreign Policy* 107 (Summer): 114–31.

Kaufmann, D., Kraay, A., and Zoido-Lobatón, P. (1999a) "Governance Matters," World Bank Policy Research Paper no. 2196, Washington, DC: World Bank.

—— (1999b) "Aggregating Governance Indicators," World Bank Policy Research Paper no. 2195, Washington, DC: World Bank.

Kaufmann, D., Pradhan, S., and Ryterman, R. (1998) "New Frontiers in Diagnosing and Combating Corruption," *PREM Notes* 7 (October): 1–6.

Kaufmann, D. and Wei, S. (1999) "Does Grease Money Speed Up the Wheels of Commerce?" NBER Working Paper no. 7093, Cambridge, Mass.: National Bureau of Economic Research.

La Porta, R., Lopez-de-Silanes, F., Shleifer, A., and Vishny, R. (1999) "The

Quality of Government," *Journal of Law, Economics, and Organization* 15 (April): 222–79.

Lambsdorff, J. (1998) "Corruption in Comparative Perception," in A. K. Jain (ed.), *Economics of Corruption*, Boston: Kluwer Academic.

Langseth, P. and Stapenhurst, R. (1997) "National Integrity System Country Studies," EDI Working Paper, Washington, DC: World Bank Economic Development Institute.

Leff, N. H. (1964) "Economic Development Through Bureaucratic Corruption," *American Behavioral Scientist* 8(2): 8–14.

Lui, F. (1985) "An Equilibrium Queuing Model of Bribery," *Journal of Political Economy* 93(4) (August): 760–81.

Mauro, P. (1998) "Corruption and the Composition of Government Expenditure," *Journal of Public Economics* 69 (August): 263–79.

Mingat, A. and Tan, J. (1998) "The Mechanics of Progress in Education: Evidence from Cross-Country Data," Policy Research Working Paper no. 2015, Washington, DC: World Bank.

Myrdal, G. (1968) *Asian Drama: An Inquiry into the Poverty of Nations*, New York: Twentieth Century Fund.

Narayan, D. (2000) *Voices of the Poor: Can Anyone Hear Us?* Washington, DC: World Bank.

Noss, A. (1991) "Education and Adjustment: A Review of the Literature," PRE Working Paper WPS 701, Washington, DC: World Bank.

Paul, S. (1998) "Making Voice Work: The Report Card on Bangalore's Public Services," World Bank Policy Research Paper no. 1921, Washington, DC: World Bank.

Plank, D. N. (1987) "The Expansion of Education: A Brazilian Case Study," *Comparative Education Review* 31 (August): 361–76.

Political Risk Services, International Country Risk Guide (CD-ROM version), access via the Joint Bank-Fund Library Network Website: jolis.

Pritchett, L. and Summers, L. H. (1996) "Wealthier is Healthier," *Journal of Human Resources* 31 (Fall): 841–68.

Reinikka, R. (1999) "Using Surveys for Public Sector Reform," *PREM Notes* 23 (May): 1–4.

Schultz, T. P. (1993) "Mortality Decline in the Low Income World: Causes and Consequence," Economic Growth Center Discussion Paper no. 681, New Haven: Yale University.

—— (1998) "The Formation of Human Capital and the Economic Development of Africa: Returns to Health and Schooling Investments," Economic Research Paper no. 37, Ivory Coast: African Development Bank.

Shi, A. (2000) "How Access to Urban Potable Water and Sewerage Connections Affects Child Mortality," World Bank Policy Research Paper no. 2274, Washington, DC: World Bank.

Shleifer, A. and Vishny, R. W. (1993) "Corruption," *Quarterly Journal of Economics* 108 (August): 599–617.

Tan, J. and Mingat, A. (1992) *Education in Asia: A Comparative Study of Cost and Financing*, Washington, DC: World Bank.

Tanzi, V. and Davoodi, H. (1997) "Corruption, Public Investment, and Growth," IMF Working Paper 97/139, Washington, DC: International Monetary Fund.

Treisman, D. (2000) "The Causes of Corruption: A Cross-National Study," *Journal of Public Economics* 76 (June): 399–457.

Ul Haque, N., and Sahay, R. (1996) "Do Government Wage Cuts Close Budget Deficits? Costs of Corruption," IMF Staff Papers, vol. 43 (December): 754–78, Washington, DC: International Monetary Fund.

United Nations Educational, Scientific, and Cultural Organization, *UNESCO Statistical Yearbook*, Paris: UNESCO.

Villegas, A., Morales, A., and Andersson, N. (1998) "Popular Perceptions of Corruption in Public Services: Key Findings of the First National Integrity Survey in Bolivia, 1998," unpublished manuscript, New York: CIET International.

Wang, J., Jamison, D. T., Bos, E., Preker, A., and Peabody, J. (1999) *Measuring Country Performance on Health: Selected Indicators for 115 Countries,* Washington, DC: World Bank.

Wei, S. (1997) "Why Is Corruption So Much More Taxing Than Tax? Arbitrariness Kills," NBER Working Paper no. 6255, Cambridge, Mass.: National Bureau of Economic Research.

World Bank (1997) *World Development Report 1997: The State in a Changing World*, New York: Oxford University Press for the World Bank.

—— (1999) *World Development Indicators*, Washington, DC: World Bank.

7 Historical antecedents of corruption in Pakistan

Aftab Ahmad

Corruption in Pakistan, no matter how one defines it, is large and pervasive in all its dimensions. Yet what makes it unique, even among the societies that are still in their formative periods, is the staggering fact that the real perpetrators of corruption have cleverly maneuvered to shift the blame to scapegoats. Both in the local as well as in the Western press, corrupt political leaders, inept political parties, and ruthless land-lords are considered as the root cause of all the ills that Pakistan faces. The reality, however, may be that with the exception of about five years in the early seventies, these players have had no effective political power since 1954. Ever since 1954, the civil service–military alliance has run the country in one way or another. Yet, one rarely comes across a criticism of this alliance. Even when they violate the country's constitution, send the elected prime ministers to the gallows or behind bars, and openly manipulate the judges of the Supreme Court, the criticism of such actions, if any, is moderated by acceptance of their assertion that once again the country has been saved from the chaos created by the elected government.

In order to understand how corruption has come to be institutionalized in Pakistan, it is necessary to identify some of the critical political developments since the partition of British India in August 1947 into two independent Dominions, namely, India and Pakistan. The partition marked a failure of the stated objectives of British policy, which was to transfer power peacefully to a united India. India was divided; a division that was accompanied by a massacre of millions of innocent people and an unprecedented mass migration. For the Congress Party of India, and for M. K. (Mahatma) Gandhi, who had effectively led this party since 1920, partition represented a failure for more or less the same reasons. For the Muslim League and Muhammad Ali Jinnah (who led the League), partition meant at best the dubious victory of having won a truncated version of Pakistan. This new nation originally included an undivided Bengal (the Eastern wing of Pakistan, which was to become the independent nation of Bangladesh in 1971) and Punjab (the Western wing of Pakistan). The details of the territorial divisions were announced the day following the partition causing the unprecedented communal carnage of at least 600,000 innocent people, and about 14 million refugees who stumbled fearfully across the frontiers of the two States. Nor was this all. A sizable territory within India under the protected ruling princes was granted the option of joining one of the two newly created dominions within a reasonable time limit. The refusal by the state of Hyderabad (ruled by a Muslim ruler but with an overwhelming Hindu population) to join India was resolved by India through a "police action." The ruler of Kashmir (ruled by a Hindu but with an overwhelming Muslim population) opted for India. Pakistan's attempt to resolve the "Kashmir problem" by force was thwarted by the Indian armed forces. Only one-third of Kashmir was "liberated"; the rest was eventually absorbed by India creating an everlasting conflict between the two dominions.

To understand subsequent political developments, it would be helpful to highlight some aspects of the social structure inherited by Pakistan at the time of its creation. The regions that constituted the state of Pakistan, both in the Eastern and the Western wings, had traditionally been the suppliers of raw materials to the industries located in other parts of India or in England. Hindus or other, non-Muslim, businessmen dominated the commercial life of these regions. The landlords and the peasants in the Western wing were Muslims. In the Eastern wing almost all landlords were Hindus whereas the peasants were Muslims. The power vacuum created by the emigration of Hindus and other non-Muslims following the partition affected the Eastern wing more severely than the Western wing. The land left behind by the Hindu landlords was redistributed among the peasants, with the result that over 50 percent of them came to own their lands in the form of uneconomic family-farms averaging 3.5 acres. In the Western wing the land holdings of the landlords remained intact, enabling the landlords to continue as a powerful political elite. They lacked, however, an effective political organization as well as an ability to govern. The bureaucracy, on the other hand, was well trained by the British as an instrument of colonial rule and was rightly referred to as the "steel frame" of their administration. Moreover, this bureaucracy was a well-knit unit, drawn as it was almost entirely from the Punjab and from the immigrants settled in Karachi. Although they had strong links with the landlords, the chaotic conditions resulting from the partition of the subcontinent as well as the growing political pressures from the Eastern wing enabled this bureaucracy to become a formidable political force in its own right, and to fill the vacuum created by the departure of the British. The army, however, also British trained and drawn mainly from the Punjab, was the most formidable political force, but its influence in the beginning remained limited. The Western wing also received, among its immigrants, Muslim traders belonging to the Memon, Bhora, and Khoja communities of

Gujrat and Bombay, who settled in Karachi. They and other commercial elements later transformed themselves into an industrial elite.

The concentration of capitalists, landlords, bureaucracy, and the army in the Western wing gradually reduced the status of the Eastern wing into a colony of the Western wing despite the fact that the Eastern wing controlled the Constituent Assembly (which acted also as National Assembly) by virtue of having 55 percent of Pakistan's population. The colonization of the Eastern wing was inherent in the power vacuum created by the partition, but the industrial elite of the Western wing could not have experienced such an unbridled growth in that region had the rules of "free enterprise" and competitive capitalism prevailed. After independence, most of the capital investments were directed at the Western wing which grew at the cost of the east. The growing disparities in the economic and social developments between the two wings are evident from the following two tables.

Table 7.1 compares the economic growth rates of the two wings. Despite the fact that there was no significant difference in population growth during the first two decades after independence, the economy of the West wing grew much faster than that of the East. Economic growth barely kept pace with the increasing population in the East while the per capita income in the West increased at a comfortable rate. Whereas the two wings were almost equal in terms of per capita income at the time of independence, the West had become much richer than the East within about twenty years. The difference in per capita incomes had grown from about 10 percent to about 64 percent over this period. Table 7.2 compares one of the determinants of economic development – growth of educational facilities – in the two wings. While educational facilities and students enrollments at all levels grew in both wings, the multiples

Table 7.1 Economic disparities: East and West Pakistan (1949–68: selected years)

	Gross domestic product 1959–60 prices (Millions of rupees)		Ratio of per capita GDP: West:East*
	East wing	*West wing*	
1949	13,130	11,830	1.10:1
1954	14,320	14,310	1.22:1
1959	15,550	16,790	1.32:1
1964	18,014	21,788	1.48:1
1968	20,670	27,744	1.64:1
Average annual growth rate	2.42%	4.59%	

Source: G. Papanek, *Pakistan's Development*, Cambridge, Mass. Harvard University Press: 317.

* Assuming that the East wing had 55 percent of the total population of Pakistan during the entire period.

Table 7.2 Educational disparities: East and West Pakistan: number of educational institutions and enrollments

	East wing		West wing	
	1947	*1967*	*1947*	*1967*
Primary level				
Institutions	20,633	28,225	8,413	33,271
Number of students	2,020,000	4,310,000	550,000	2,740,000
Secondary level				
Institutions	3,481	4,300	2,598	4,563
Number of students	53,000	107,000	51,000	153,000
College level				
Institutions	50	173	40	230
Number of students	19,000	138,000	13,000	142,000
University level				
Institutions	1	2	2	4
Number of students	1,600	8,000	700	10,000

Source: Haque (1969): 13.

between the years of 1947 and 1967 are almost twice as large in the Western wing as they are in the Eastern wing.

Foreign economic and military aid has played a significant role in the political developments of Pakistan. Pakistan started receiving economic aid from the United States in 1951. In the same year Ghulam Mohammad, a top bureaucrat, succeeded Khawja Nazimuddin as the Governor General of Pakistan. In the beginning, the economic aid consisted mainly of grants, but by 1955 Pakistan was firmly in the orbit of the United States receiving large amounts of grants, loans and military aid. By this time, Pakistan had become a key member of the American regional security and defense pacts – Southeast Asian Treaty Organization (SEATO) and Central Treaty Organization (CENTO). As part of its obligations, Pakistan allowed the United States a military base in the Western wing and the use of its civilian airfields for espionage flights. One such flight, the ill fated U-2 plane shot down by the Soviet Union, led to a major international crisis in 1960.

It was during this period that the bureaucracy consolidated its powers and took steps to ensure that elected officials would not undermine these powers. Soon after independence, a Constituent Assembly had been created (which also functioned as National Assembly until the new constitution could be adopted) to frame a constitution for the nation. The Constituent Assembly published a draft of Pakistan's new constitution that had been approved by the Assembly. This draft would have rested much of the political power in the hands of elected representatives and would have given more powers to the East wing of the country due to its larger share of the population. The ruling bureaucratic elite, surprised that various factions within the leading political party, Muslim

League, had managed to reach a compromise on the thorny issue of division of powers between the two wings, managed to oust the party from power with some help from the foreign donors. The draft was to be formally voted on October 24 1954. On that date Pakistan's Governor General, Ghulam Mohammad, dismissed the Constituent Assembly and ordered the police to bar members of the Assembly from entering the meeting hall. In the following year, Chief Justice of Pakistan, Mohammad Munir, legitimized the dissolution in a majority decision of the court on grounds that

> that being the legal position, it follows that Pakistan being a Dominion and the Governor General being the King for the purpose of the Government of the Dominion, he is possessed in the matter the same powers as in the absence of a statute were or are exercisable by the King.
>
> (Jennings 1955: 293)

The bureaucracy had the strong tacit backing of Pakistan's aid-donors in the industrialized world. Media coverage at the time provides some clues to this approval.

- The *New York Times* in its coverage of the recent changes had heralded the Assembly's work on the new constitution as a "key to the way the changing Muslim world may go politically in the next few years." In its attempts to discover the significance of the dissolution on October 25 and 28 1954, however, it limited itself to quoting unidentified constitutional lawyers who had confirmed that the Governor General had the power to dissolve the Assembly and had found his proclamation as being "complete in itself." No authority was cited to support this opinion except to say that the Governor General's action fitted into "the highly involved and complicated structure of the British law." The paper also reported that Ghulam Mohammad had the backing of the army and the civil service, and that the regime was friendly to the United States.
- *Time* magazine (April 11 1955) described Ghulam Mohammad as the "Reluctant Dictator." The magazine claimed that he had put his civil servants to work on what Pakistan's Constituent Assembly had failed to achieve for seven years – a constitution. "A man disabled by a stroke, half paralyzed, and trained by crack British civil servants to rule by law, Ghulam Mohammad does not really like being a dictator." *Time* intimated that Ghulam Mohammad wanted to convene the Assembly and hold elections but was dissuaded by his advisors, who had reportedly argued that "restoring democracy would mean restoring chaos."
- *The Economist* (London, October 30 1954) approved of the dissolution.

Immediately after the dissolution, *The Times* of London seemed somewhat at a loss to grasp the situation. By November 1 1954, however, it had come to the conclusion that the legacy of the Raj, "the trained administrators of the old Civil and Provincial Services with the army behind them" had served as the "remedy" for the plight facing Pakistan. "Any thing must be better than a system which allowed the Civil Service and the army to be exposed to the risk of manipulation by self-seeking and largely self-appointed political party caucuses" (*Times* November 1 1954: 11).

Ghulam Mohammad by now had at his disposal the emergency and police powers of the state with little constitutional restraint on how they were to be used. The inclusion in his cabinet of the Commander-in-Chief of the armed forces, General Ayub Khan, as Defence Minister further secured his position. His powers were strong enough that in 1959, despite the opposition of the regional politicians, he was able to convert the four provinces of the Western wing into one unit, named as West Pakistan and the Eastern wing as East Pakistan. His hand-picked Prime Ministers (three in four years) were chosen and replaced at his pleasure. In effect, Ghulam Mohammad ruled in the same manner as the Viceroy did during the British Raj, though with one big difference. The Viceroy was ultimately answerable to the British Parliament while Ghulam Mohammad was not.

The army meanwhile had increased in strength and was growing in importance behind the political scene. The ever-present opinion that India was a threat to Pakistan's existence, and the continuing dispute over Kashmir with India, made it ill-advised for any Pakistani government to deny the army a sizable portion of national resources. US military assistance in response to the Cold War pacts signed by Pakistan eventually converted Pakistan's army into the paramount political force in the country. In 1958, the army asserted its hegemony by staging a coup in order to prevent the scheduled general elections. The leader of the coup, General Ayub Khan, later revealed in his autobiography that he had consulted officials in Washington, including CIA chief Allen Dulles, before declaring martial law in the country (Ayub Khan 1967: 59). Pakistan's dependence on American aid was so colossal that 35 percent of its first Five-Year Plan and 50 percent of its second plan were supported by external loans and grants. Nonetheless, for the next ten years Pakistan's economy made great strides and was often cited (in the World Bank reports) as the "showcase" of non-Communist development. Such reports, however, conveniently ignored the inherent weaknesses of the model of economic development followed by Pakistan. This model sought unbridled growth through the agency of a handful of immigrant capitalists. These immigrants, treated as entrepreneurs, enjoyed not only a "tax holiday" of up to ten years and non-unionized labor, but were also protected against competition through price controls and selective licensing, more so with regard to their investments in East Pakistan. As a result, by 1965 twenty families of West Pakistan came to control 80 percent of the banking, 70 percent of the insurance and 60 percent of the industrial assets of Pakistan (Haq 1966). In the process the army, by now in its own right the top elite in the country, became the great defender of the propertied classes and a formidable deterrent to possible social adjustments.

By 1965 there was significant reduction in the economic and military assistance caused by strains in the Pakistan–US relationship as a result of Sino-Pakistan "friendship." Nonetheless, the army found itself powerful enough to risk a military solution to the lingering Kashmir problem. The resulting war with India, however, did not help Pakistan. The Kashmir problem, instead of being solved, was aggravated. Chinese help to Pakistan during the war in the form of amassing its threatening troops at the Indian border, and the signing of a cease-fire agreement at Tashkent under Soviet auspices brought further strains in the Pakistan–US relationship. The economic strains caused by the war and the diminishing economic and military aid hastened the inevitable consequences of Pakistan's ruthless economic policies. In the process, existing regional strains and disparities were intensified with a force eventually erupting in the massive countrywide upsurge that lasted for over five months in 1968 and overthrew Ayub Khan's ten-years-old dictatorship. The imposition of martial law by his successor, General Yahya Khan, with a firm commitment to free elections eased the situation for a while. General Yahya Khan fulfilled his promise by holding elections in December 1970 – the first countrywide elections in Pakistan's history.

The results of the elections, however, created a huge dilemma for the army. The Awami League (AL), whose top members along with its leader Sheikh Mujibur Rhaman had suffered long jail terms on charges of treason during Ayub Khan's regime, won almost all National Assembly seats in East Pakistan giving it a simple majority nationwide. The AL's "treason" had emanated from its six-point program of regional autonomy, which was essentially a Bill of Right for East Pakistan. The program, however, also included the right to negotiate foreign aid and trade for East Pakistan, which threatened the army's hegemony as well as the investments in East Pakistan by West Pakistan's entrepreneurs. Furthermore, its program of replacing the Central Civil Service by proportional representation from the two wings of Pakistan ran counter to the interests of West Pakistan's bureaucracy. The AL had won the election on the platform of its six-point program of regional autonomy and seemed in no mood to compromise. The Pakistan People Party (PPP) recently founded by Zulfiqar Ali Bhutto, an elite landlord and a key cabinet minister during Ayub Khan's regime, won the largest number of National Assembly seats in West Pakistan. The army was convinced that it would be impossible to perpetuate West Pakistan's dominance over the country once the AL six-point program was incorporated in the constitution by the AL-dominated Assembly. The army had two options: it could nullify the elections or it could refuse to validate the constitution when it had been passed. Considering the nationwide popular sentiment for a return to democracy, both alternatives seemed poor choices. Consequently, the army chose the military solution to resolve the issue once and for all. The PPP, now representing West Pakistan's interest, went along with the army.

The dream of achieving regional autonomy within the union of Pakistan died with the first blast of cannons by Pakistan's army in East Pakistan on March 25 1971. The military's offensive had already liquidated or put out of action the entire leadership of the AL. Others fled to India to form a "Provisional Government." The reign of terror continued until the Indian armed forces entered East Pakistan to aid the growing resistance movement. The ensuing war with India was a disaster for Pakistan. Pakistan achieved a cease-fire by accepting a humiliating unconditional surrender to the Indian armed forces, leaving behind every thing it owned in East Pakistan including more than seventy thousand troops as prisoners of war. East Pakistan declared itself an independent country adopting the name of Bangladesh.

Pakistan was now confined to the territories of West Pakistan where the one unit, formed by Ghulam Mohammad, had already been undone in order to restore the original four provinces. For the next five years Pakistan was ruled by a civilian government, headed by Zulfiqar Ali Bhutto whose PPP now enjoyed a majority in the National Assembly. It was for the first time since the appointment of Ghulam Mohammad as Governor General in 1951 that the army or the bureaucracy had little say in the political affairs of the country. From the outset, Bhutto had daunting problems on his hands: over 70,000 soldiers as prisoners-of-war in India, a shattered economy and a confused nation with devastated morale and, above all, a grudgingly envious army and indifferent bureaucracy. The prisoners-of-war were brought back without conceding much more than a promise of détente in respect of the Kashmir dispute. Through an Islamic Conference held in Karachi, a dialogue was initiated with Bangladesh. A democratic constitution was passed unanimously by the members of the National Assembly. Sooner than expected the nation's morale was back and the past seemed almost forgotten. The PPP felt confident of its popularity and called elections earlier than the end of its mandate. The election results justified the PPP's confidence. The PPP won against a coalition of ten opposition parties, giving it far more seats both in the National and Provincial Assemblies, than it had before. With democracy entrenched in a unanimously passed constitution and a stronger mandate from the people than ever before, Bhutto and his PPP seemed invincible for at least the next five years. This, however, was not to be. Whatever Bhutto and his PPP had secured for themselves proved no match for the hostile civil-military alliance, emboldened by the expressed displeasure of the American government against Bhutto's flirtation with the so called Islamic atom bomb. The decline of the powers of democratic forces started with allegations by the defeated parties of fraudulent election practices by the PPP government. Normal protests gradually snowballed into rowdy demonstrations, as the police looked the other way. Bhutto finally agreed with the coalition of the opposition parties to annul the elections and reschedule new ones, providing the army with the opportunity it had been awaiting. On July 5 1977 the Chief of Army Staff, General Zia-ul Haq staged a coup against Bhutto and took over the government. To calm a bewildered nation, General Zia solemnly promised on public television to hold elections within ninety days of his take-over and then return to the barracks. General Zia did no such thing. He later arrested Bhutto, tried him on questionable murder charges and eventually sent him to the gallows. He stayed in power till his accidental death in 1987.

Never before was the Pakistan–US relationship so close as during the ten years of General Zia's rule. Destiny chose Pakistan to play an active role in the geopolitics concerning the growing Soviet influence in Afghanistan. The Russian invasion of Afghanistan opened the floodgates of economic and military assistance to Pakistan. In addition, unaccountable amounts of American arms and financial aid passed through Pakistan for the freedom fighters in Afghanistan. Pakistan was also encouraged to help the freedom fighters to generate funds through smuggling of heroin and other contraband from Afghanistan. Large funds poured in to train thousands of young freedom fighters in the makeshift "jihad" oriented schools. All this enabled Zia to destroy all the prerequisites for revival of democracy, leaving no mechanism intact for any grassroots political movement at the national level. The regular inflow of funds from American sources as well as drug money from the Afghan connections made almost everyone blind toward the fast growing rot that Zia's policies were gradually creating within Pakistan's body-politic. Afghani refugees, drug culture, money laundering, illegal arms traffic, widespread armed robberies, and kidnapping were almost nonexistent in Pakistan before Zia. Corruption was not so rampant and widespread as it has become ever since. In the absence of any significant criticism of his policies at home or in the West, coupled with the constant inflow of unaccountable American funds, Zia was able to camouflage the rot by buying the cooperation of conflicting interests.

The withdrawal of the Russians from Afghanistan followed by the end of the Cold War changed it all. The army decided to allow a weakened parliamentary government, stripped of its sovereignty, to run the country. The crippled political parties, having little funds, time, and skills, instead of developing an effective economic agenda, chose an easy path in order to acquire the elected positions. Almost all of them wooed and nominated the existing political elite – a powerful group dominated by absentee land owners having sufficient funds (largely because income from agriculture is exempt from taxes) – and "close connections" with the bureaucracy to extract votes. Once elected their primary objective was to get back their political investment with interest compounded at prohibitive rates. It would be hard to find any significant difference between the make up of the ruling and the opposition parties, which replaced each other several times over through dismissals and new elections.

Elected governments, however, had little control over the national budget or the administration. The former was dictated by the army and the latter by the bureaucracy. The turnover of political parties in power continued until the last elected assembly succeeded in giving itself sovereignty by means of effective changes in the Constitution. By this time, unfortunately, the elected politicians had already demeaned the ideas of democracy so thoroughly in the public's mind that the most recent army take over in October 1999 met very little resistance from the masses.

Separating politics from religion is not an easy task in any developing society, but Zia consolidated his powers by cleverly manipulating religious factions for his political ends. His ruthless exploitation of religious sentiments unleashed unprecedented religious fanaticism not only in the masses, but also in a significant part of the army and the bureaucracy. His support of the Taliban in the form of training in makeshift religious schools in Pakistan vindicated his strategy especially in view of the Taliban's military success – against the Russians as well as other factions of "freedom fighters" in Afghanistan. In fact, even among the people with Western education there is a growing number who no longer give much credence to democracy or to other Western thoughts. The Western press, which only in the recent past had glorified Zia almost on all counts, seems largely responsible for such erosion. Cynicism, confusion and, above all, lack of any other viable alternative to democracy, have driven them to seek solutions to the country's plight through early Islamic traditions. This is a far cry from the days prior to the dissolution of the Constituent Assembly by Ghulam Mohammad. Then, even the "ulema" (religious scholars) including Moulana Modudi, the most powerful spokesman of them all, were willing to compromise with the machinery of parliamentary government. While it is true that the "ulema" were not enthusiastic for democracy, they nevertheless supported the draft constitution and protested against its destruction at the hands of Ghulam Mohammad.

It would be unfair, however, to characterize the role of the bureaucracy and the army in only negative terms. There is no doubt that it was the dedicated efforts of these institutions which not only helped Pakistan to survive, but also enabled the ruling Muslim League to find time to formulate a draft constitution. Their acceptance of American aid and directives were not so flagrant as to set them apart from others. One could go so far as to say that their initial conspiracy to replace democracy by the political system they knew best was, in large part, due to a clash of ideologies. Nothing positive, however, comes to mind when one reviews Zia's take over and his subsequent policies. Even the army and the bureaucracy, insofar as their inherent functions are concerned, have become casualities of his regime. Today the army is the richest elite in Pakistan. Army officers directly or indirectly own not only the choice urban and agricultural lands, but also a large part of major manufacturing and resource industries. Their housing, health, education, and other amenities are far above what is available to the rest of the population. The bureaucracy is not far behind. For obvious reasons, these institutions are no longer capable of delivering the goods as they were in the past. Devotion to work and professional integrity have long been compromised by a relentless pursuit to amass wealth by any means, whatsoever. In a nutshell, Zia has succeeded not only in uprooting democracy but also in severely damaging the intrinsic qualities of its own power base. No longer does it seem unthinkable that a brute force like the Taliban may eventually take over the country, destroying all institutions developed in the past several centuries.

With the exception of Bhutto's five years, it is the army, not a general or a family, that has in fact been ruling Pakistan since 1954. In the process, the army, closely assisted by the bureaucracy, has been transformed into the defender and protector of the propertied classes. They are the real elite and power broker in Pakistan. It is they who have kept the masses under "control," for the mutual benefits of the urban industrialists, traders, and white-collar professionals. The landlords have at best remained at the fringe and are kept intact only to maintain and support the status quo. The most conspicuous are the proverbial "vaderas" (a popular term for the big landlords of Sindh) and "sardars" (a similar term for the big landlords of Baluchistan). Even these landlords, despite their dominant positions within their respective ethnic communities, do not wield much power at the national level. Political leaders are only allowed, if at all, to play roles within preset limits, and are ousted as and when they tend to act otherwise. Since the army is drawn mainly from the Punjab, which has over 55 percent of Pakistan's population, its political hegemony is difficult to challenge. The same is true, to a large degree, of the bureaucracy. Nonetheless, the country's economy and the resulting social conditions pose a serious challenge to army rule. From the outset, Pakistan's economic growth was interdependent and inter-linked with foreign aid, military assistance, grants, and loans. Since only a fraction of this was utilized for national development, Pakistan had never enjoyed broad-based economic growth. The bulk went to fatten the elite, such as the army, the bureaucracy, and the urban industrialists and traders; or to such unproductive projects as the multi-billion dollar new Federal capital, Islamabad. For example, in ratio to the GNP, Pakistan's expenditure on health, education, or training has always been one of the lowest among the developing countries; although the opposite is true with regard to its expenditure on defense. Nevertheless, so long as the foreign inflow included a generous portion of grants and interest-free loans the situation seemed tolerable. Eventually aid and grants dried up and the interest-bearing loans became the only recourse to sustain an unbalanced economy, which has kept all its proverbial eggs in one basket. As a result, in ratio to the GNP, Pakistan's debt servicing cost has grown to be one of the highest among the developing countries. Nor is that all. Since the early 1980s, the Afghan connections have provided Pakistan with a huge underground economy generated from the illicit dealings in narcotics, fire-arms and other contraband. The incessant inflow of foreign luxury goods, automobiles, and housing material, financed and sustained through money laundering or similar other devious means, has brought new strains on indigenous growth, not to mention the ever-widening gap between the rich and the poor. Since the government has no legitimate share in such an economy, the country's infrastructure has gone from bad to worse. Expensive imported automobiles ply on roads full of pot-holes, stinking garbage and leaded-gas pollution, while luxurious housing suffers from power shortages and minuscule water supplies. One can imagine the plight of the common man, when even to the elites, basic needs such as drinkable water, breathable air, child education, proper medical care and so on pose considerable problems. Drug and firearms traffic now have a growing home market, pushing crime and corruption to new heights, and touching almost every one's life. As a result there is a noticeable increase in the flight of capital, skilled work force, professionals, and trained managers. Add to this growing religious fanaticism, ethnic and sectarian killings, and, above all, ever-lasting conflict with India over Kashmir, which has taken a new turn since Pakistan's nuclear tests in May 1998. General Musharruf, the current army ruler of Pakistan, believes that nuclear deterrence has ensured Pakistan's security and created a strategic balance in a region that has seen three wars in the last fifty-three years.

There is no doubt that the problems Pakistan is facing today are enormous and complicated. Nonetheless, in a large part, they seem to have grown gradually from misplaced goals and wrong priorities established for national development as a whole. It seems unlikely that any one person or elite group will be able to set it right. Such a rule, at best, can provide only temporary relief.

Understandably, Pakistan today is undergoing a phase of acute frustration, which could take the country in any direction. One may only hope that the fear of total destruction of their cherished institutions might induce the army and other elite groups to recognize and accept the ultimate power and aspirations of the people. Once this is accomplished, it should not be so difficult for Pakistan to manage its affairs through normal constitutional means and to develop a broad based self-sustained economy.

Bibliography

Ayub Khan, M. (1967) *Friends not Masters: A Political Autobiography*, New York: Oxford University Press.

Economist (1954) London, October 30.

Haq, M. (1966) *The Strategy of Economic Planning: A Case Study of Pakistan*, Karachi: Oxford University Press.

Haque, A. O. (1969) "Education Disparities in Pakistan," Government of Pakistan, *Forum on Education*, Islamabad (December 20).

Jennings, Sir W. I. (1955) *Special Reference number 1*, Federal Court of Pakistan.

Papanek, G., Schydlowsky, D. M., and Stern, J. J. (1971) *Decision Making for Economic Development: Text and Cases*, Boston: Houghton Mifflin.

Time (1955), April 11.

Times (1954) London, November 1.

Part IV

Solutions and future research

8 Measuring corruption
Numbers versus knowledge versus understanding

Michael Johnston

Introduction

Other than the question of definitions, few issues have so thoroughly stymied the comparative study of corruption as that of measurement. Types and amounts of corruption vary among, and within, societies. Theory tells us that these contrasts reflect political and economic influences, history, and culture, and in turn affect societies and their development in important ways. But the difficulty of measuring corruption has long made it difficult to make such comparisons, to test hypotheses, and to build sound, comprehensive theories.

For many years, this problem was of concern mostly to academic analysts. But recently a variety of forces have put corruption back on the international policy agenda. These include, *inter alia,* the globalization and growing competitiveness of the world economy, and a resulting awareness within international aid and lending agencies, and on the part of private business, of the costs of corruption. Other influences include movements to ban international bribery by domestic legislation (the US Foreign Corrupt Practices Act), or by international agreements (the OECD Anti-Bribery Treaty, and the OAS Anti-Corruption Convention); concern about the cost and efficacy of international development programs, and over the role corruption might play in perpetuating poverty; and the end of the Cold War, which reduced tolerance for corruption among ideological allies.

This revival of interest has spurred innovative attempts to measure corruption, often as a part of more general efforts at reform. Both, however, often reflect the worldviews of business and development interests. "Corruption" as an operational concept is becoming synonymous with bribery, its impact judged increasingly in terms of economic development. Few would dispute the importance of those concerns, but they have fashioned a new orthodoxy about corruption mirroring the broader "Washington consensus" over trade, aid, and development. With that has come a tendency for rich comparative concepts and findings to be overridden by a narrower vision treating corruption primarily as a problem of political and economic liberalization. The indices and research that have resulted may draw upon the detailed knowledge of many people and groups, but ironically may also narrow our understanding of the problem. Not only does this vision disregard important variations, in the course of "explaining" corruption; as the momentum behind reform builds, there is a growing risk that scarce opportunities will be wasted because of policies that are insufficiently adapted to local realities, and to the complexity of corruption itself.

In this discussion I will consider the measurement issue on several levels. One issue is the quality of the indices themselves – and there are important strengths as well as shortcomings. Another will be their impact upon the policy and analytical debates, with an emphasis upon definitions as well as upon analysis and reform. "Second-generation" measures, and ideas for further improvements, will also come in for discussion. Finally, I will survey the prospects for better comparative research and a richer policy debate. The purpose of my critique is not to suggest that the new corruption scales are radically wrong; indeed, there is little reason to think they are. Nor is it to criticize the motives behind the various statistical indices. Rather, it is to emphasize the continuing need for a richly comparative and historical view of corruption, focusing upon many varieties of the problems and drawing upon diverse kinds of evidence and theory.

What makes corruption so difficult to measure?

In principle, social scientists ought to be able to measure anything (Babbie 1995: 110). But this is more easily said than done, and it is a long way from essential concepts and nominal definitions to the events or artifacts included in operational measures.[1] Many concepts are categorizations of, or inferences from, phenomena that may themselves be difficult to identify and observe. Consider "democracy" (Collier and Levitsky 1997): we know it when we see it, but the concept remains essentially contested (Gallie 1965). Over time the concept has a way of "creeping" away from its starting point, necessitating a rethink of what it means (Collier and Levitsky 1997). Reaching consensus over definitions, let alone measurements, would be difficult. One result is that at times we study things mostly because they are easily counted. A more subtle danger is *reification* (Babbie 1995: 116–18) – thinking about operational measures as though they were the concept itself.

Measurement becomes all the more difficult when that which concerns us is hidden. We know corruption exists, but direct witnesses are few; often, those with direct knowledge have an interest in keeping it secret. Where corruption is most serious the officials charged with control are themselves compromised; in such settings reporting corruption becomes an exercise in risk and futility. Violence or intimidation may be used to see off investigators and keep others quiet. Statistics on conventional crimes are notoriously inaccurate; how can we measure an activity that is usually clandestine?

The issue is even more complex because of an old problem – that of definitions. If we study corruption at a general level – particularly, if our concern is commonly repeated syndromes – it may make sense to examine the core cases and not worry much about cases at the margins. But when it comes to counting and measurement the margins become critical – and there is much disagreement as to where those boundaries fall. Add to this the complex relationship between corruption and scandal (Moodie 1980, Markovits and Silverstein 1988): public reports and controversies may tell us more about the *appearance* of corruption – and thus, about political conflicts, or about journalistic practices – than about its actual extent.

The indices: notable strengths, continuing weaknesses

First-generation measures

A variety of corruption measures, differing in breadth, methodology, and quality, are now available; still others are under development. Some of the longest-running efforts at measurement have been mounted by firms providing risk assessments to international business. These, some available on a proprietary basis only, include surveys by Political and Economic Risk Consultancy,[2] the Institute for Management Development,[3] Political Risk Services,[4] *The Economist* Intelligence Unit,[5] and Business International (now a part of *The Economist* group). Others are produced by advocacy groups such as the World Economic Forum[6] and Freedom House,[7] survey organizations such as Gallup,[8] publications such as *The Wall Street Journal*, and groups of analysts, sometimes working in affiliation with international organizations. Some rely upon sample surveys of the public at large, or of international business executives; others depend upon expert assessments. Not surprisingly, sample sizes vary widely. Some ask respondents to rate overall levels of corruption on a scale; others ask about bribes, extortion, or other irregularities in specific governmental functions; others tap respondents' own experiences of corruption. All are aspects of a particular country's corruption situation, broadly defined; what is less clear is whether different kinds of questions about a variety of countries, reported in different units, produce results that are broadly comparable.

Other sorts of data have also been used in the comparative study of corruption. In the United States, for example, the Public Integrity Section of the US Department of Justice regularly publishes data on corruption convictions in federal courts (Schlesinger and Meier 2000). Economists have used measures of economic problems that, while not offered as corruption scales *per se*, tap into closely-related problems, such as data on "black-market premiums" or the quality of countries' institutions (Knack and Keefer 1995). A different approach is the international compilation of criminal justice data by the United Nations Crime Prevention and Criminal Justice Division.[9] These data encompass many countries and a long time span; on the negative side, reliance on official statistics raises questions of comparability across countries' definitions of corruption, court systems, and investigatory efforts.

Corruption versus perceptions of corruption

Most first-generation indices measure perceptions of corruption – comparisons among specific countries, or ratings on an absolute scale – and many depend upon the views of business people. Given the lack of harder indicators, the fact that much corruption arises in the context of business deals, and the extent to which these people move about the global economy, this approach is a natural one. Moreover, perceptions of corruptness are significant in their own right, influencing foreign policy, aid, investment, and lending decisions. They also factor into political interactions, particularly as regards democratization issues. In other ways, however, appearances can be deceiving.

I focus here primarily upon Transparency International's Corruption Perceptions Index (CPI) – the most widely-used and, in many respects, the most ambitious effort to measure and compare perceived levels of corruption.[10] The CPI – a kind of "poll of polls" – has won worldwide attention and aided a variety of analytical studies (for a useful survey see Lambsdorff 1999b).[11] Coverage has expanded from forty-one countries in 1995 to ninety-nine in the 1999 version. Seventeen surveys are now used to calculate the CPI; databases for individual countries range from the minimum of three required for inclusion (eleven countries) to thirteen for Hong Kong, Hungary, South Korea, and Russia, and fourteen for India. (By contrast, in the first CPI (1995) there were no more than seven data sources for any country, and two – Colombia and Argentina – had but two ratings.) CPI methodology has become increasingly sophisticated, and TI publishes a comprehensive "framework document" (Lambsdorff 1999a) and list of data sources on its website.[12]

These ratings, and the scholarship and public debate they have spawned, have seemed to confirm much of what we had long suspected. Corruption rankings are worst for poor, undemocratic, and unstable countries. Multivariate analysis employing CPI data (and others) has produced solid evidence that corruption significantly slows and distorts economic development (Mauro 2000) and reduces foreign direct investment (Wei 1997). It is also linked to inflation (worse where inflation is high and variable – see Braun and Di Tella 2000), and weak political and administrative institutions (Knack and Keefer 1995), and is marginally worse where political competition is weak (Braun and Di Tella 2000, Johnston 2000). Corruption is worse, again, where ethnolinguistic divisions are severe (Mauro 1995, Easterly and Levine 1996).

Like any social-science measure, the CPI has strengths and weaknesses. Its value in sparking new research and public debate is beyond dispute. So are the occasional misuses of the data, though that fault lies principally with users rather than with those devising the scales: Transparency International has been careful to emphasize the CPI's limitations. The CPI's reliability has been commendable, as we shall see. Its precision and validity are more problematical; while difficulties in these areas are inevitable, they also identify challenges for improving our measures. A validity issue common to nearly all first-generation indices – a tendency to equate corruption with bribery, and to focus more upon high-level corruption than the so-called "petty" varieties – will come in for discussion later on.

Reliability

Reliability is the strongest point of the CPI. Rather than employing just one or a few indicators, the data reflect the views of thousands of individuals who encounter corruption in differing ways in a range of countries, and are gathered in a variety of ways.

Given the links between corruption and basic political, economic, and institutional processes, a reliable index should return broadly consistent values from one year to the next. And such is indeed the case. Table 8.1 presents the correlations among the CPI scales published at the time of writing. If these correlations were weak or inconsistent we would have

Table 8.1 Pearson correlations among CPI scales

	1995	*1996*	*1997*	*1998*
1996	0.9770 (41) P=0.000			
1997	0.9354 (42) P=0.000	0.9689 (47) P=0.000		
1998	0.9450 (42) P=0.000	0.9663 (53) P=0.000	0.9880 (52) P=0.000	
1999	0.9386 (42) P=0.000	0.9594 (53) P=0.000	0.9820 (52) P=0.000	0.9933 (85) P=0.000
	Coefficient (Cases) 1-tailed significance			

reason to doubt the CPI's reliability, but the consistency across time is striking.

A few qualifications are in order, however. Coefficients could also be *too* strong: levels of corruption are likely to change, even if gradually, and to change in differing ways from one country to the next. A reliable scale should reflect these changes, too. Thus, is the coefficient of almost 0.94 between 1995 and 1999 scores, for example, too strong? There is no real way of knowing. Moreover, nine of the seventeen component measures in the 1999 CPI are actually three surveys taken in the same, or very similar, ways three years running (1997, 1998, and 1999). While this broadens the number of respondents, and does insulate the scores from short-term fluctuations caused by sensational scandals, this method might also magnify the errors and biases in particular surveys, thus undermining the CPI's responsiveness to real changes. Comparability is an issue too: scores for countries with thirteen or fourteen surveys must include most or all of the repeated measures – meaning that their scores reflect perceptions over several years – while those based on just a handful of surveys will not.

The correlations shown here cannot tell us whether year-on-year differences reflect changes in "real" levels of corruption or the addition of new data improved the measurements, or whether other methodological difficulties have introduced more error. They give little immediate reason to doubt the CPI's reliability, but do raise the question of whether an *annual* index that, in early versions, extended ratings to two decimal places – as opposed, say, to a more general ranking published every three to five years – exaggerates the apparent significance of small variations of unknown origins.

Precision

The precision of the CPI and similar scales is difficult to evaluate. It is not obvious what units of measurement *any* corruption scale ought to use, or how we might expect observations to be distributed. While the many measures folded into the CPI contribute to its reliability, they yield results expressed in significantly different ways. Some produce perceptions of how corrupt a whole society is, while others deal with particular agencies or functions of the state. Indeed, what we mean by "more" or "less" corruption is less obvious than it may seem, a problem that is reflected in the various surveys. Some ask about perceptions of the "problem," or of its "pervasiveness," "level," "number of cases"; CPI architects defend these as comparable assessments of the "degree" of corruption (Lambsdorff 1999a: 7), but others might question this, particularly in differing linguistic settings. Some ratings are anchored on absolute scales, while others are ordinal comparisons only (judgments that country X is more corrupt than others, or that there are "a lot," "a few," or "no" cases of corruption among particular officials). One, the Freedom House ranking, was not even expressed numerically in its original form. Sample sizes, ranges, and distributions vary considerably, and thus sampling distributions and standard errors are likely to differ as well. Rendering these data comparable – and specifically, averaging ordinal-level comparisons into an interval- or ratio-level overall ranking – inevitably produces results shaped by the assumptions of the statistician as well as by actual perceptions or events. One specific result of these difficulties is that while we often treat CPI data as ratio- or interval-level, variations across all values – say, the difference between 5.0 and 6.0, versus 8.4 and 9.4 – may not be consistent.[13] The problem may be most difficult at the extremes – the high- and low-corruption cases that interest us most, and whose rankings draw most attention.

Closely related to this are the differing lists of countries to which various component measures apply. Ideally we would have the same large number of corruption measures for every country, but we do not. The architects of the CPI have, in recent years, required a minimum of three corruption surveys before a country can be included – an approach minimizing the error that might result from relying on just one or two ratings. But the missing data are not randomly distributed; countries with poor institutions and governance also tend to have the fewest scales available. Thus, those with the worst corruption might well have the least data, while others slightly better off, where at least *some* surveys have been conducted, may be wrongly viewed as the world's most corrupt societies (Kaufmann, Kraay, and Zoido-Lobatón 1999a: 22–3). TI regularly warns against interpreting CPI results in that way, but variations in amounts and quality of data among countries raise validity and reliability issues, possibly reducing the former while artificially inflating the latter to some degree.

A different precision problem concerns the reporting of results. CPI scores are reported on a 0-to-10 scale (with low scores referring to high levels of corruption, and vice versa) in tenths of points, and, for the 1995 through 1997 CPIs, in *hundredths* of points. It seems unlikely that this sort of implied precision is justified; at the very least, reporting to only one decimal place beginning in 1998 was an appropriate change. What would be an appropriate level of precision? Since the CPI does not have a true zero point, and if we are not certain that variations are consistent across all values, an argument can be made that it is essentially ordinal-level, and ought to be reported in broad bands (perhaps "low," "low-medium," "medium," and so forth) rather than in numerical points.

Perhaps the most serious drawback of the CPI and similar indices is what might be called the "single-number problem." It is a precision issue, but one with validity and reliability implications as well. Actual corruption varies in many ways: there are many forms – a validity issue discussed later – and contrasts within most societies. When respondents judge the amount of corruption in a society, are they responding to the same things, or do their judgments reflect *qualitative* variations from one case to the next? How much nepotism or patronage is equivalent to a certain level of bribery in road construction? Is that bribery comparable in *significance* to similar practices in arms contracting? No single national score can accurately reflect contrasts in the types of corruption found in a country, or the contrasts between (say) Northern and Southern Italy, across Russia, or among Minnesota, Alabama, and New Jersey. Some countries have high-level corruption, others find it lower down the political or bureaucratic hierarchies, and still others see most abuses in electoral politics and patronage. It may be seen as a major concern even where absolute levels are likely moderate to low (as in New South Wales); elsewhere, corruption enjoys official protection. In some countries the problem centers around international trade, while in others it is home-grown. Obviously any account of corruption, be it a case study or a data point, will be a simplification, and the CPI's architects have no control over the interpretations that result. But we might still ask how much understanding is lost by collapsing complex variations – qualitative as well as quantitative – into single-number ratings.

Validity

The CPI, and many of the measures upon which it is based, represent a clear advance over the anecdotal evidence and hypothetical cases that dominated earlier phases of research, and over the diffuse and emotional claims often marking public discussions. Its results are plausible: it is difficult to dispute the notion that Canada is less corrupt than Poland, and that Poland is less corrupt than Kenya. In addition, the CPI and similar scales relate statistically to others in ways that make theoretical sense – evidence for construct and predictive validity.

Problems arise, however, with the basic approach of using perceptions as our operational measure. Setting aside the difficulties inherent in measuring perceptions of *anything,* we must remember that perceptions are not the same thing as corruption itself. They may reflect the open-ness of corruption, rather than its actual extent. The two may differ considerably: indeed, Rose-Ackerman (1996) has observed that as corruption problems worsen in a country, the major dealings tend to become fewer in number, to involve higher stakes, and to take place closer to the top. We can easily imagine one country in which corrup-tion takes place openly, in small-to-moderate transactions, and another with less frequent, but large, well-concealed deals at the top of the state structure, perhaps under the protection of the very officials and agencies nominally charged with bringing it to light. Where corrupt officials and their clients operate with impunity, informants and prying journalists might be silenced by intimidation. The few visiting business people who do gain access to such dealings might quickly acquire a stake in keeping their true perceptions to themselves. Corruption might distort politics, the economy, and development, and yet this country might score better on the CPI that its neighbor, where less serious corruption is practiced more openly.

Other subtleties complicate the rankings. What is being perceived as more or less serious? How much do judgments reflect levels of corruption, and how much are they reactions to *trends*? That is, might sudden revelations in a society where the problem had not been regarded as serious lead to harsher judgments – or, to less reliable changes in ratings – than would levels of corruption that have been consistently high for many years? Does extensive corruption refer to the number of cases, the sums changing hands, impact upon politics or the economy, or cases involving particularly important officials or programs (Rose-Ackerman 1999: 4; Lambsdorff 1999a: 7–8)? Perceptions could reflect general impressions, or ethical expectations, of whole societies – of inefficiency or official impunity, poverty, or a weak civil society – rather than knowledge of corruption as such. What appears to be corruption might actually be scandal stirred up by feuding factions. Some judgments might reflect culture shock (particularly if one's basis for comparison is a low-corruption society), language limitations, or sheer dislike of a country or its regime.[14] The perceptions of outsiders – even if they rest upon a shared definition – might tell us little about the *significance* of corruption: what a case or allegation *means* in its context. A seemingly minor case might be freighted with significance lost upon outsiders or ordinary citizens unfamiliar with elite conflicts. Or, a generally well-governed country with a free press and independent judges might produce numerous reports of corruption, while in another – where the press is intimidated, officials lead insecure lives, and international donors and lenders are threatening sanctions because of poor governance – corrupt figures might become unusually skillful at covering their tracks. Finally, do we trust the honesty of visitors' reports? Some might be less than candid because of their firms' or agencies' – or their own – involvement in corrupt activities (though the large sample sizes and respondent anonymity of several of the CPI component surveys likely mitigates this problem). Others who have not done well in business might exaggerate corruption to explain away their failures.

Another validity problem is similar to the "single-number" issue. League-table rankings effectively treat corruption as a single generic process or problem, inviting statistical analyses that impose a common model upon (and within) widely-varying societies and cases.[15] Qualitative differences are reduced to matters of degree. Consider, for example, the changing calculus of daily life – and of reform – implied when corruption is the rule rather than the exception, is facilitated by well-organized groups holding political or economic monopolies (Johnston 1998), or is backed up by force. Then, corrupt figures face few meaningful limits, and can practice extortion or outright theft more easily, rather than making quid pro quo deals. The losers from such corruption are more likely to respond in evasive or illicit ways (Alam 1995), rather than directly confronting it as they might where corruption is the exception and the rule of law is secure. To a degree this problem can be eased by incorporating corruption indicators into the best theoretical models we can. But nonetheless, as Luis Moreno Ocampo, a former Argentine prosecutor, has put it, "corruption in Sweden and Nigeria are just not the same. To use the same word for completely different situations can only generate confusion" (Ocampo 1993).

A *"bribery bias"?*

If corruption indices tend to impose a single model upon corruption, what is it? To a significant degree it is that of bribery. Several of the components of the CPI specifically ask respondents to judge the extent of bribery, or of demands for bribes. Others implicitly emphasize bribery by sampling business people instead of, say, poor farmers. (In that connection, three component measures ask recipients the extent to which corruption harms the business environment, confusing measurement with the question of consequences, and inviting connections between corruption and broader economic problems.) Nepotism, official theft, and fraud, *political* corruption such as patronage, so-called "petty corruption" such as police shakedowns of stall holders at local markets, and election fraud may not fit the bribery model (or the daily experiences of business people) so neatly, and may thus be underestimated.

Again, qualitative differences are collapsed into matters of degree. Bribery may be the main form of corruption in international business, and may be what springs to most minds when "corruption" is mentioned, but in some respects it is a special case. In a strict sense, bribery is a quid pro quo on *comparatively* free and equal (if illicit) terms. It differs from extortion, where officials force deals that may be anything but free and are rarely equal. Bribery seems most likely to dominate where corruption is moderate to moderately high, illicit deals are a matter of course, and participants are not frequently punished. Where the risk of punishment is high, or (by contrast) where powerful officials act with impunity, things may be different: in the former, bribe payers may have to add a "risk premium," while in the latter they are at the mercy of officials. In some corruption exchanges, such as patronage and nepotism, considerable time may elapse between receiving the quid and repaying the quo, and the two may be difficult to link or compare to each other. And other forms of corruption – electoral fraud, embezzlement, or using official resources to operate an under-the-table business – are not exchanges at all. Respondents to the CPI's component surveys may be well aware of these variations, but their knowledge cannot be conveyed in any single rating.

Why do these problems matter?

First-generation corruption measures have helped move the debate forward, and have framed new hypotheses for further work. None has been proposed as the final word on measuring corruption; and, to discuss their weaknesses is ultimately to return to the inherent difficulties of measuring corruption.

Still, the difficulties outlined earlier do matter. Existing indices help us least in the countries we care about most: those with the worst corruption problems. Even if country rankings make sense, causes, effects, and corrupt processes exist at several different levels of aggregation. Thus developing careful, nuanced accounts of corrupt processes remains a central task for comparative analysts. Without such foundations, the significance of any ranking is open to debate. A 1999 re-analysis of CPI data by TI representatives in Latin America and the Caribbean (TILAC 1999), for example, emphasized the range of variation in ranking across the Americas, and compared scores for the *region* to those of other parts of the world, with results that made Latin American corruption appear not quite as exceptional, and the worst cases less typical of the region, than we might have assumed. Perhaps it makes most sense to say that corruption indices have definite uses, but are just one form of evidence among many others and may be more useful for framing hypotheses than for providing conclusive answers.

As noted at the outset, many of the current scales reflect the outlooks of international business, and of the aid and lending institutions that have put corruption back on the policy agenda. There is nothing wrong with this, and the field is richer today for the efforts of such groups. But theirs are partial visions nonetheless; knowing how corruption – conceptualized as bribery – affects development – expressed in GDP figures or in terms of governance indicators – is valuable knowledge, but there is much more to be said. Years ago, for example, Huntington (1968) proposed that corruption might be a preferable alternative to violence; in the process, making the important point that in judging its effects we must make comparisons to its real alternatives, not just to ideal processes and outcomes. Statistical indices cannot settle that sort of question by themselves; we will also need historical, linguistic, political, and cultural evidence, and knowledge of forms of corruption beyond the bribery paradigm. Classical concerns of theory – the nature of accountability and justice, the sources and benefits of good politics, the dynamics behind cooperation, the emergence of normative frameworks, and strong civil societies – are parts of that picture too. No index could be expected to reveal these subtleties, but they are no less important for being less easily quantified.

These, again, are more than methodological niceties. Perceptions of corruption do shape important decisions, but the danger is that they will lead to an "echo chamber" problem in which officials and investors repeat what they hear from each other, in effect, and in which anecdotes and perceptions acquire false authority through repetition. Analysts can make good use of perceptions of corruption, but there must also be ways to anchor perceptions in less subjective information about societies.

Better numbers, or better understanding?

It is unlikely that we will ever have valid, reliable, precise, subtle, and broadly comparable data on corruption – much less on all of its various forms. But even if we had, they would be only one aspect of the broader and richer comparisons that are needed both for analysis and reform. Understanding the varying forms of corruption, their links to deeply-embedded causes, and their consequences requires many kinds of evidence, and theoretical approaches sensitive to a range of variations among societies. Reforms and more general development efforts need similar foundations. A number of attempts have been made to improve our measurements of corruption, and I will note a few of those below. But the real challenge for the next stage of corruption research is not just to improve our measurements, but rather to build a richer understanding of the phenomenon, and to show why such an understanding is essential.

Second-generation measures

The first-generation indices elicited strong reactions. Journalists pounced upon the CPI as a rating of the world's most corrupt countries, even though TI explicitly warned against that interpretation. International agencies and many scholars quickly put the data to work, while others were more critical. Governments joined the fray, some crying foul as negative ratings threatened their countries' images and economic prospects.

The result was a new set of initiatives that could loosely be termed "second-generation" measures. A variety of sample surveys, for example, have focused upon businesses, households, and individuals, and their experiences of corruption (bribes paid, bureaucratic harassment, and the speed and quality of public services). Surveys are subject to many of the same validity, reliability, and precision problems discussed earlier, but provide a level of detail that first-generation scales cannot (and were not intended to) offer. A variety of organizations, including the US Agency for International Development, have sponsored such surveys. The most elaborate is the World Bank Institute's 1999 Business Environment and Enterprise Performance Survey (BEEPS) carried out in twenty transitional states in the former USSR and Eastern and Central Europe (Hellman, Jones, Kaufmann, and Schankerman 2000). The data, based on a seventy-item survey of business firms, and on some supplementary questions, were gathered in 1999 (for a description of methods, see ibid.: 1–8). The survey approach allows considerable control of data gathering, and in particular it allows researchers to consider different varieties of corruption. Cross-national surveys involve obvious linguistic problems; other difficulties of comparison, such as a tendency for respondents in various countries systematically to under- or overestimate the corruption with which they deal, must be taken into account too. On the latter point, however, the BEEPS survey asks respondents' views on verifiable aspects of the business environment, such as exchange-rate fluctuations, as well as about corruption. For the former, perceptions can be checked against valid indicators, allowing an intelligent guess as to whether respondents systematically over- or understate the latter. BEEPS-style projects are formidably expensive, and while including a wider variety of corrupt practices and situations than most other indices, still approach the problem from the standpoint of businesses and lenders. Nonetheless, they are an extremely promising addition to the growing number of corruption measures, and the 1999 data have already begun to produce intriguing comparative studies of some of the countries where corruption problems are of most concern (see, for example, Hellman, Jones, and Kaufmann 2000).

In 1999, Transparency International, responding in part to the criticisms of countries rated negatively in the CPI, and in part to the growing realization, as the OECD anti-bribery treaty took shape, that the *sources* of bribes needed to be studied as well, devised a "Bribe Payers' Index" (BPI).[16] The BPI, based on Gallup survey data gathered in fourteen "emerging market" countries, ranked nineteen leading exporting countries in terms of their own firms' propensity to pay bribes to "senior public officials." The results were quite different from those of the CPI: countries such as Sweden, Australia, Canada, the United Kingdom, and the United States came off much less favorably in this index. The BPI has made its share of headlines, but here again questions are being raised. The new index does not appear to control for the size of the "home economies" of bribe-payers, or for their countries' prominence (or lack of it) in trade, either overall or within particular regions. There is no distinction made as to the gravity of cases in which a country's firms might be involved. It is not clear which country would be blamed for bribes paid by (say) an Indonesian employee of a Thai subsidiary of an Anglo-Dutch corporation that is part of a multi-national consortium bidding on a major arms contract. Again we have the problem of the differences between perceptions and corruption itself: are respondents basing their judgments on actual knowledge of corruption, upon hearsay, or upon their general opinions of particular countries? The BPI is a new measure; it does raise an important issue, and again Transparency International has provided an extensive "framework" document.[17] It seems likely that this and other measures focusing on the sources of bribes will be the focus of continued work over the years to come.

Kaufmann, Kraay, and Zoido-Lobatón (1999a) have constructed a sophisticated index of "graft" as a part of a broader measure of the quality of governance (ibid.: 2 *passim*). They use thirty-one component measures that allow the inclusion of 166, 156, and 155 countries, respectively, in aggregate indices of the rule of law, government effectiveness, and graft (ibid.: 2; data are described in Kaufmann *et al.* 1999b). The statistical approach is an "unobserved components" model (Kaufmann *et al.* 1999a: 1–2, 8–14; see also Greene 1990: ch. 17), treating country data as a linear function of governance – which remains unobserved, but is assumed to be normally distributed across countries – plus a "disturbance term" reflecting both error resulting from the different samples of countries available for the various indicators, and error in the indicators themselves. This approach allows estimates of standard errors, and (under certain assumptions) of confidence intervals, for the three governance indices.

Unlike the CPI, which excludes countries with fewer than three corruption surveys, this approach is more inclusive. The rationale is that data are likely to be more plentiful for countries with better governance, and that excluding those for which data are scarce has the effect of omitting many of the worst-governance cases, as discussed before. Supporting this view is a comparison made by Kaufmann *et al.* (1999c: 23–4, Fig. 8: 46) between preliminary estimates of "probity" (calculated using the same unobserved-components approach on a somewhat smaller database) and 1998 CPI scores. The CPI produced systematically lower estimates which are most likely to be the result of excluding countries with fewer than three surveys.

Kaufmann *et al.* found that even given some strong assumptions, standard errors for their governance indicators (including graft) were very large. It was possible to identify a handful of countries at the good- and bad-governance extremes, but results for the vast majority did not differ statistically from the global means. For most countries, the data did not support confident judgments that probity, bureaucratic quality, and rule of law were particularly high or low – much less allow fine comparisons using a single-number index (Kaufmann *et al.* 1999a: 2, 15–19). Moreover, averaging "noisy" individual measures together, by any of several methods, means that statistical models including aggregate governance indicators are likely to understate their relationships with other variables by 10 to 15 percent (Kaufmann *et al.* 1999c: 21–6). Finally, the assumption of a linear relationship between governance itself and the component measures may not be sustainable (Kaufmann *et al.* 1999a: 22–4). As with the CPI, we are thus not sure that "real" variations are equal across all identical intervals of the indices. In the end, probably the most a realistic corruption measure can do is to identify bands of cases likely to have broadly comparable levels of corruption (for a critical evaluation of the methods used by Kaufmann *et al.*, see Lambsdorff 1999a: 18–20).

A different approach (Hall and Yago 2000) gets at corruption by way of its correlates and consequences. It focuses upon the concept of "opacity" – the opposite of transparency or, in this context, restrictions upon the open flow of information essential to orderly, efficient markets. Opacity has many forms in practice, ranging from false accounting to intimidation, and serves "to ensure the secrecy of corrupt or questionable practices" (ibid.: 1). A statistical model is developed that incorporates corruption in several different ways: CPI figures are included as an estimate of corruption, along with macroeconomic data and various measures of institutional quality. The data are used to account for the varying interest rates paid by governments as they float bonds on the international market. Those with poorer institutions and higher levels of opacity pay higher costs – a "premium" – to borrow money. Estimating the size and sources of these costs is, in effect, a way to compare the seriousness of these countries' corruption problems. The authors calculate an "institutions premium," a "corruption premium," and a "graft premium" – the latter based on the graft index calculated by Kaufmann *et al.* – for each of thirty-five countries. These estimate "the shortfall each country had from the perfect transparency score" (ibid.: 5). The results are strong and consistent: poor-quality institutions, corruption, and graft are linked to significantly higher costs of borrowing – estimated at over $130 billion per year for the sample of thirty-five economies. These are indirect measures of corruption, to be sure, but they have the virtue of incorporating perceptual scales into a range of harder indicators. But while the corruption and graft premia are both consistent with the perceptions tapped by CPI – and, in practical terms, are likely influenced by such perceptions, as noted earlier – construct validity, reliability, and precision are augmented by the ways lenders continually evaluate countries' economic performance and debt-service prospects. Corruption itself remains difficult to measure, but the notion of building indices on more reliable measures of other variables closely related to it is a very promising one.

Conclusion: better research, better policy

Two major issues remain. One is a shortcoming with all of the measures now available. The other reflects the range of forces shaping the past decade's work.

As for the first: how much guidance do corruption indices give reformers? Can those fighting corruption in a society look to CPI scores for evidence of progress, and for guidance in shaping their strategies? In all likelihood they cannot. CPI data do exhibit impressive reliability, but as noted before we still do not know how well they track changes in levels of corruption. Perceptions may outrun, or lag behind, actual trends. Any comprehensive anti-corruption strategy will likely work better with some varieties of the problem than with others, and yet a single-number index will not be able to tell us much about those contrasts, and thus, much about which aspects of the strategy are working and which are not.

What is likely to happen to perception scores for a country that has begun to make meaningful progress against corruption? There are several possibilities: at the very least, progress will be uneven, and thus recognized more quickly by some observers than by others. In that event, the uncertainty (variance, or standard deviation in some versions) of CPI scores might widen considerably while the scores themselves change in ways that would be difficult to interpret. More likely, a successful anti-corruption campaign would produce revelations of wrongdoing, convictions, and new allegations. This is all the more likely in a democratizing country with citizens, journalists, and opposition figures feeling more free to speak out, and contending factions using corruption allegations to settle old scores. In that setting, effective anti-corruption efforts would likely cause perceptions to *worsen* markedly, at least in the short run. Finally, a campaign that begins to break up corrupt networks may well lead to a short-term surge of overt, smash-and-grab corruption as elites, uncertain about their hold on power, take as much as they can, as fast as they can take it (Scott 1972, Knack and Keefer 1995). Once again, CPI ratings may worsen. Surveys, whether on the BEEPS scale or smaller, are probably the best way to gauge anti-corruption progress. But they are expensive, and may not reveal much about progress against the deeper causes of corruption, or *why* observed trends are occurring.

Can we devise relatively inexpensive measures that are still sensitive to changing levels of corruption, and can give useful guidance to anti-corruption efforts? One way might be to focus less on measuring corruption itself and more upon scaling its correlates. We have good reasons to think that a variety of conditions and phenomena are closely linked to corruption. Many of these have been measured at a considerable level of validity, reliability, and precision, and in ways that do not reify perceptions and anecdotes as broader trends. Serious corruption is deeply embedded, and causality can be difficult to disentangle; still, we might construct a pair of indices approximating causes and effects. Loayza (1996) has employed a similar approach in studying informal economies, a measurement challenge resembling corruption in many respects. On one side we could incorporate measures of major problems giving rise to, and sustaining corruption – poor-quality institutions, lack of political competition, a lack of openness in the economy, inflation, and weak guarantees of civil liberties and property rights, for example – as well as those that make corruption easier to conceal (such as Hall and Yago's measurements of "opacity"). A parallel index of consequences might include factors such as capital-to-labor ratios in key aspects of the economy, budget-composition indicators (Mauro 2000), statistics on the efficiency of tax collection, "black-market premiums" in foreign exchange, trends in aggregate development, indicators of various forms of capital flight (or even of conspicuous consumption?), and so on. Both indices could be based upon an unobserved-components model; both could be tailored to include likely correlates of different forms of corruption. A focus upon specific countries or regions over time would reduce the risk of distortions caused by the differing data available in various countries. The result could be indices complementary to those now available, yet sensitive to changes and to the deeper causes and effects of corruption.

There are some obvious problems here. Endogeneity and simultaneity make causes and effects of corruption difficult to separate: are ineffective tax collection or a "black-market premium" results of corruption, or do they create incentives that cause it? This approach, while it might reveal distinctive aspects of corruption in particular societies or regions, would not produce "headline numbers" for broad cross-national comparisons, though as the discussion before makes clear, such comparisons face major difficulties to begin with. The statistical risks inherent in merging disparate indicators would remain. So would problems of reliability and precision: how, for example, should the components of such indices be weighted? Should we use a regression model that predicts CPI or other scores for some initial point in time and weight measures by their statistical power (along with control variables) to predict our "effects index," or changes in it? If so, how should we weight the components of the effects scale?

As with the CPI and other measures, there would also be questions as to how to report the results. Are annual results extended to decimal places appropriate? Would they raise expectations that cannot be met or, because of the long-term nature of basic reform, lead to disillusionment? Would reporting results in broader "bands" create the illusion that nothing is changing? On the other hand, if reforms really are likely to produce the *appearance* of increased corruption in the short-run, solid evidence that underlying changes are more gradual might be very valuable to anti-corruption agencies facing press and political scrutiny.

The second problem is a needless, and ultimately false, bifurcation in the corruption debate, generally expressed as a gap between "theory" and "practical" research. This too is linked to reform, but has deeper roots, reflecting the outlooks and interests that have shaped many first-generation measures and their uses. Usually the implication is that broadly comparative work – particularly that aimed at developing conceptual frameworks and broad-based explanations – falls into the former category, while the statistical approaches and reform orientation defining the "new consensus" embody the latter. Research and reform are indeed distinct enterprises, but the most troubling aspect of this bifurcation is the frequent implication that comparative research is irrelevant – or a positive hindrance – to "practical" insights about corruption.

This distinction, of course, quickly breaks down under critical examination: sound theory will always have to be tested against the best evidence available, while reforms or empirical research not guided by theory are pointless, and may do more harm than good. But it may damage both the analytical and the reform agendas. The scholarly tradition is distorted by an overemphasis upon the narrow range of factors included in the so-called "practical" arena – perhaps most clearly illustrated by the ways corruption indices reduce complex cases to single numbers and encourage cross-sectional statistical approaches that impose a single model upon widely divergent cases. Policy-makers may lose sight of the historical origins of corruption, and thus of some of the forces and conflicts sustaining it; of the cultural and linguistic factors shaping the social significance of corruption as well as responses to reforms; and of the many opportunities – indeed, the necessity – to carefully choose policies and judge their effects in the context of local realities. In such a setting scholars – seeking "relevance" – may produce work that is atheoretical, ahistorical, and devoid of comparative insight; a collection of case studies without richness or context. There is also the concern that policy-makers, rejecting the need for a subtle and contingent analytical framework, will support one-size-fits-all remedies or "toolkit" reforms that do not reflect the kinds of things comparativists have long known about the societies in question.

There is no valid reason why the theoretical/practical bifurcation should exist. Indeed, as emphasis shifts away from putting corruption back on the international policy agenda – a task for which indices such as the PCI have proven very well-suited – and instead shifts toward action against it, the need for theory, comparisons, and subtle, often qualitative sorts of evidence becomes greater, not less. Broad-based comparative frameworks merging quantitative evidence with qualitative knowledge, and with linguistic, cultural, and historical evidence, would serve both traditions well. Reform and analysis will always remain distinct enterprises, but as Hall and Yago's work on "opacity" suggests, the shortcomings of perceptual measures become less critical the more they are augmented with other evidence. Comparative frameworks may generate more precise hypotheses to the extent that they draw upon quantitative evidence. Here, in a way, the second-generation corruption measures help show the way forward: as they become more elaborate they are more and more dependent for their meaning upon complex models, and become increasingly distant from "corruption rankings." There is no reason why that trend cannot be carried further, with statistical analysis of corruption questions becoming one component in broader comparative frameworks that have linguistic and cultural subtlety, and qualitative and historical depth, along with the kind of breadth that cross-sectional statistical data can provide.

There is no doubt that the effort to measure corruption has been worthwhile. It has helped set to rest a variety of questions that had long kept the scholarly debate going around in circles, and has framed others in more precise and comparative terms. Even to devise a critique of the existing measures, and of the corruption-as-bribery paradigm underlying much of the recent empirical work, is to identify fresh comparative challenges. The potential of any research to produce rich *and* useful insights depends fundamentally upon careful design and honest application, not upon the apparent simplicity of its methods or results. The task now is to bring evidence of many sorts together into discussions of corruption that can match the comparative reach of most statistical indices with the complexity of corruption itself, and of the societies it affects most.

Notes

1 A discussion of basic problems in measurement appears in the Appendix.
2 www.asiarisk.com
3 www.imd.ch
4 www.prsgroup.com
5 www.eiu.com
6 www.weforum.org
7 www.freedomhouse.org
8 www.gallup-international.com
9 See www.uncjin.org/Statistics/WCTS/wcts.html#globalreport and the agency's *Global Report on Crime and Justice* (Oxford: Oxford University Press, 1999).
10 www.transparency.org/documents/cpi; see also the very useful Internet Center for Corruption Research (www.gwdg.de/~uwvw/) established at the University of Göttingen by Prof. Johann Graf Lambsdorff, the CPI's author.
11 See, for the 1998 CPI, www.gwdg.de/~uwvw/PRESS98/Press98.html
12 www.transparency.org/documents/cpi/cpi_framework.html
13 I include myself in the term "we" here: see Johnston 2000.
14 On the subtleties of the language of corruption, see Génaux 2000 and Moroff and Blechinger 2000.
15 I am particularly indebted to Mushtaq Khan for his comments on this point.
16 www.transparency.org/documents/cpi/bps.html
17 www.transparency.org/documents/cpi/bpi_framework.html

Appendix

The basics of measurement

The discussion in this appendix draws heavily upon Babbie (1995: 121–9).

Validity raises the question of whether our data actually measure what we claim they do. Concepts themselves do not exist in the real world, or have "real definitions" (Babbie 1995: 116; see also Hempel 1952). They are, rather, constructs useful for categorizing objects or events, and for drawing out attributes we think they share. Thus our empirical measures can never be better than approximations, and the literature abounds with "measurements" that draw on something in addition to, or other than, that which they claim to measure – or that are grounded in nothing at all. As Babbie (1995: 127–8) explains, we can assess the validity of a measure in several ways. Does it possess *face validity* – that is, does it have anything to do with the concept we have nominally defined? An index that excludes extortion while counting street crimes might return higher values for places we think are more corrupt, but it does not measure what we mean by "corruption." Does it possess *criterion-related* or *predictive* validity, in the sense of predicting changes in other variables that theory tells us should be linked to our concept? For example, corruption measures should statistically "predict" the credit ratings lenders give to various governments. Or, a measure might be related to other variables in ways that are consistent with what we know about those factors, even if it does not "predict" them – an attribute called *construct validity*. We might, for example, expect extensive corruption where institutions are of poor quality (Knack and Keefer 1995) and ethno-linguistic fragmentation is severe (Easterly and Levine 1996). A measure possessing *content validity* works well across diverse manifestations of a concept: corruption ratings ought to reflect the incidence of all the major varieties of corruption, not just one or a few. Finally, a concept might have *reference-group validity* – that is, be judged sound by people with extensive knowledge of whatever we wish to measure.

Reliability refers to the question of whether a particular measure returns consistent results. A corruption scale that rates Zimbabwe (say) as an 8 on a scale of ten one year, 2 the next, and 5 the year after that, is of little use: theory suggests that such wide variations are unlikely. No social-science measure will be completely reliable, but we can improve our results through careful construction of indices using good data, and by repeated testing.

Finally, *precision* refers to the fineness of the units in which a measure is expressed. In general, the more precision the better: we would have little use for a "yes/no" corruption variable. High-, medium-, and low-corruption categories would be better, and numerical rankings more precise yet. A related issue is *level of measurement*: some measures are *nominal*, grouping cases into categories among which there is no particular relationship (the continent where a country is located, for example). Others are *ordinal*, grouping cases into categories that can be ranked higher or lower in terms of some shared attribute. We might, for example, place countries into high, middle, and low GDP-per-capita groups; all in the "high" category would be more affluent than all in the "middle" group, but there would be considerable variation within groups and no consistent variation among groups. *Interval*-level measurements array cases along a common dimension marked off into units of identical size, but without a point indicating the complete absence of the attribute. The Fahrenheit scale, for example, has an arbitrary zero point: a 1 degree difference is identical across all values, but 40 degrees is not twice as warm as a reading of 20. We might survey several countries asking whether officials are venal or public-spirited, and express the results at the interval level (say, +5 to −5). Such a measure could not, however, tell us a particular country has a total absence of public spirit or that it is twice as venal as another. Finally, *ratio*-level data also array cases along a dimension marked off in units of identical size, but include a true "zero point." Here, expressions of proportion are appropriate: a country with 50 million residents is twice as populous as its neighbor with 25 million.

Other things being equal, higher levels of precision and measurement are desirable. But there is such a thing as false precision: while it is more useful to know that a country's population density is 255 people per square mile than that it is moderate, it is neither useful nor statistically appropriate to express that measure as 255.348906346 people/mi². Indeed, one measurement can be more precise, but less accurate, than another: data telling us country X's population density is 255 people/mi² may be less accurate than an ordinal ranking of "moderate" if the true figure is 75 people/mi². Level of measurement is an important statistical issue: it is tempting to treat ordinal data as interval-level, for example, but the results can be misleading.

Bibliography

Alam, M. S. (1995) "A Theory of Limits on Corruption and Some Applications," *Kyklos* 48(3): 419–35.

Babbie, E. (1995) *The Practice of Social Research* (7th edn), Belmont, Calif.: Wadsworth.

Braun, M. and Di Tella, R. (2000) "Inflation and Corruption," Working Paper 00–053, Cambridge, Mass.: Harvard Business School, Division of Research.

Collier, D. and Levitsky, S. (1997) "Democracy with Adjectives: Conceptual Innovation in Comparative Research," *World Politics* 49 (April): 430–51.

Easterly, W. and Levine, R. (1996) "Africa's Growth Tragedy: Policies and Ethnic Divisions," Washington, DC: World Bank, Policy Research Department, Macroeconomics and Growth Division.

Gallie, W. B. (1965) "Essentially Contested Concepts," *Proceedings of the Aristotelian Society 56.*

Génaux, M. (2000) "Early Modern Corruption in English and French Fields of Vision," in A. J. Heidenheimer and M. Johnston (eds), *Political Corruption*, New Brunswick, NJ: Transaction.

Greene, W. (1990) *Econometric Analysis*, New York: Macmillan.

Hall, T. and Yago, G. (2000) "Estimating the Cost of Opacity Using Sovereign Bond Spreads," Working Paper, Santa Monica, Calif.: Capital Studies Group, Milken Institute.

Heidenheimer, A. J. and Johnston, M. (2000) *Political Corruption*, New Brunswick, NJ: Transaction.

Hellman, J. S., Jones, G., and Kaufmann, D. (2000) "Seize the State, Seize the Day: An Empirical Analysis of State Capture and Corruption in Transition," draft of paper prepared for the Annual Bank Conference on Development Economics (April), Washington, DC: World Bank, www.worldbank.org/wbi/governance/working_papers.htm

Hellman, J. S., Jones, G., Kaufmann, D., and Schankerman, M. (2000) "Measuring Governance, Corruption, and State Capture," (April), Washington, DC: World Bank, www.worldbank.org/wbi/governance/working_papers.html

Hempel, C. G. (1952) "Fundamentals of Concept Formation in Empirical Science," *International Encyclopedia of Social Science* 2(7).

Huntington, S. P. (1968) *Political Order in Changing Societies*, New Haven: Yale University Press.

Johnston, M. (1998) "What Can Be Done About Entrenched Corruption?" in B. Pleskovic (ed.), *Annual World Bank Conference on Development Economics 1997*, Washington, DC: World Bank: 149–80

—— (2000) "Party Systems, Competition, and Political Checks against Corruption," in A. J. Heidenheimer and M. Johnston, (eds) *Political Corruption,* New Brunswick, NJ: Transaction.

Kaufmann, D., Kraay, A., and Zoido-Lobatón, P. (1999a) "Aggregating Governance Indicators," (August), Washington, DC: World Bank, www.worldbank.org/wbi/-governance/working_papers.htm

—— (1999b) "Governance Matters," World Bank Policy Research Working Paper no. 2196 (October), Washington, DC: World Bank, August version at www.worldbank.org/wbi/governance/working_papers.htm

—— (1999c) "Aggregating Governance Indicators," (August), Washington, DC: World Bank; unpublished.

Knack, S. and Keefer, P. (1995) "Institutions and Economic Performance: Cross-Country Tests Using Alternative Institutional Measures," *Economics and Politics* 7(3): 207–27.

Lambsdorff, J. G. (1999a) "The Transparency International Corruption Perceptions Index 1999: Framework Document," (October), Berlin: Transparency International, www.transparency.org/documents/cpi/cpi_framework.html

—— (1999b) "Corruption in Empirical Research: A Review," www.gwdg.de/~uwvw/

Loayza, N. (1996) "The Economics of the Informal Sector: A Simple Model and Some Empirical Evidence from Latin America," *Carnegie Rochester Conference Series on Public Policy* 45: 129–62.

Markovits, A. S. and Silverstein, M. (1988) *The Politics of Scandal: Power and Process in Liberal Democracies*, New York: Holmes and Meier.

Mauro, P. (1995) "Corruption and Growth," *Quarterly Journal of Economics* 110(2): 681–712.

—— (2000) "The Effects of Corruption on Growth, Investment, and Government Expenditure," in A. J. Heidenheimer and M. Johnston (eds), *Political Corruption*, New Brunswick, NJ: Transaction.

Moodie, G. C. (1980) "On Political Scandals and Corruption," *Government and Opposition* 15(2): 208–22.

Moroff, H. and Blechinger, V. (2000) "Corruption Terms in the World Press: How Languages Differ," in A. J. Heidenheimer and M. Johnston (eds), *Political Corruption*, New Brunswick, NJ: Transaction.

Ocampo, L. M. (1993) "*En Defensa Propria: Como Salir de la Corrupcion?*" *Suramericana*, Buenos Aires.

Rose-Ackerman, S. (1996) "When is Corruption Harmful?" Washington, DC: World Bank.

—— (1999) *Corruption and Government: Causes, Consequences, and Reform*, Cambridge, UK: Cambridge University Press.

Schlesinger, T. J. and Meier, K. J. (2000) "Variations in Corruption among the American States," in A. J. Heidenheimer and M. Johnston (eds), *Political Corruption*, New Brunswick, NJ: Transaction.

Scott, J. C. (1972) *Comparative Political Corruption*, Englewood Cliffs, NJ: Prentice-Hall.

TILAC (Transparency International for Latin America and the Caribbean) (1999) "Another Form to Look at the TI Index: Latin America as an Example," unpublished.

Wei, S. (1997) "How Taxing Is Corruption on International Investors?" National Bureau of Economic Research Working Paper 6030, Cambridge, Mass.: National Bureau of Economic Research.

9 Legislating against corruption in international markets

The story of the US Foreign Corrupt Practices Act

Wesley Cragg and William Woof

The passage of the Foreign Corrupt Practices Act (FCPA) by the US government in 1977 was a watershed event in the fight against corruption in the post-war era. Its criminalization of bribery on the part of US citizens and corporations conducting business overseas, and its provisions for mandatory self-regulation through internal control mechanisms, maintenance of transaction records, and other accounting practices made it unique: between the passage of the Act in 1977 and the adoption of the OECD anti-corruption convention in 1997 no other nation initiated similar legislation.[1] Recent studies, however, raise significant questions about the efficacy of this American initiative. Concerns have taken a number of forms. In 1999, Transparency International released the results of a survey ranking nineteen leading exporting countries by the degree to which their companies were perceived to be paying bribes abroad.[2] The United States ranked ninth of nineteen countries in the resulting "Bribe Payers Index." Accompanying the United States in ninth position was Germany, a country where, until very recently, bribes paid to foreign public officials were both legally acceptable and deductible as legitimate expenses for taxation purposes. A number of other studies have looked critically at the structure of the Act itself, its enforcement provisions, its reliance on self-regulation and efforts undertaken by American multinational companies to ensure compliance with its provisions.

This chapter examines questions and concerns raised by these studies. We trace the forces that led to the Senate investigations that in turn resulted in the passage of the FCPA in 1977. We examine the structure of the FCPA, its connection to legislation enacted in the 1930s designed to build transparency into the trading of securities on American stock exchanges, and exemptions related to the protection of the national security interests of the United States. Our analysis of the effectiveness of the legislation will focus on the role given to self-regulation, the response of American corporations to that role, and the history of enforcement between 1977 and 1995. We conclude that the Act has not had a significant positive impact on actual standards of international business conduct of American corporations collectively, at least with respect to the bribery of foreign public officials. We trace the reasons for this to the impact of US foreign policy on the enforcement of the FCPA, the impact of globalization on the willingness and the capacity of American corporations to meet their obligations (and their interpretation of those obligations), and finally the intersection of foreign policy concerns and competitive pressures and their implications for compliance and enforcement.

Our conclusions are important for two reasons. First is the growing consensus worldwide that corruption has been exacerbated by the phenomenon of globalization, while seriously damaging the capacity of developing countries to realize the economic and social benefits on which justifications of globalization have been built. Second, in 1997, the industrialized world was finally persuaded to follow the lead of the United States and endorse an OECD convention modeled on the FCPA criminalization of the bribery of foreign public officials. With the entry into force of this convention in February 1999, a new chapter has been added to the fight against corruption in international business transactions. How effective the convention will be in controlling the supply side of corruption will depend in part, we surmise, on what can be learned from the American experience with the enforcement of the FCPA.

Historical overview of the FCPA

The post-Second World War era witnessed the extraordinary growth of American power and influence. Apart from obvious examples such as the Peace Corps and the Marshall plan, important new global institutions such as the United Nations and the World Bank were created and functioned with strong US support and sponsorship. To a large degree, this was made possible by the sheer economic power that US corporations were able to exert worldwide within the structure of the international financial framework established by the Bretton Woods Agreement of 1944. The US dollar, the value of which was fixed to the price of gold, became the world's base currency against which all other national currencies were measured. The international stature of the dollar was backed up by US worldwide industrial dominance, which was reflected in the fact that the US accounted for 40 percent of the world's industrial output and 20 percent of its exports. The subsequent worldwide demand for dollars as the means for financing world trade gave the American government and American multinational corporations the power to establish international standards of business conduct.

Reports that the International Telephone and Telegraph Corporation (ITT) had offered the US Central Intelligence Agency (CIA) $1 million in 1970 to block the election of Marxist presidential candidate Salvador Allende in Chile were the first clear indication that something was seriously amiss. The CIA declined the offer. However, in 1972 when the story became public knowledge, the Senate Committee on Foreign Relations formed the Subcommittee on Multinational Corporations headed by Senator Frank Church with a mandate to investigate this issue. The Church Subcommittee concluded that ITT had not acted unlawfully. It did not leave the matter there, however. What was not to be condoned, it stated, was "that the highest officials of the ITT sought to engage the CIA in a plan covertly to manipulate the outcome of the Chilean presidential election. In doing so the company overstepped the line of acceptable corporate behavior" (US Congress, Senate, Committee on Foreign Relations 1973). The standard that had been breached was therefore an ethical, not a legal standard of international business conduct for American corporations.

Had the ITT incident been an isolated event, it would not have had the impact it did. Unfortunately, it was not. As allegations of corporate misconduct overseas emerged from the Watergate investigations, it became increasingly clear that the practice of questionable payments to foreign government officials by US firms was widespread. The Allende government demand of $1 million from multinational corporations as protection against expropriation was one example (*Wall Street Journal* 1977).[3] The contributions of Gulf Oil to the Korean government were another.[4]

As the ITT case came to its conclusion in mid-1973, the mandate of the Church Subcommittee was expanded to investigate the questionable activities of a variety of US multinationals that were coming to light as a result of the Watergate investigations.[5]

Subsequent investigations by the Church Subcommittee were able to establish the widespread nature of questionable payments, to date the practice from the early 1960s, and to show that the size of questionable payments had grown substantially through the late 1960s and early 1970s. For example, Lockheed Aircraft Corporation, which by February 1976 had felt itself compelled to pay out more than $200 million in questionable payments, had been able to resist a $100,000 kickback requested on the sale of four Jetstars to the government of Indonesia in 1965 (US Senate 1975: 356–9, 366–8). Gulf Oil's payments to the Democratic Republican Party of Korea increased from $1 million in 1966 to $3 million in 1970, followed by a further solicitation for $10 million (Jacoby *et al.* 1977: 107).

It was argued in Senate hearings that US companies had to pay bribes to compete with foreign multinationals that were out to win market share from their US competitors. The weakening of the US dollar relative to European currencies in the early 1970s greatly strengthened the hand of European firms seeking new third world operations. Since European corporations could deduct bribes as business expenses for tax purposes, an option not available to their American competitors, competitive pressures may well have encouraged them to escalate the level of bribery to win business away from US competitors.[6] This was not an insignificant problem, for, by the mid-1970s, some US corporations were earning half their pre-tax profits from foreign operations. Maintaining market share was therefore a matter of strategic importance. There was therefore considerable pressure on companies competing in international markets to win acceptance for the view that, if American companies were to remain competitive, they had to accept prevailing "local" standards of business conduct however distasteful they might appear to an American public. These arguments were in the end rejected by US legislators. However, they did illustrate the pressures an increasingly competitive international business environment was creating for multinational companies.

Those for whom bribery was a rational response to international business competition faced two powerful counter arguments requiring a legislative response. First, was the commitment of the Securities and Exchange Commission (SEC) to the importance of maximizing the disclosure of relevant financial information for stockholders; the second was concern for the implications of corrupt practices by US corporations for American foreign policy.

The SEC commitment to ensuring financial transparency for the benefit of investors had, by the 1970s, a long legislative history dating from the dark days of the Depression in the 1930s. The Securities Act of 1933, the Securities Exchange Act of 1934, and other New Deal legislation were intended to maximize transparency of corporate conduct and to enhance the reporting of relevant information to both investors and securities enforcement agencies. The problem was that no provision had been made in any of this legislation for payments to foreign officials, much to the consternation of SEC officials called in to investigate potential violations of federal securities law during the Watergate crisis. The Watergate investigations exposed the efforts of Nixon's Committee to Re-elect the President to illegally solicit campaign contributions from corporations during the 1972 federal election. But the Watergate investigations also revealed corporate slush funds used not only to aid Nixon but also to make questionable payments to foreign parties. This practice turned out to be widespread: over 400 corporations eventually admitted to making irregular or questionable payments totaling more than $300 million.

The SEC recognized that the general acceptance accorded by the US business community to the practice of overseas bribery challenged long accepted principles of ethical securities trading in the United States.[7] On the other hand, the SEC was concerned with proposals that were not within its enforcement capacities.[8] Its response was to launch a Voluntary Disclosure Program in 1975 placing the onus on US corporations governed by federal securities law to identify and report material foreign payments of a questionable nature. Since existing law did not include foreign payments, it was left to each corporation to determine what payments it felt were "material," that is, significant enough to be reported to its stockholders. Monitoring, investigating, and reporting were to be conducted by audit committees comprised of directors who were not corporate executives and not linked to suspect transactions (SEC 1975: 6–13). By the mid-1970s, committees of this kind had been a common feature of American corporate governance for almost thirty years and had proven useful in eliciting voluntary corporate efforts to improve audit standards and accountability.

In addition to concerns about securities trading, the various investigations also raised concerns about the conduct of American foreign policy. It was inevitable, therefore, that as the various Senate hearings wound their way towards their conclusions, the question of effective remedies would come to the fore. The SEC pressed for provisions that would continue to put the onus on corporations to monitor themselves and therefore reduce its own enforcement role (*Wall Street Journal* 1976, May 19: 5; June 23: 2). The Church Subcommittee, for its part, drafted Bill S. 3379 requiring disclosure of all overseas payments made by US corporations, annual reports by the State Department to the House and Senate listing the nations in which these payments were made, the particulars of US foreign policy objectives in these states, and payment disclosures to the stockholders of the applicable corporations. The Ford Administration opted for a disclosure bill that would require the reporting of payments to the Department of Commerce with subsequent reporting (at the discretion of the State Department) to the foreign governments in question, which in turn could choose to initiate prosecution against offenders under its own laws.

The Ford administration proposals, with their emphasis on disclosure, were repudiated by Senator William Proxmire, the chairman of the Senate Committee on Banking, Housing, and Urban Affairs. Proxmire argued that Ford's "Foreign Payments Disclosure Act" would grant to multinational firms the US government's tacit approval of overseas bribery practices (*Los Angeles Times,* June 15 1976: 2). Proxmire then advanced his own legislation, Bill S. 3133, which advocated criminalizing bribery payments and amending the 1934 Securities Exchange Act to include bribery as a prohibited practice.[9] These amendments included a disclosure requirement for all payments over $1,000 to foreign officials. The SEC protested this requirement on the grounds that it would make the revised Act impossible to monitor. Proxmire then revised his bill into the form that would become the FCPA and agreed to drop his disclosure provision, favoring the SEC's proposal to make companies legally responsible for establishing accounting controls and detecting suspect transactions. The result was shared responsibility for enforcement since suspect payments by firms not covered by securities laws would now become the responsibility of the Department of Justice.

Proxmire was quite explicit in justifying his approach to anti-bribery legislation. Mere disclosure in his view was insufficient. What was required, he argued, was "a national policy against corporate bribery that transcended the narrower objective of adequately disclosing material information to investors" (US Senate 1976: 1–9). "[A] strong anti-bribery law" that criminalized the bribery of foreign public officials, he reasoned, "would help US multinational companies resist corrupt demands" (ibid.).

Proxmire's position irritated some business leaders, who felt that the proposal by the Ford administration for a multilateral agreement by UN member states, that is to say, an international anti-bribery treaty, was a preferable option. It was their view that a multilateral agreement or treaty would bolster the existing "Foreign Payments Disclosure Act," and provide legal uniformity to international markets while allowing multinationals to avoid the dilemma of risking US government prosecution in situations where they followed local practices with a view to gaining or retaining market share. Top US government officials, including Henry Kissinger and Elliot Richardson disagreed. They argued that the proposals for an international treaty were not practical and would never garner approval from all members of the international community.[10]

A code of conduct drafted by the OECD as well as a code developed by the United Nations Commission on Transnational Corporations containing anti-bribery provisions also met with resistance from multinationals, as corporate leaders believed that any uniform code of a general nature was unrealistic and would be too restrictive (UN ESCOR 1983).[11] Proxmire himself was also sceptical that a general OECD code would do much good,[12] arguing that bilateral treaties would be more likely to complement his criminalization proposals.[13] He concluded: "The Committee [on Banking, Housing, and Urban Affairs] firmly believes . . . that an American anti-bribery policy must not await the perfection of international agreements, however desirable such arrangements may be" (US Senate 1976: 1–9). The urgency lay not in the enforcement of US securities laws. Rather, Proxmire left no doubt that the crucial importance of the FCPA lay in the domain of US policy:

> Bribery of foreign officials by some US companies casts a shadow on all US companies . . . [and] creates severe foreign policy problems. The revelations of improper payments inevitably tend to embarrass friendly regimes and lower the esteem for the United States among the foreign public. It lends credence to the worst suspicions sown by extreme nationalists or Marxists that American businesses operating in their country have a corrupting influence on their political systems.
>
> (US Senate 1976: 1–9)

The link to US foreign policy objectives was therefore a central feature of the FCPA from its inception.

The Foreign Corrupt Practices Act became law in 1977 at the conclusion of deeply disturbing hearings whose effect was to challenge the moral authority of American political institutions and leadership. The Act prohibited payments made directly or through an intermediary with a view to influencing a foreign official in the performance (or non-performance) of authorized duties and functions in exchange for unwarranted benefits or considerations. Prohibited bribe recipients included foreign government officials and all foreign political parties and candidates (as well as all intermediaries for people in these positions). Officers of foreign businesses without political or governmental connections were excluded from these provisions. The Act's proscriptions against bribery were accompanied by accounting stipulations regarding transaction recording and internal control as well as disclosure requirements respecting changes in ownership of businesses subject to FCPA jurisdiction. These provisions were designed to prohibit corporate slush funds that had been discovered to be instrumental in disbursing irregular payments to agents, government officials, and political parties.

The original Act was focused on criminalizing payments to high-level foreign officials, rather than those who performed "clerical" or "ministerial" functions. Thus, so-called "grease" payments or facilitating payments were not excluded as such, but excluded by means of association with the position descriptions of low level officials whose job responsibilities would center on routine duties.[14] This focus on the stature of the foreign officials in question allowed the Act to facilitate prosecution based on "reason to know" standards, under which corporate officers could be deemed to have a reason to know that payments were being made for the purposes of bribery.

Finally, the original Act was divided between corrupt practices by companies registered as issuers of securities and those "domestic concerns" that did not issue securities. This division facilitated a division of responsibility with respect to the enforcement of the Act. The SEC would be responsible for civil enforcement of accounting standards with respect to issuers of securities while the Justice Department would be concerned with criminal violations of the Act.

The Act was subsequently amended in 1988 as part of the Reagan administration's Omnibus Trade Act. New "corporate friendly" provisions in this Act made prosecutions more difficult by stipulating that officers of firms offering bribes must be proved to have direct knowledge that payments were being used for illicit purposes (as opposed to the old "reason to know" standard) and by accommodating payments lawful in host countries or made contractually to agents in reasonable exchange for legitimate promotional services. Facilitating payments were also explicitly defined and were excluded regardless of the stature, position, or role of the foreign official making them. Although these changes restricted the scope of the FCPA, the actual number of potential FCPA cases investigated increased after passage of the Omnibus Trade Act, in part because the amendments defined more clearly the legal obligations of corporations.[15] Changes in the foreign policy priorities of the Bush administration also had an impact in this regard, a subject we discuss in some detail later in the section entitled "The political economy of FCPA enforcement."

Designed to maximize the disclosure of relevant information to stockholders in US corporations and to establish an elevated standard of business practice for US firms overseas, the 1977 Act was grounded in the belief that the twin disasters of the Vietnam War and Watergate had cost America the moral authority that went with its role as the leader of the free world. The tone of moral outrage and the urgency of moral reform would constitute a major theme of the Carter administration.

The SEC, self-regulation, and the FCPA

Time and again in pre-FCPA hearings, the SEC made it clear that its chief motivation in placing the burden of enforcement on the self-regulatory activities of corporations themselves rested on the fact that it lacked the resources to effectively enforce anti-bribery requirements of the amendments to securities laws that had been incorporated into the FCPA. The agency was only too happy to enthusiastically promote corporate principles of "new governance" requiring high standards of accountability grounded on the work of independent audit committees. These would oversee stricter policies using enhanced systems of internal control for monitoring international business conduct. Hence, the SEC was not reluctant to support amendments to securities laws requiring higher standards of self-regulation that depended upon effective systems of internal control.

Corporations, on the other hand, had little reason to share the SEC's enthusiasm for "the new governance." Given unremitting pressure for improved profitability, US multinationals could not afford to treat their overseas operations as a minor theatre of operations where experiments in morality could be conducted. Because of tax and cost differentials, there was too much profit to be made from foreign operations at a time when domestic profits at home were under siege. American corporations were generally opposed to the FCPA because of the belief that it would result in the loss of business to less scrupulous foreign competitors.[16] The FCPA legislation would also complicate established provisions in securities law with respect to suspect transactions. Although the use of agents to transact business with foreign governments was not prohibited, the FCPA also held corporations using agents responsible for ensuring that these agents respected the anti-corruption provisions of the US legislation. This burden was made explicit by the "reason to know" provisions of the 1977 Act, the purposes of which were to

> create a standard of negligence that imposes a duty on corporate management to inquire about possible improper or illegal payments. It is thus hoped that the anti-bribery provisions would produce accountability, and that to avoid criminal accountability, self-enforcing preventative mechanisms would be introduced at the corporate level.
>
> (Shaw 1988: 792)

The "reason to know" provisions were thus integral to Senator Proxmire's original vision of the purpose of the FCPA. The goal was to block the use of "plausible deniability" as a defense for questionable transactions that slipped past "reasonable" internal control mechanisms required by the Act.

The FCPA's unilateral "supply side" approach to controlling corruption placed a considerable legal and moral burden on US multinational corporations as an analysis of early SEC investigations and legal actions reveals.[17] Members of the business community criticized this burden as unfair since it placed anti-bribery restrictions on American companies in increasingly competitive international markets under conditions of corruption over which many believed they had no control.[18] It is not surprising, therefore, that many in the US business community supported the efforts of the Reagan administration throughout the 1980s to soften the application of the FCPA by eliminating the "reason to know" provisions of the Act.

It is clear that the FCPA posed both competitive and control challenges for US corporations competing in international markets. The nature of those challenges is revealed by enforcement measures undertaken by the SEC. SEC v Katy Industries, Inc., which was brought within six months of the passage of FCPA, established "reason to know" as an important principle and set the stage for later significant SEC cases, the most important of which was SEC v Ashland Oil, Inc., in 1986.[19]

Ashland Oil first came to the attention of the SEC as a result of investigations conducted by the Office of the Special Prosecutor in connection with the Watergate hearings (SEC 1975: 160–6). From the early 1960s to detection in 1973, Ashland was found to have made extensive political contributions (estimated at $300,000) to the ruling party of the African nation of Gabon, a former French colony with a long history of corrupt activity (Kugel and Gruenberg 1977).[20] These payments were made primarily to gain access to authorities for the purpose of gaining normal permits for business operation. Company officers were aware that the payments were illegal. However, they believed that the relevant laws would not be enforced because such payments were an accepted business practice.

The SEC cited Ashland for breakdowns in internal control procedures and accounting practices, which were attributed largely to rapid corporate growth and expansion of operations overseas. The commission recognized that demand determinants constituted a key factor in the initiation of payments acknowledging that "political contributions . . . in some instances were made in response to real or apparent pressure from public officials or their close political associates" (SEC 1975: 160–6). The SEC found, nonetheless, that the specific actions of company officers were serious enough to warrant dismissal, even while acknowledging that violations of federal prohibitions against political contributions had become a common corporate practice. The commission recommended against dismissal, however, on the condition that the officers in question provided an appropriate settlement with the corporation to compensate shareholders for these unwarranted expenditures. This outcome reflected the fact that the SEC was in the end satisfied with the effectiveness of the internal control procedures that were implemented by Ashland to prevent any recurrence of such payments. To use their words: "We believe that the policies, operating procedures and structural changes recommended in this Report provide such safeguards and that the monetary settlement recommended herein provides a reasonable recovery for the Corporation" (ibid.). Subsequent events belied this confidence, for, five years later, the Company found itself again the subject of an SEC investigation.

This second investigation determined that in 1980, Ashland purchased a majority interest in Midlands Chrome, a mining firm operating in Zimbabwe (a purchase made shortly after that nation's independence) that proved to be unprofitable. The purchase price of $29 million was made to an organization controlled by an official of the government of Oman. In December 1982, Ashland contracted with the government of Oman for the delivery of 20,000 barrels of crude oil per day at a discount of $3 per barrel below the spot market price. This concession in itself would have generated some $40 million in profits for Ashland. The company claimed that the contract was granted in exchange for "technical services rendered" to the Omani government, but the company's CEO had allegedly told his board of directors in 1980 that the Midlands Chrome acquisition "had the potential for being more than offset by a potential crude oil contract" (Shaw 1988: 789–90).[21]

The SEC investigation concluded that Ashland was guilty of improper accounting and defective internal control mechanisms that failed to detect the illegitimacy of what the company purported to be *bona fide* transactions under the terms of the Omani contract. It would seem that over the five years intervening between the two investigations, little had changed.

A second case, SEC v Montedison, which was filed as a civil injunctive action in November 1996, offers additional insights into enforcement of the accounting provisions of the FCPA.[22] Montedison, an Italian company with listings on the New York Stock Exchange and 6 percent ownership by US investors, was charged with failure "to devise and maintain a system of internal control" and with materially misstating its financial condition for the fiscal years 1988–91 (Aronoff 1998). The company had attempted to conceal payments of $398 million, much of which, according to the SEC, was intended for bribes to Italian politicians. It was alleged that Montedison's financial statements and records materially overstated the company's assets with the consequence of misleading investors. Although in violation of the FCPA, the company's conduct was consistent with current business practices of other Italian firms involving misstatement of assets for tax purposes and covert payments to Italian politicians.

Montedison was charged under the accounting provisions of the FCPA and not under the anti-bribery provisions, since Italian officers of an Italian company were bribing Italian politicians. However, since the American Depository Receipts (ADRs, namely that portion of Montedison stock registered for sale to US investors under the provisions of the 1934 Securities Exchange Act), resulted in 6 percent ownership of the company by US investors, the SEC could claim that the concealment of bribes in Italy resulted in a misstatement of its financial condition, thus misleading US investors. Under accounting provisions of the FCPA, Montedison had a legal obligation to maintain internal controls required to identify any material irregular transactions ($398 million) and report them to the SEC.

Two other cases investigated by the SEC involved outright falsification of financial records. SEC v Triton Energy Corp. *et al.* revolved around the payment of $450,000 in bribes to independent agents in order to influence Indonesian officials on the company's behalf using false invoices for non-existent services (Zedlin *et al.* 1997: 7).[23] In another case, American Eurocopter was discovered to have paid $10 million to an Israeli agent through the outright falsification of company records. Payments involving the improper transfers of funds through corporate affiliates had been concealed by the destruction of records.

This review of the application by the SEC of the accounting provisions of the FCPA raises two questions. First, did the accounting provisions of the FCPA effectively deter companies falling under its provisions from engaging in corrupt business practices in their international operations? Second, did the self-regulation requirements of the accounting provisions lead companies falling under its provisions to establish effective approaches to self-regulation?

Because of the nature of corruption, evidence relevant to answering the first question must by necessity be indirect. The only clear evidence pointing to the effectiveness of the FCPA in discouraging the use of bribery by US corporations in international business transactions, is the Transparency International Bribe Payers Index. That study, reported in 1999, suggests that from the perspective of those surveyed, the reputation of US companies falling under the Act was not significantly different from companies not facing similar legal restraints.[24]

Nothing arising from this review of the accounting provisions of the FCPA would suggest that the results of the Transparency International survey are inaccurate or misleading. Confidence that accounting provisions could be an effective mechanism of enforcement was based on the experience of the SEC with the self-regulatory provisions of securities laws dating to the 1930s. The effect of the FCPA, however, was to change radically the context in which the law would apply. First, the FCPA put the burden of compliance squarely on the shoulders of the companies falling under its authority while giving those companies wide latitude in establishing the accounting provisions required in their own particular case. Second, unlike other securities laws, the FCPA required that American companies regulate their conduct in settings where foreign competitors were not similarly constrained. US corporations were virtually unanimous in their opposition to the unilateral character of the legislation.[25] The setting was, as a result, not particularly conducive to effective self-regulation.

The pattern of enforcement of the accounting provisions that emerged did little to counteract initial lack of enthusiasm for the law on the part of the business community. Between 1977, when the FCPA was enacted, and 1995, only seven charges were laid under the accounting provisions and only three cases were brought under the revisions to Section 30A of the revised Securities Exchange Act (made part of the FCPA) which prohibited payments to foreign officials by issuers of securities (under "reason to know" provisions). It seems implausible to suggest that the circumstances under which the companies that were charged operated were unique or that the companies in question were significantly different from other US companies similarly engaged in international markets. Neither is there any indication that the FCPA deterred US companies from doing business in notoriously corrupt countries.

In short, there is nothing about the history of the enforcement of the accounting provisions of the FCPA that would suggest that they constituted a significant general deterrent to corrupt business practices on the part of US companies engaged in international markets.[26]

Did the self-regulation requirements of the accounting provisions lead companies falling under its provisions to establish effective approaches to self-regulation? A 1981 survey by the US General Accounting Office of 250 companies selected randomly out of *Fortune* magazine's top

1,000 companies indicated that 60 percent of them had made explicit changes in their codes of conduct because of the FCPA, while 75 percent had updated their internal accounting controls (Geo-JaJa and Mangum 1999: 6).[27] But a 1995 study by Wayne State University in Detroit, Michigan, raises doubts as to the effectiveness of these enhancements (Spalding and Reinstein 1995: 23–35). From a survey of 109 randomly selected companies listed on the New York Stock Exchange, it was found that while 93 percent of firms had a code of conduct, only 36 percent had anti-bribery provisions in their code and less than 9 percent had internal control or monitoring procedures designed to ensure that the code was adhered to (ibid.). In stressing the need for corporate boards to ensure FCPA compliance through audit committees, the authors note: "While management is responsible for establishing internal controls, most violations of the FCPA occur when management overrides these controls" (ibid.). The authors of the Wayne State study concluded that it is not sufficient to merely establish such controls as part of operating procedures. Rather, "audit committees (established in each corporation and including outside directors as members) should obtain management's written assurances that they have met the FCPA's requirements" (ibid.). Clearly, the accounting provisions of the FCPA were not successful in persuading American companies to adopt these kinds of operating provisions.

Our story, however, is as yet incomplete. The FCPA had very significant political dimensions and these must now be considered in order to fully assess its effectiveness as a tool of law enforcement, as well as a means of corporate self-regulation.

The political economy of FCPA enforcement

As we have seen, available evidence provides little reason to believe that the FCPA led American companies collectively to adopt standards of conduct with respect to the bribery of foreign public officials that were significantly different from their international competitors. We have also seen that there is little about the history of the enforcement of the accounting provisions by the SEC that would cast doubt on this conclusion. Is there any reason to believe that the enforcement efforts of Justice Department officers were more vigorous or effective than their SEC counterparts? And if not, why was enforcement so ineffective?

There is little evidence to suggest that the pattern of enforcement by the Department of Justice deviated significantly from that of the SEC. Only sixteen prosecutions for bribery were initiated between 1977 and 1995. It would appear that significant efforts at enforcement did occur in the two years immediately following enactment. Following the inauguration of President Reagan, enforcement patterns changed. Enforcement of the FCPA was relaxed, funding for the two principal enforcement agencies was considerably reduced, and efforts by the Reagan administration to alter the "reason to know" provisions of the Act were initiated.[28] How are these events to be explained and what was their impact on the effectiveness of the FCPA and on the standards of conduct of American companies in the international business arena?

It is clear from the hearings of the Church Subcommittee and the Watergate investigations that it was widely assumed by the American public and their leaders, that the international business activities of American corporations would conform to high standards of conduct, while aligning with the national interests of the United States and the expression of those interests in American foreign policy. Comments of the Under-Secretary of State, Robert S. Ingersoll and Senator Proxmire illustrate the central role of this view, although from opposing political perspectives. In the course of expressing in Senate hearings deep concern that Congressional testimony would damage America's international image, Ingersoll commented:

> I wish to state for the record that grievous damage has been done to the foreign relations of the United States by recent disclosures of unsubstantiated allegations against foreign officials. . . . It is a fact that public discussion in this country of the alleged misdeeds of officials of foreign governments cannot fail to damage our relations with these governments.[29]

Proxmire similarly was explicit about foreign policy considerations in justifying the need for legislation that would impose anti-bribery obligations on American corporations as indicated by his observation that:

> Bribery is simply unethical. It is counter to the moral expectations and values of the American public, and it erodes public confidence in the integrity of the free market system. Bribery of foreign officials by some US companies casts a shadow on all US companies. It puts pressure on ethical enterprises to lower their standards and match corrupt payments, or risk losing business. . . . Bribery by US companies also undermines the foreign policy objectives of the United States to promote democratically accountable governments and professionalized civil services in developing countries.
>
> (US Senate 1976: 1–9)

It is not surprising, therefore, to discover foreign policy considerations also played a significant role in the FCPA's subsequent enforcement.

The Watergate revelations had led to increasing surveillance of American multinationals by the SEC and to the subsequent establishment of the Foreign Corrupt Practices Act. But it also led to the desire, both in

Congress and more widely among the American public, to re-establish America's moral authority both at home and abroad. The resignation of Richard Nixon under the shadow of impeachment and the election of Jimmy Carter reflected this mood. The Carter administration issued a "moral equivalent of war" against corruption and on behalf of human rights around the world. US firms were pressured to follow strict environmental and safety standards with respect to products and equipment shipped to developing nations, while Carter cut off aid and curtailed trade with nations with poor human rights records such as Guatemala, Nicaragua, Honduras, and the Philippines.

But Carter's administration also became associated with the questionable management of the US dollar, which fell victim to a severe currency crisis during late October 1978.[30] The crisis was averted and the dollar's recovery was engineered under the stewardship of Paul Volcker as head of the US Federal Reserve. Jimmy Carter was subsequently defeated by Ronald Reagan in the presidential elections of 1980, which were again dominated by a debate about regaining international respect and reasserting American leadership internationally. Under Ronald Reagan, however, American foreign policy shifted to a focus on financial and military concerns governed by an intense preoccupation with defeating Communism and winning the Cold War based on a strategy of *realpolitik*.

Privileging *realpolitik* over human rights and other ethical concerns meant that the Reagan administration was prepared to overlook the failure of its foreign allies to maintain a strict division between private and public interests (a *sine qua non* in the war against corruption), just as the Nixon administration had failed to maintain a clear distinction between its political interests and its responsibilities for public administration during the Watergate debacle.

The extent to which Reagan's subordinates were prepared to push their *realpolitik* agenda was amply demonstrated by the Iran-Contra affair. Frustrated by the provisions of the Boland Amendment, by which the US Congress officially prohibited funding of the Contra insurgents in Nicaragua, the Reagan administration circumvented constitutional prohibitions against appropriations of government funds by the Executive branch without Congressional approval. Under a covert scheme directed by members of the National Security Council, the US sold weapons to Iran (which was officially considered to be a pariah nation at the time) and secretly diverted the sales of these weapons to the Contras.[31] The transactions involved payoffs to Saudi and Iranian arms dealers, who in turn procured financing for the deals through bribes paid to a branch manager of the Bank of Credit and Commerce International.[32] Two major principals in the affair, Richard Secord and Albert Hakim were alleged to have used over $2 million out of the inflated commissions paid for the arms sales for their personal benefit

(US Senate 1992: 105). Lt. Col. Oliver North, who headed the operation, was able to destroy much of the documentation pertaining to the
case (records that it was alleged might have directly implicated President
Reagan in the scandal) once it was clear that the operation was losing
its cover. Despite legal requirements that accountability in government
operations was to be maintained through provisions that all covert operations conducted by US intelligence agencies must be directly authorized
by the President and funded by Congressional appropriations, North's
operation proceeded without Presidential or Congressional authorization
and without disclosure to the appropriate Congressional committees as
stipulated in Section 501 of the National Security Act. North and his
operatives then sought to obstruct Congressional investigations and
made false and misleading statements to Congressional committees. As
the Congressional report on the matter notes: "These were not covert
actions, these were covert policies; and covert policies are incompatible
with democracy" (ibid.: 107).

The relevance of the Iran-Contra Affair for our study lies in the fact
that government agents violated many of the principles of the Foreign
Corrupt Practices Act by conducting overseas business transactions facilitated by bribery and then falsifying the accounting transactions and
destroying records to prevent appropriate disclosure.

It is hard to believe that a political environment that harbored policies
and activities of this nature had no impact on the enthusiasm with which
the FCPA was enforced and adherence to its underlying principles encouraged. It is therefore not surprising that, under the Reagan administration,
very few prosecutors in the Department of Justice fraud section were
authorized to conduct FCPA cases (Geo-JaJa and Mangum 1999: 3).[33]
Cutbacks in funding to the principal enforcement agencies (the SEC
and the Department of Justice) no doubt also served to strengthen
prevailing attitudes.

Is there evidence that foreign policy considerations intersected with
the few FCPA cases that were prosecuted under Reagan's tenure? While
the evidence is inevitably circumstantial, one cluster of cases in which
prosecution did occur, and two cases in which it did not, suggest a
pattern that is hard to ignore.

The interlocking cases of Ruston Gas Turbine and Crawford
Industries, involving company efforts to bribe officials of Pemex,
Mexico's national oil monopoly, with respect to the sale of compression
equipment systems, were brought to trial almost immediately after the
American government concluded a massive bilateral agreement in
August 1982 with the Mexican government.[34] Is there a connection
between these temporally parallel sequences of events?

On July 14 1981, a Federal Grand Jury subpoenaed transaction
records between Ruston and Pemex. On September 22 1982, one month
after the Mexican agreement, Ruston pleaded guilty to one count of

violating the FCPA and agreed to pay a $750,000 fine. Two weeks later, on October 2 1982, the Grand Jury indicted Crawford Industries, International Harvester, Ruston's president, and seven others on FCPA violations, all of whom (except for International Harvester, which was guilty only of conspiracy charges with respect to the activities of its division, Solar Turbines International) would later be found guilty. Crawford, Ruston, and International Harvester were also charged with conspiracy to violate the FCPA, to which charge International Harvester would later plead guilty.[35]

On December 15 1982, after Ruston requested the return of documents subpoenaed by the Grand Jury, it was disclosed that the US government had released the contents of these documents to the Mexican government without Ruston's permission. These documents then provided the foundation for a civil action launched on October 23 1983 by Pemex against Ruston and eighteen other defendants with claims to damages totaling more than $45 million. The documents related to charges raised in the US District Court Texas that included the violation of anti-trust laws, conspiracy to commit fraud and bribery and violations of the Racketeering and Corrupt Organizations Act.

Ruston responded by claiming that the US government had violated federal rules of criminal procedure. The District Court denied Ruston's motion for discovery and Ruston appealed. The US government then distanced itself from the case and avoided formally addressing Ruston's complaint that rules of criminal procedure had been violated by the government.[36] The Appellate Court took note of the curious fact that the US government "had not taken a position with respect to the District Court order" dismissing Ruston's motion. Neither could the Appellate Court understand the grounds taken by the District Court in not ruling on Ruston's behalf, given that all the precedents relevant to the issue were favorable to Ruston. Because of vagueness with respect to the full presentation of evidence by the District Court, however, the Appellate Court did not grant Ruston's motion for discovery but remanded it back to the District Court requesting that it supply reasons for not ruling on Ruston's behalf. Most significantly, the Appellate Court noted that the US government had released this privileged documentation to Pemex "pursuant to both an order of the District Court and *an agreement between the government and the Federal Republic of Mexico*" (our emphasis), thereby flagging the conjunction of a major foreign policy initiative with a complex legal action linked to an FCPA prosecution.[37]

The foreign policy initiative was a response to the 1982 Mexican debt crisis. A sharp decline in export earnings, a rapid increase of flight capital, and a 40 percent rise in external debt in 1981 had forced the Mexican government to double the price of certain food staples and to accept an IMF-dictated peso devaluation of 40 percent. The US government, deeply concerned about the possibility of domestic discontent in

Mexico and the specter of a massive increase of illegal aliens into the southern US states, organized an agreement that was an exemplar for President Ronald Reagan's new policy of bilateral relations. To end Mexico's currency crisis, the Americans advanced $3 billion in new credit: $1 billion as an advance on future oil purchases from Mexico (at a price discounted well below OPEC benchmarks), $1 billion to finance desperately needed imports, and a further $1 billion in loan agreements from the Federal Reserve that would help Mexico service its foreign debts. Statements by US Assistant Secretary of State for Inter-American Affairs Thomas Enders in August 1982 clearly indicated that Mexico would now be expected to follow US foreign policy more closely. (Mexico had been providing Nicaragua's Sandinista government with oil on credit (Naylor 1987: 63–4).)

Is this an instance where the foreign policy interests and enforcement of the FCPA did in fact intersect? The evidence is circumstantial. It is, nonetheless, persuasive. The fact that the agreement between the American and Mexican governments was cited by a court in legal proceedings directly related to an FCPA prosecution highlights this inter-section. There is little doubt that the transaction records between Pemex and Ruston released to the Mexican government played a role in subsequent civil proceedings involving a financially significant claim for damages against Ruston and the other defendants involved. Ironically, the action was brought by a government that was itself thought to be seriously corrupt. Not surprisingly, therefore, the role of corruption in the peso crisis was publicly debated. Taking American companies to court on grounds of corruption would have the potential for shifting blame for corrupt business practices from the Mexican government to foreign multinational corporations, prepared to corrupt Mexican officials in the pursuit of business opportunities. It is true that any shifting of blame would point back to American corporations. But it is also possible that the shapers of government policy were becoming aware of the potentially destabilizing impact of corruption on development and political stability in Mexico.[38] If that is so, then prosecuting American corporations under the FCPA, and releasing information with damaging implications for their financial liabilities would also have a place in a policy framework designed to stabilize a government and economic system seriously threatened by a financial crisis. The intervention in the peso crisis was a clear indication of the importance attached to relations with Mexico by the American government. A strong signal to the American business community with respect to activities likely to exacerbate Mexican problems would clearly not be out of place in that environment.

Another factor influencing enforcement of the FCPA was the explicit exemption from prosecution provided for firms collaborating with agencies such as the CIA (Central Intelligence Agency) or the DEA (Drug

Enforcement Agency) on matters affecting the interests of the United States. The Act reads:

> With respect to matters concerning the national security of the United States, no duty or liability ... shall be imposed upon any person acting in cooperation with the head of any Federal department or agency responsible for such matters.
>
> (Foreign Corrupt Practices Act 1977: Sect. 102 (3) A)

Inserting this provision was not inconsistent with past practice. At the time the FCPA was enacted, US multinational corporations had had a long history of involvement with the CIA, by providing their facilities for international transfers of funds to finance CIA operations, for example (Naylor 1987: 312–13). The history of activities on the part of the American multinational oil company, Exxon, in Italy is a good illustration of the evidence of this involvement. Investigations of questionable payments by Exxon's Italian subsidiary, Esso Italiana, conducted by Exxon as part of the SEC disclosure program, led to the admission by senior executives of the US parent company that $27 million in secret contributions had been advanced to Italian political parties between 1964 and 1971. Further investigations revealed the previously unknown fact that an additional $29 to $31 million in secret payments had been advanced by a former managing director of Esso Italiana using secret bank accounts and other off-book record keeping. (Exxon was then cited by the SEC for deceptive accounting practices and inadequate internal controls.) It is likely that the bulk of these secret payments went directly or indirectly to the Italian Christian Democratic Party to counter the strong influence of the Italian Communist Party, a battle that had received constant and concerted assistance from the CIA since the end of the Second World War.[39]

Neil Jacoby concludes that the fact that Exxon's senior management approved of the use of deceptive accounting practices (deceptive in American practice) in order to make campaign contributions in Italy, opened the door for abuses in accounting practices in Italy to occur. That is to say, the managing director of Esso Italiana was able to advance additional funds clandestinely following precedents established when the company had violated its internal control procedures to allow the original payments.[40]

Whether CIA involvement with American multinational corporations continued after the passage of the FCPA in 1977, and when and how often the "national security" exemption clause was clandestinely invoked to protect US multinational firms from FCPA prosecution, can only be a matter of conjecture. However, there are cases where prosecution did not take place for which the national security exemption clause is a plausible explanation. One example involves Lockheed

Corporation, which was implicated in alleged payments of $1.1 million made to Prince Bernhard of the Netherlands from 1960 to 1962. In the early 1970s prior to FCPA passage, Lockheed, who had employed Yoshio Kodama as an agent for procuring business in Japan at the same time that Kodama was a CIA agent (1958–72), was also implicated in bribery scandals with the Japanese government (Seagrave 1988: 363, 374–5; Jacoby *et al.* 1977: 162–4). There were no FCPA prosecutions against Lockheed during Reagan's tenure. However, in June 1994, almost as soon as FCPA enforcement activity was revived by the Clinton administration, new charges were leveled against Lockheed Martin with regard to $600,000 in bribes paid to an Egyptian parliamentarian over the sale of C-130 aircraft to that country (Rossbacher and Young 1996: 13).

A second, more significant potential example of a missed FCPA prosecution can be found in the case of Westinghouse Corporation and its construction of a nuclear reactor facility in the Philippines. The story provides a cautionary tale as to how US bilateral and multilateral relations with deep historical roots with a developing nation could, and apparently did, profoundly impact the norms of business conduct for multinationals operating there.

A US colony since 1898, the Philippines was granted independence in 1946 after being occupied by the Japanese during the Second World War. The Americans, who strongly valued the military importance of the Philippines, had, during their administration of the islands, supported a highly autocratic government and, by implication, a regimented class-based land tenancy social system. They were thus deeply concerned with the possibility that the government they supported might be overthrown following independence. The significance of US government concerns are conveyed in a 1950 National Security Council memorandum addressed to President Truman, which read:

> Failure of the Philippines to maintain independence would discredit the US in the eyes of the world and seriously decrease US influence, particularly in Asia. . . . Denial of the Philippines to communist control depends not only upon military measures but even more upon prompt, vigorous political and economic action. . . . The deterioration of the economic system has caused widespread feelings of disillusionment.
>
> (Seagrave 1988: 140)

Truman's government responded with the establishment of a strong CIA presence in the Philippines, to the point where the islands eventually provided the agency with its largest telecommunications base in the Far East.[41] The strategic importance of the country was heightened during the Vietnam War with the result that a corrupt Marcos regime received strong bilateral support from both the Johnson and Nixon administrations. After the declaration of martial law in 1972, bilateral aid declined. World Bank support continued, however, throughout the 1970s in spite of allegations of growing corruption. This support gave the Philippines credibility with US multinational banks and lending agencies, which in their turn ended up financing the most ambitious industrial project attempted by the Marcos regime.

In return for its support, the World Bank demanded export-oriented growth, which in turn required the development of a reliable supply of electric power. Both General Electric and Westinghouse Corporation, the two key players in the US nuclear industry, stepped forward with proposals for two 600-megawatt nuclear power plants. Both firms had broad experience in building nuclear facilities in Europe and Asia. General Electric, the more prosperous of the two firms, had developed a code of conduct that addressed FCPA requirements in an exemplary manner.[42] Subsequent events suggest that Westinghouse, a company struggling at the time to improve its overall revenues and profits, was not averse to using questionable payments in winning the support of the Marcos government.[43]

After nine months of researching the Philippine situation, General Electric submitted its proposals to the country's National Power Corporation. However, the decision then came from Marcos that the contract was to be awarded to Westinghouse without competitive bidding, even though subsequent analysis of the two offers led National Power (a Philippine government agency) to the conclusion that General Electric's proposals were superior on all counts (Seagrave 1988: 290). Of concern was the decision of Westinghouse to retain the services of a Marcos insider, Herminio Disini, as an agent for a "commission" of $17 million.[44]

Once again, the United States government worried about the impact of Philippine affairs on its own national image. The US Ambassador to the Philippines, William Sullivan, warned Secretary of State Henry Kissinger:

> I stressed that the embassy considered that a great deal of American prestige was riding on the Westinghouse performance, and that therefore we intended to follow the project closely. I pointed out that this was in effect the Filipino Aswan Dam, being the largest and most expensive construction project ever undertaken in this country.
> (Seagrave 1988: 290)

When the contract was signed in March 1976 the cost of construction had spiraled to $1.1 billion (Beaver 1994: 272–3). The US Export–Import Bank, which had already financed the construction of nuclear power facilities overseas on numerous occasions, stepped in with $272 million in direct loans and $367 million in guarantees on

National Power Corporation bonds. (The bank would ultimately provide $900 million in loans to the project (Boyce 1993: 321).) The US embassy proved true to its word and sent warnings to Washington that the cost overruns were inflated and that there was evidence of payoffs (ibid.: 343, fn. 30).

Irregularities began to surface publicly when Marcos selected the Bataan peninsula, site of an industrial zone largely controlled by his associates, as the location for the plant, despite warnings that the area was located near major geological fault lines and a dormant volcano. Westinghouse began construction on the site before technical reports on potential risks were finished. The International Atomic Energy Commission advised a moratorium on construction in 1978 pending a further safety study, but both Marcos and Westinghouse pressed the Philippine Atomic Energy Commission to authorize continuing construction (Seagrave 1988: 292). After the Three Mile Island episode in the US in 1979, Marcos himself ordered a halt to the project (June 1979) and a new review concluded that the project was unsafe. Once Westinghouse agreed to needed changes in line with those put into effect in the US by the Nuclear Regulatory Commission after Three Mile Island, project costs soared to $1.8 billion. The US Commission refused to issue Westinghouse an export license for nuclear components until May 1980 due to safety concerns at the plant. The license was finally issued after Westinghouse launched a lawsuit against the Commission (Beaver 1994: 275).

Events surrounding the Philippine project were of concern for the Carter administration because of newspaper reports in early 1978 linking the Westinghouse contract with the cronyism and corruption of the Marcos regime, whose human rights violations had already been the subject of Congressional investigations (ibid.: 274). Since the reports were published so shortly after the passage of the FCPA, it seemed that the effectiveness of the law would shortly be put to the test. However, a joint investigation by the SEC and the Justice Department concluded that there was no evidence of irregularities in Westinghouse's relationship with the Philippine government, even though the SEC reported that a Westinghouse district manager in the Philippines had destroyed six volumes of documents pertaining to the project.[45]

The appropriateness of the commission payments made by Westinghouse throughout the life of the contract has been the subject of on-going speculation. In reports filed in 1976 with the Securities and Exchange Commission under its disclosure program, Westinghouse claimed that during the fiscal years 1971 to 1975 it expended only $243,000 in questionable payments set against total 1974 revenues of $5.838 billion and gross five year revenues (1971–5) of $25.729 billion. Yet in 1978, Westinghouse reached a plea agreement with the Department of Justice with respect to misrepresentations of payments to foreign officials regarding "matters within the jurisdiction of the Export–Import Bank," and it is difficult not to speculate that this plea agreement directly pertained to the Philippine nuclear plant.[46] It took almost a decade for Westinghouse to disclose the $17 million payment to retain the services of Herminio Disini. Westinghouse has claimed that the commissions paid in the course of its contract for the nuclear generating facilities were proper and that no US laws were violated, but the company's assertions have been challenged by other sources within the Philippine government who claim that commissions of $50 million were actually paid, out of which Marcos himself received $30 million (Seagrave 1988: 291). In a later action initiated by the Aquino government in Federal District Court in Newark, NJ in December 1988, it was claimed that Westinghouse ultimately paid Disini and his companies $80 million for work that was never completed.[47]

The plant was finally completed in February 1985 under a cloud of charges that final construction was rushed leaving the plant in an unsafe condition. The charges were the subject of two UN International Atomic Energy Agency investigations that reported contradictory conclusions. The divergent reports led to an investigation into the plant's financing and construction, which in turn prompted the Aquino government to file suit against Westinghouse in US courts.[48] Westinghouse appealed for arbitration, which was granted by a federal judge. The arbitration case was heard by the International Chamber of Commerce which ruled in December 1991 that there was insufficient evidence to support charges of bribery against Westinghouse. The federal court refused a Westinghouse petition to dismiss the case, however, arguing that the arbitration was not binding and that the court would judge the case on the "preponderance of evidence," rather than "clear and convincing proof" (Beaver 1994: 277). Westinghouse then opted for an out of court settlement, agreeing to pay the Philippine government $100 million under an agreement that allowed Westinghouse to claim that the taint of bribery had been removed from the company.[49]

The Philippine government, for its part, agreed to pay $400 million to upgrade the plant to full safety standards, for which Westinghouse would rebate $300 million out of revenues generated by plant operations. However, the successor government of Fidel Ramos decided to take the case back to federal court with the result that the final plant cost was pushed to $3 billion. The government finally abandoned its legal claims in 1999 when it decided to dismantle all the nuclear components of the plant and sell the assets, with the plant itself to be converted to a science park. The plant never produced electricity and it is estimated that it will take until 2018 for the Philippine government to retire all outstanding debts incurred by the project (*Guardian*, September 7 1999).

Throughout this long series of events, Westinghouse managed to sidestep FCPA prosecution despite strong evidence presented in US federal court by the Philippine government based on Westinghouse documents that referred to Disini as "the front man for Marcos" and made reference to "the fix being in" (Beaver 1994: 277). Neither can the failure to initiate legal action under the FCPA be explained by the FCPA's five year statute of limitations since evidence, including events cited during the federal trial, as well as the company's reluctance to disclose commissions, indicates that questionable payments continued well into the FCPA period.

What then explains the failure of both the SEC and the Department of Justice to test accusations against Westinghouse in court? Is it possible that the security provisions of the FCPA were invoked to protect Westinghouse from prosecution? The answer to this question can only be a matter of speculation since any decisions in this regard are not a matter of public record. However, there is circumstantial evidence suggesting grounds for CIA involvement. An offer by the Soviet Union to take over the plant from Westinghouse during the late 1970s, an offer rejected by Marcos, would certainly have raised national security issues. William Casey, the CIA director during the Reagan administration, was also the head of the US Export–Import Bank when it approved the original loans to the Westinghouse project in the Philippines. As director of the CIA, Casey took full advantage of President Reagan's predilection to give his cabinet members and agency directors wide latitude in running their own operations and thus expanded the role of the CIA from a mere intelligence gathering service into an organization that played a strong role in formulating foreign policy (Sloan 1999: 94–102). These incursions into the foreign policy domain created acrimony with the State Department, which frequently questioned the reliability of CIA reports to President Reagan (Fischer 1997: 88–90). Casey's contempt of congressional restrictions on foreign policy played a major role in the Iran-Contra scandal and in the questionable relationships the CIA established with the Bank of Credit and Commerce International, which subsequently collapsed amid charges of rampant corruption (Truell and Gurwin 1992: 126–8).[50] With respect to the Westinghouse affair, it seems reasonable to assume that Casey may have used his considerable influence to block FCPA prosecution and might well have granted the company an authorized, if covert, exemption from prosecution according to the terms of the Act itself. It is possible, therefore, that Westinghouse escaped prosecution under the FCPA for reasons of national security. In any event, the Westinghouse story illustrates the complex economic and political environment that surrounded FCPA enforcement.

Conclusion

Available evidence suggests that while the FCPA together with other influences has resulted in more comprehensive codes of conduct and enhanced scrutiny of standards of corporate governance, it has not had a significant positive impact on actual standards of international business conduct of American corporations collectively, at least with respect to the bribery of foreign public officials.[51] How is this outcome to be explained? Several reasons emerge from this and other studies to which we have referred.

Review of the debates leading to the passage of the FCPA indicates clearly that support for legislation was motivated by two distinct but related considerations: standards of international business conduct and American national interests. Under the imperatives of Watergate and the mandate of the Carter administration, these concerns were seen as justified and mutually reinforcing. It would appear in retrospect, however, that high standards of business conduct were not always compatible with the protection of national interests as they found expression in the foreign policy of ideologically diverse presidential administrations.

Division of enforcement responsibilities between autonomous agencies may also have been a complicating factor. A related consideration was the decision to rely on self-regulation in an intensely competitive international business environment in which sharply conflicting standards of conduct was clearly in play. Self-regulation in American securities evolved in a relatively stable legal environment, with uniform rules for all players for reasons widely accepted as fair and reasonable. None of these factors was clearly applicable to the FCPA between 1977 and 1995. The standards imposed were not a part of an overarching international legal framework. There was no pretense at creating a level playing field. There was little support for the legislation in the business community at the time. And there was neither national nor international consensus on the reasonableness of the rules.

It is arguable that the FCPA would have been an ideal piece of legislation during the 1950s. It was consistent with Bretton Woods agreements requiring that the United States play the role of impartial enforcer of international finance, responsible for providing a sound currency as the basis of an international monetary system built on a regime of fixed exchange rates and the internal fiscal discipline that such a regime demanded from each nation, particularly the United States. Unfortunately, the historical record shows that the United States was not successful in achieving a standard of impartiality that could be made compatible with its own foreign policy objectives. The efforts of the Carter administration to reestablish this moral standard through the FCPA and other policy objectives were undermined by its failure to reestablish the strength of the US dollar in international finance. The Reagan administration succeeded in this latter endeavor, but in the process instituted a policy of *realpolitik* that abandoned all pretense of exporting any US standards of human rights or ethical business practices. Indeed, it would appear that the Reagan administration effectively abandoned enforcement of the FCPA except in cases like Ruston, where quid pro quo in US bilateral relations with foreign governments was at stake.

In conclusion, our study indicates that the FCPA was not effective at raising the standards of business conduct either at home or abroad with respect to the bribery of foreign government officials, or in encouraging the voluntary establishment of accounting and internal control standards. During the Reagan era, enforcing the criminalization of bribery would appear to have been compromised in cases where bilateral relations with an important anti-communist ally meant turning a blind eye to corruption in that country. American multinational corporations did establish important, profitable operations in countries where it is widely thought to be the case that bribery was tolerated and possibly encouraged. Foreign policy considerations may well have resulted in a reordering of corporate priorities away from the ideals of "new governance" set by the SEC during the 1970s, encouraged in some instances, this analysis suggests, by the national security exemptions of the FCPA. A lack of uniform standards resulting from the self-monitoring character of the accounting provisions of the FCPA would have been facilitated by this reordering.

Concluding postscript

It is possible that this has all changed. The new wave of FCPA prosecutions during the second term of the Clinton administration, due in part, no doubt, to the efforts of the OECD and other international organizations to join the war on corruption through the establishment of multilateral conventions and guidelines, suggests that a more optimistic view of the future effectiveness of the FCPA may now be warranted. It is true that international markets have become even more intensely competitive. Furthermore, sharply conflicting standards of conduct remain in play. However, the OECD convention is a step toward a more uniform international legal framework for responding to bribery. The new rules are widely endorsed as reasonable and fair and have the support of large segments of the international business community. A new standard of monitored self-regulation has also been put in place by the OECD convention, although its target is national governments, not multinational corporations.

Whether these developments will have a decisive impact on standards of international business conduct remains to be seen. What history tells us, it is now widely recognized, is that the cost of failure for human development is likely to be very high and the path to success painstaking and complex.

A final word with respect to the FCPA is also in order. We have concluded that as a unilateral attempt to raise general standards of business conduct in the global marketplace, the FCPA has had little general positive impact. It would be a mistake to conclude, however, that it was therefore either a failure or a mistake. It might rather be seen as a striking, and perhaps even bold and courageous, first attempt to address a problem the seriousness of which the American business community, the international business community, and other governments at the time were not prepared to acknowledge. Neither was the FCPA without effect. Almost certainly it encouraged some American companies to implement strict anti-bribery policies. General Electric[52] and Colgate-Palmolive (which cited the FCPA in successfully resisting demands for bribes from Chinese officials) may well be examples.[53] This impact on individual companies is also part of the experiment from which there are lessons to be learned. For those companies that responded in the spirit of the Act as well as their managers and agents, the FCPA quite possibly provided a useful reference point for explaining and justifying, in a morally inoffensive fashion, their refusal to offer bribes in environments where bribery was expected, demanded, or commonly practiced.

Other lessons are also forthcoming. It is not at all clear that companies that respected the spirit of the FCPA were placed at a competitive disadvantage, all things considered. It is true that, almost certainly, contracts were lost as a result. But it is also possible that setting high standards of conduct was a competitive advantage in some instances. For governments, civil servants, and other companies anxious to ensure that moneys expended purchased the quality of goods and services specified in contracts, turning to companies with a track record of integrity would have obvious advantages. In the end, a hard and fast balance sheet recording the costs and benefits of observing or failing to observe the standards pointed to by the FCPA is out of reach. Nonetheless, what should be clear is that failure to respect the spirit of the law was not without its costs; and the decision to respect the law was not without its benefits for the companies involved.

It would also be hard to deny that the existence of the FCPA gave the issue of corruption a public profile for almost two decades that almost certainly it would not otherwise have had. Whatever their attitude to the acceptability of bribery, American corporations operating internationally could not simply ignore the law's existence or its objectives. Whatever the complications it created for their operations, it ensured continuing awareness of a growing problem and considerable political pressure to address it in international *fora*. The resulting political pressures were not homogeneous or unidirectional. In some cases their effect was to encourage modifications designed to weaken the law's rigor as the amendments of 1988 evidence. However, the Act also created pressure to extend the law through international treaties and UN action. There can be no doubt that these pressures played a significant role in negotiations leading to the OECD anti-bribery convention of 1997, and its subsequent entry into force in 1999.

Finally, the FCPA has served as a testing ground for efforts designed to improve standards of conduct in global markets. It is true that the FCPA generated remarkably little critical research in the first decade of its operation. However, with the passing of the Cold War, attention has refocused on the economic and social dimensions of standards of international business conduct. Resulting research has led to increasingly firm conclusions about the damaging impact of grand bribery on international development. Much of this research has almost certainly been stimulated by political pressures designed to see anti-corruption legislation in the US either scrapped or internationalized. Patterns of research are affected by political and legal initiatives. Once again, it would be hard to deny that research into the effects of corruption is one of the beneficiaries of the FCPA.

Notes

The authors of this chapter would like to acknowledge the capable research assistance of Ruth Rosen.

1 The Swedish penal code did, however, outlaw the bribery of foreign officials at the same time as the passage of the FCPA. Swedish Penal Code, SFS 1977; 103 (January 1 1978).
2 See note 24 for details.
3 Asserted by former US Ambassador to Chile, Edward M. Korry, in testimony before the Senate Subcommittee on Intelligence Activities, also chaired by Senator Frank Church.
4 The Counter Intelligence Corps (CIC) had established the practice of financial contributions to pro-US politicians in Japan, Korea, Thailand, and Indonesia as early as 1948.
5 The Church Subcommittee investigation was focused largely on five US multinationals: Lockheed, Northrop, Exxon, Gulf, and Mobil.
6 US corporations were prohibited by Section 162(c) of the Internal Revenue Code from deducting out of taxable income specific types of payments that would, in effect, include kickbacks or payments to government officials. Moreover, under the Tax Reform Act of 1976, any US corporation deriving income from such questionable payments was denied certain foreign tax credits and deferrals (Jacoby *et al.* 1977: 68–9).
7 Surveys of businessmen conducted in 1975 by the Conference Board and the Opinion Research Corporation showed that 50 percent of them accepted foreign payments as necessary in countries that accepted the practice (Kugel and Gruenberg 1977: 5).
8 At the time of the Watergate hearings, some 9,000 corporations regularly filed disclosure documentation with the SEC pursuant to the 1933 and 1934 Securities Acts. These disclosure requirements entailed reporting material information (e.g., executive salaries, significant transactions, etc. deemed important to disclose to shareholders).
9 US corporations were prohibited by Section 162(c) of the Internal Revenue Code from deducting out of taxable income specific types of payments that would, in effect, include kickbacks or payments to government officials. Moreover, under the Tax Reform Act of 1976, any US corporation deriving income from such questionable payments was denied certain foreign tax credits and deferrals (Jacoby *et al.* 1977: 68–9).
10 In a speech to the American Bar Association in Montreal on August 11 1975, Kissinger noted: "A multilateral treaty establishing binding rules for multinational corporations does not seem possible in the near future" (Jacoby *et al.* 1977: 223–4).

11 In 1979, a UN Committee, formed for the purpose of drafting an International Agreement on Illicit Payments, drafted a treaty prohibiting overseas bribery that had the backing of the Carter administration. Neither the treaty nor the conduct code was ever adopted.

12 The following quotation from the report of his committee comments on the option as follows:

> The recent OECD code of conduct, for example, provides that "Enterprises should not render, nor should they be solicited or expected to render, any bribe or other improper benefit, direct or indirect, to any public servant or holder of public office." While this code might prove marginally useful, the Committee notes that bribery of public officials is already illegal under the laws of most countries. Clearly, where countries do not vigorously enforce their domestic bribery laws, there is little likelihood that a redundant, voluntary code will have significant impact. In order to facilitate enforcement of the proposed anti-bribery statute, the Committee does expect the State Department to continue efforts to negotiate treaties and bilateral agreements providing specific cooperative law enforcement arrangements, including exchange of information and records, and extradition of fugitives. Binding bilateral enforcement agreements will produce more results than voluntary codes.
>
> (US Senate 1976: 1–9)

13 The US had at the time mutual assistance treaties with Holland, Switzerland, Greece, Nigeria, and Colombia. These agreements provide for cooperation in investigations, document sharing and compelling witnesses to testify in foreign jurisdictions.

14 The Act reads:

> As used in this section, the term "foreign official" means any officer or employee of a foreign government or any department, agency or instrumentality. Such term does not include any employee of a foreign government or any department, agency or instrumentality thereof whose duties are essentially ministerial or clerical.
>
> (FCPA Sec. 103 (b))

15 Cf. *Foreign Corrupt Practices Reporter,* Business Laws Inc., Chesterland, Ohio. In short, prosecutions became more difficult because "reason to know" could not be as easily ascribed to corporate officers as before. On the other hand, ambiguities pertaining to the interpretation, jurisdiction and/or enforcement of the 1977 Act were clarified.

16 A vigorous academic debate has been conducted over the years as to how much business has actually been lost to US firms because of FCPA restrictions. There is no room in this chapter to pursue the issue here. A report issued by the US Information Agency (USIA) estimates that in a two-year period from 1994 to 1996 bribery was a factor in 139 international commercial contracts valued at $64 billion. The USIA estimates that American firms lost thirty-six of these contracts worth $11 billion. The agency believes that these numbers are conservative and that bribing companies win approximately 80 percent of contract decisions (National Export Strategy Report 1996).

17 In fact, the FCPA governed not just corporations headquartered in the US. Its provisions also extended to companies whose shares traded on American stock exchanges though its actual reach in this regard remained a matter of controversy up to the entry into force of the OECD legislation which has had the effect of making this aspect of the FCPA a dead letter.

18 For a contrary view, see the analysis in deGeorge (1997: 553).

19 SEC v Katy Industries, Inc: No. 78C-3476 (ND I11. August 30 1978). Settled by consent decree. SEC v Ashland Oil, Inc.: 18 Sec. Reg. & L. Rep. (BNA) 1006 (July 11 1986).

20 Ashland's revenues in fiscal 1974 were reported as $3.45 billion. Gabon had invested its entire social security fund in the corrupt Bank of Credit and Commerce International. The entire fund was lost when regulators closed the bank in 1991. (Cf. Passas 1994.)

21 Another description of the Ashland case can be found in Rossbacher and Young (1996).

22 SEC v Montedison, Civ. A. no. 1:96 CV 02631 (DDC November 21 1996).

23 SEC v Triton Energy Corp. *et al.* no. 1:97 CV 00401, 1997 WL 94141 (DDC February 17 1997).

24 The Bribe-Payers Survey was commissioned by Transparency International and carried out by Gallup International Association, which conducted in-depth interviews with private sector leaders in fourteen emerging country economies. Detailed information about the survey is available on the Transparency International website (www.transparency.org).

25   Whatever their various views of the FCPA, executives of American multi-nationals have been all but unanimous in their wish for a level playing field, repeatedly urging the US government to take actions to inter-nationalize the FCPA prohibitions or to persuade other nations to adopt similar laws.

(Glynn *et al.* 1997)

26 The emphasis here is on the impact of the FCPA as a general deterrent. As we acknowledge in the final sections of the chapter, there is evidence that the FCPA did both motivate some companies to avoid bribing to gain or retain business and did serve to strengthen the hand of others determined to resist the practice quite independently of the existence of legal sanctions.

27 See also Romeneski (1982).

28 When the complete listings of enforcement actions, administrative proceed-ings, and so on (as well as actual FCPA cases prosecuted) are examined, an interesting trend emerges. Twelve cases were initiated during the last three years of the Carter administration (after the passage of the Act), despite the apparent ambiguities in the law and despite the difficulties encountered by the SEC and the DOJ in working out their joint enforcement responsibilities. During the eight years (1981–9) of the Reagan administration, only twenty-three cases were initiated (allowing for the overlap of Pemex and other cases). The totals pick up during the Bush administration (thirty-five cases), but really explode during the Clinton years, when 225 cases were initiated (February 1993–October 1999).

29 Robert S. Ingersoll, Statement before the Subcommittee on Priorities and Economy in Government of the Joint Economic Committee, US Congress, March 5 1976.

30 An excellent account of the crisis can be found in Mayer (1981: 228–64).

31 These were among the facts revealed in the course of the Irangate inquiry.

32 The particulars of this bribery came out in 1992 during Senate testimony on the BCCI affair (Truell and Gurwin 1992: 136).

33 By way of contrast, under the Clinton administration, all prosecutors in the Department of Justice fraud section were given this authority. Cf. *National Law Journal* 1997: B16 and Schmidt and Frank 1997 in *National Law Journal* 1997: B18. It should also be pointed out that the Reagan adminis-tration dismissed a long outstanding anti-trust suit against IBM early in

Reagan's first term, as well as minimizing the role of the Export–Import Bank in financing exported goods manufactured in the US.

34 FR-735-2d-174; FR-754-2d-1272; FR-720-2d-418.

35 International Harvester owned a company, Solar Turbines International, that was implicated with Ruston and Crawford in the bribery of Pemex.

36 FR-735-2d-174.

37 Ibid. Other court records indicate that Pemex "was cooperating with the United States Justice Department in the investigation and prosecution of these defendants" (643 F. Supp. 3d 922). Nonetheless, Pemex itself was found in contempt of US court requests to release documentation required by Crawford Enterprises for its own defense. For its part, Ruston, as part of its plea agreement, agreed to provide any and all documents pertaining to the offshore movement of funds involved in the Pemex transaction.

38 The negative impact of corruption on economic development and political stability in developing countries has now been well established as is shown by the other contributors to this volume.

39 Pope Paul VI had a longstanding fear of Communist influence in Italian politics, dating back to his tenure as Bishop of Milan after the Second World War. He maintained close ties to the CIA during his own pontificate. The Vatican and the CIA collaborated in supporting Italy's Christian Democratic Party (Naylor 1987: 78).

40 It may be just a coincidence that large multinational American companies like Exxon and Mobil were making payments to Italian political parties at the same time that the American government was directly supporting the Italian government and its ruling party (Naylor 1987: 78). The Church Subcommittee, however, was critical of this explanation offered in evidence given to the Senate Subcommittee on Multinational Corporations by Mobil Executive Vice-President Everett S. Checket, claiming that the political contributions of Mobil's Italian affiliate were intended to obtain special favors, not to support the democratic process in Italy (Jacoby *et al.* 1977: 168). The fact that the US Embassy in Italy was apparently already well aware that Esso Italiana was making political contributions, well before it became an issue for the Church Subcommittee, would seem to support the Church Subcommittee's skepticism in this regard. The fact that the US Embassy knew that Esso Italiana was involved in prohibited activity in Italy may also suggest CIA involvement. In this case the CIA might well have been aware of the extra contributions that were not disclosed to Exxon's executive management.

41 After Marcos' downfall in 1986, the CIA received $10 million from the Reagan administration, earmarked specifically for Philippines operations (Seagrave 1988: 410, 422).

42 Cf. note 52.

43 William Beaver reports on Westinghouse's troubles as follows:

> An obvious question is why did the two companies approach the Philippines so differently? Was General Electric simply a more ethical firm that refused to make grease payments? Perhaps, but a more basic explanation might be that Westinghouse simply needed the business more. Nuclear power had turned out to be an enormous success for the Pittsburgh firm – supplying about one-quarter of the company's profits at a time when the corporation, as a whole, was in trouble. A series of miscalculated ventures into such areas as low income housing, record clubs, and long-term uranium contracts had not panned out. For instance, in 1975 Westinghouse barely made a profit at all, with only a 2.8 percent return on sales. If the company's nuclear business went sour

things could have been worse. On the other hand, business could not have been better at General Electric. Revenues were more than double those of Westinghouse, while General Electric's earnings were nearly triple those of its arch-rival. *Business Week* attributed General Electric's lead over its arch-rival to aggressive international expansion and sound acquisitions, all tied to first rate strategic planning.

(Beaver 1994: 273)

44 The initial budget for the project in 1974 was $500 million.
45 It has been suggested that this outcome is due in no small part to a desire to avoid embarrassment to both the US government and its nuclear industry (Seagrave 1988: 291).
46 Based on 8K and 10K reports submitted to the SEC for this period. This was the fifth lowest amount of questionable payments of the thirty-four companies with revenues of $1 billion or more who did report questionable payments to the SEC. (GTE, with just slightly lower revenues, reported questionable payments of $13.075 million (cf. Jacoby *et al.* 1977: 120).) It should also be noted that on November 11 1978, a notice of plea agreement was filed whereby Westinghouse agreed to plead guilty to undisclosed FCPA related charges on the condition that the Department of Justice waive all further criminal charges on the matter (*FCPA Reporter*).
47 This action was part of a civil suit raised against Westinghouse in Federal District Court in Newark NJ in December 1988 which claimed damages of $6.6 billion, or three times the final cost of the nuclear plant.
48 In its US court action, the Aquino government claimed that the bribery had effectively nullified the contract.
49 In William Beaver's words:

> Westinghouse would pay the Philippine government $100 million in cash, goods, and services. "The bottom line is we got $100 million to deal with the bribery issue," stated an American lawyer for the Filipinos. Westinghouse denied that the payment had anything to do with bribery, noting that the International Chamber of Commerce had cleared the company of such charges.
>
> (Beaver 1994: 277–8)

50 Cf. Fischer (1997: 88–90), Iran-Contra Affair Executive Summary, 98.
51 For example, the implementation of the sentencing guidelines.
52 General Electric is an interesting case. Patrick Glynn, Stephen Korbin, and Moises Naim note that "General Electric has produced what US officials regard," according to a State Department official interviewed by one of the authors, "as a model company ethics code, designed to insulate the firm completely from FCPA violations" (Glynn *et al.* 1997: 19). Jack Walsh, the company's CEO has been quoted as claiming that it was a mistake to think that a willingness to bribe was essential to success in international markets. It is no doubt possible to trace an element of this stance to GE's involvement in a very serious corruption case involving one of its international sales managers: US v. Herbert B. Steindler, Rami Dotan, and Harold Katz, Cr. no. 1-94-29, S.D. Ohio, March 1994. General Electric agreed in July 1992 to a settlement with the Justice Department of $59 million in civil damages and $9.5 million in criminal penalties with respect to $41 million in US military funding to the government of Israel which was embezzled and laundered through European banks by Steindler (a senior GE employee), Dotan (an Israeli air force general), and Katz (their lawyer). The eighty-nine-count indictment leveled against these three individuals included only six that pertained to

the FCPA, and these involved GE company funds that were fraudulently disbursed through subcontractors for testing of jet engines that was never actually conducted. (Dotan was paid out of these funds to exercise his influence with the Israeli government to use GE in future contracts, but there was no evidence that GE was aware of this.) GE's settlement with the Justice Department thus pertained entirely to the embezzlement of US government funds and not to the FCPA. GE's internal response as a company to the scandal was to fire several senior level managers for their failure to ensure that the anti-corruption policies of the company were adhered to. In the intervening period, GE has become one of the strongest multinational corporate voices for the development of corporate, national, and international anti-corruption programs, policies, and laws.

53 In January 1992 Colgate-Palmolive opened a plant in Guang Dong, China, without resorting to bribery (Rossbacher and Young 1996: 12).

Bibliography

Aronoff, A. (1998) "Anti-bribery Provisions of the Foreign Corrupt Practices Act," United States Department of Commerce, www.ita.doc.gov/legal/fcpa1.html

Beaver, W. (1994) "Nuclear Nightmare in the Philippines," *Journal of Business Ethics* 13.

Boyce, J. K. (1993) *The Philippines: The Political Economy of Growth and Impoverishment in the Marcos Era*, Honolulu: University of Hawaii Press.

deGeorge, R. (1997) "International Business Ethics: Russia and Eastern Europe," in T. L. Beauchamp and N. E. Bowie (eds), *Ethical Theory and Business* (5th edn), Upper Saddle River, NJ: Prentice-Hall.

Fischer, B. A. (1997) *The Reagan Reversal: Foreign Policy and the End of the Cold War*, Columbia, Mo.: University of Missouri Press.

Geo-JaJa, M. A. and Mangum, G. L. (1999) "The Foreign Corrupt Practices Act's Consequences for US Trade: The Nigerian Example," *Africa Economic Analysis*, David Eccles School of Business and Dept. of Economics, University of Utah, www.afbis.com/analysis/corruption.htm

Glynn, P., Korbin, S. J., and Naim, M. (1997) "The Globalization of Corruption," in K. A. Elliott (ed.), *Corruption and the Global Economy*, Washington, DC: Institute for International Economics.

Jacoby, N. H., Nehemkis, P., and Eells, R. (1977) *Bribery and Extortion in World Business: A Study of Corporate Political Payments Abroad*, New York: Macmillan.

Kugel, Y. and Gruenberg, G. (1977) "International Payoffs: Where We Are and How We Got There," in Y. Kugel and G. Gruenberg (eds), *Selected Readings on International Payoffs*, Lexington, Mass.: D. C. Heath.

Los Angeles Times (1976) June 15.

Manchester Guardian (1999) September 7.

Mayer, M. (1981) *The Fate of the Dollar*, New York: New American Library.

National Export Strategy Report (1996) "U.S. Government Report on Transnational Bribery," September 14, usinfo.state.gov/topical/econ/bribes/txt0924.htm

Naylor, R. T. (1987) *Hot Money and the Politics of Debt*, Toronto: McClelland and Stewart.

Passas, N. (1994) "I Cheat Therefore I Exist? The BCCI Scandal in Context," in W. M. Hoffman *et al.* (eds), *Emerging Global Business Ethics*, Westport, Conn.: Quorum.

Romeneski, M. (1982) "The FCPA of 1977: An Analysis of its Impact and Future," *Boston College International and Comparative Law Review*: 5.

Rossbacher, H. and Young, T. (1996) "The Foreign Corrupt Practices Act Within the American Response to Domestic Corruption," Fourteenth International Symposium on Economic Crime, Jesus College, Cambridge, September, home.pacbell.net/rossbach/foreign.htm

Schmidt, W. C. and Frank, J. J. (1997) "FCPA Demands Due Diligence in Global Dealings," *National Law Journal* (March 3), B16, B18.

Seagrave, S. (1988) *The Marcos Dynasty*, New York: Harper and Row.

Securities and Exchange Commission (SEC) (1975) *Report of the Special Committee to the Board of Directors of Ashland Oil, Inc.*, June 26: 160–6.

Shaw, B. (1988) "Foreign Corrupt Practices Act: A Legal and Moral Analysis," *Journal of Business Ethics* 7.

Sloan, J. W. (1999) *The Reagan Effect: Economics and Presidential Leadership*, Lawrence: University Press of Kansas.

Spalding, Jr., A. D. and Reinstein, A. (1995) "The Audit Committee's Role Regarding the Provisions of the Foreign Corrupt Practices Act," (23–35) *Journal of Business Strategies* 12(1) (Spring).

Truell, P. and Gurwin, L. (1992) *False Profits: The Inside Story of BCCI, the World's Most Corrupt Financial Network*, New York: Houghton Mifflin.

UN ESCOR (1983), U.N. Doc. E/1983/17 Rev.1.

US Congress, Senate, Committee on Foreign Relations, Subcommittee on Multinational Corporations (1973) *"The International Telephone and Telegraph Company and Chile, 1970–1971, Report to the Committee by the Subcommittee,"* June 21.

US Senate (1975) Subcommittee on Multinational Corporations, *Hearings*, Part 12, May–September.

—— (1976) Committee on Banking, Housing, and Urban Affairs, Report no. 94–1031 to accompany S.3664, July 2.

—— (1992) Select Committee on Secret Military Assistance to Iran and the Nicaraguan Opposition, and House Select Committee to Investigate Covert Arms Transactions With Iran, "The Iran-Contra Affair: Executive Summary of the Report of the Congressional Committees Investigating the Iran-Contra Affair," in *Essentials of Government Ethics*, P. Madsen and J. Shafritz (eds), New York: New American Library.

Wall Street Journal (1976) May 19: 5 and June 23: 2.

—— (1977) January 12.

Zedlin, M., Bullock, J, and DiFlorio, C. (1997) "Transparency, Integrity and Good Governance: Navigating Global Markets Under the Foreign Corrupt Practices Act and the OECD Convention on Combating Bribery of Foreign Public Officials," Price Waterhouse LLP and American Corporate Council Association, www.acca.com/networks/FCPA3.html

10 Controlling power and politics

Arvind K. Jain

Corruption becomes possible when those in positions of power fail to keep their public and private interests separate. There would be no need for monitoring or control of such separation if those in power were pathologically honest. This, however, is rarely the case. There would also be no need for such monitoring if the markets – for labor, capital, and commodities – were perfect. Perfect markets would allow prices and wages to adjust and allow misuse of powers to be "bought out." Since this is also not the case, societies that delegate powers to politicians, legislators, and administrators must develop strategies to control and separate use of public power for public use from that for private use, that is, corruption. These strategies must be incorporated in the system that allocates these positions of power, and in the checks and balances that are installed as part of that system. Hence the importance of the "politics" of corruption and, hence, of this volume. Political systems must minimize incentives for misuse of power as well as account for imperfections in the markets that allow the misuses to persist.

Efforts at reducing corruption will have little impact unless they are directed at the essence or core of corruption, rather than at the activities that are manifestations of corruption but are confused with the activity itself. Bribery, for example, is a manifestation or form of corruption; the essence of corruption is the ability of a bureaucrat or a politician to take advantage of its powers. Recent events in France have illustrated this point quite well. France was ranked twentieth out of ninety countries in the Transparency International's "Corruption Perception Index" for the year 2000, placing the country in the company of other Western European countries. While this index, as Johnston points out in his second contribution in this volume, is quite reliable in what it measures, it relies largely on perception of acts of bribery. Does this then mean that the French political system can be considered to be among the more-or-less corruption-free systems around the world? Developments in the later half of 2000 would challenge this contention. President of the country, Jacques Chirac, son of a former president, Jean-Christophe Mitterand, and a former president of France's highest legal body, Roland Dumas,

have all become embroiled in corruption scandals. The problem, according to one scholar, was that "[A] culture of so-called arrangements
permeated government, allowing the system to function and the political
class to manipulate public institutions and the private sector according to
its needs" and the political leaders "feigned ignorance of corrupt practices while continuing to benefit from them" (Mény 2001). It required
much more than preventing briberies for the system to begin to resolve
the problem.

Readings in this volume and elsewhere (some of which are summarized
in Jain 2001) point to at least three areas where efforts to reform political
systems must focus. First, it appears that systems that allow open
exchange of information and expression of interests lead to superior
quality of governance. A number of studies (Johnson *et al.* 1998, Ades
and Di Tella 1997, Van Rijckeghem and Weder 1997) show that civil
liberties, protection of citizens' rights, and equality of citizens lead to less
corruption and more efficient economies. Treisman (2000) has observed
that common law systems have less corruption than code law systems.
Kaufmann (1998) shows, however, that "left" and "right" regimes are
equally prone to corruption. Why would the nature of the regime not
make a difference to the level of corruption but the nature of the legal
system would? We do not know the answer to this question yet. Rose-
Ackerman's dissection of various types of democratic systems in this
volume, as well as her analysis in Rose-Ackerman (1999), however, indicate that the answer may lie in checks and balances that political systems
build into the processes of selection of individuals who assume positions
of power. One channel for these checks and balances is the freedom with
which information is made available and disseminated in the society.
Combined with a few observations taken from the behavior of investors
in the financial markets, there may be important lessons for the design
and reform of the political systems. Investors in financial markets seem to
pay a lot of attention to the quality of information and governance. This
is evident from the following.

- Evidence indicates that financial markets intermediate larger volume
  of funds when investors are given direct control over the people who
  are going to manage their money (La Porta *et al.* 1997).
- The importance given to information asymmetry in corporate management shows consistently that people show more trust in managers when
  the managers provide clear information about their activities. In the
  same vein, it appears that markets place higher value on firms that
  allow transparency in the process of selection of investment projects –
  by relying on external markets for funds – compared to firms that place
  greater reliance on "internal" markets for these funds (Scharfstein and
  Stein 2000). Administrators who allow their decisions to be scrutinized
  appear to be valued by the public.

• Investors put a premium on firms whose managers are willing to tie their compensation to the performance of the firm – thus opening them to scrutiny.

Clearly openness of systems leads to better information analysis and better decision-making. The first step in reforming the political systems, therefore, may be recognizing that information about the behavior and decisions of those in power must be open to scrutiny. Any attempt by administrators at maintaining confidentiality must be resisted. The openness must extend to how decisions are made and whose voices are heard in the process of decision-making.

Along with the openness of information, political systems must be open to the entry of competing groups in the contest for political positions. Rose-Ackerman's analysis of democratic system and Ahmad's description of the workings of Pakistan's political system indicate that systems that allow entry of competing groups as well as competition within each competing group seem to have more success in combating corruption than systems where entry into politics is restricted to close knit groups.

The two propositions mentioned above – openness of information and of political systems – are offered here as hypotheses. Future researchers may want to address these questions.

Second, political reform must include channels for participation of all citizens in the decision-making process regardless of who actually occupies the positions of power. Ades and Di Tella (1997) and Johnson *et al.* (1998) have shown that protection of citizens' property rights lead to lower corruption levels. An interesting observation of Rose-Ackerman's analysis of the democratic systems is that systems which allow legitimate channels for interest groups to exert influence and represent their interests in the political arena may end up with less corruption. Kurer, in his contribution in this volume, has shown that political systems which fail to allow citizens a voice in protecting their rights will force them to resort to corruption. It would appear that reform strategies may depend upon the maturity of the political system. Mature political systems, especially democracies would require a reform of the process by which interest groups acquire access to decision-makers (see later in the chapter on this point). Emerging political systems would require development of mechanisms that would allow interest groups to be formed and have a voice in the political processes.

Third, mechanisms for controlling misuse of power must be strengthened. This must include penalties for misuse of political power – which may have been perpetuated with the use of the coercive powers of the state that accompany positions of power. Although this example does not relate to corruption, trials and tribulations faced by the ex-dictator of Chile, Agusto Pinochet, will force at least some dictators to be more careful with citizens' rights. Such international actions should be extended to acts of corruption. At the present time, there is little that governments can do to recover loot from corrupt leaders of the past. Unlike some recent international actions against past profiteering by private entities from the miseries of others – relating mostly to the activities of Swiss banks and German companies during the Second World War – governments in the Philippines and elsewhere have had little success in recovering even a small part of the wealth accumulated by previous dictators. International laws protect leaders who accumulate personal wealth at the cost to the societies they have governed. The balance must change from the attitude of "possession is 90 percent of the law." The situation is not helped when laws do not protect those who provide information about corruption.[1]

The most important reform of the political system may have to do with control of the process by which a society's political leaders make decisions that affect the economic welfare of the entire society. Two aspects of this process need attention. First, attention must be paid to the process of decision-making, and second, decision-makers must be held responsible for their decisions.

First, take the issue of how decisions are made. As Johnston points out in his first contribution in this volume, a broad definition of corruption includes situations where wealth owners are allowed disproportionate influence over the political decisions of the society. Economics dominates politics. Tanzi and Davoodi in their contribution in this volume analyze the allocation of government budgets and taxation from the perspectives of large versus smaller enterprises in an economy. They find clear evidence of political structures' preferences for larger enterprises in spite of the contributions that small enterprises make for economic growth. The bias in the allocation of funds may be caused by systems of campaign financing which favor large organized groups over smaller unorganized groups. Smaller firms may also have less to gain from corruption since they may not be able to enjoy the economies of scale resulting from changes in administrative decisions.

Second, there is the issue of responsibilities of the decision-makers. Besides the discussion of the process of selection regarding the nuclear plant in the Philippines (in the contribution by Cragg and Woof), and the analyses of the governments' decisions on public expenditures (Tanzi and Davoodi's contribution), as well as on health and education (analysis by Gupta, Davoodi, and Tiongson in this volume), there are many studies that show that most systems do not hold politicians sufficiently responsible for their decisions. Mauro (1995, 1997), Ades and Di Tella (1997) and Tanzi and Davoodi (1997) show that the self-interest of politicians will lead them to make decisions that are not in national interests. Why are some political systems better at controlling the tendency of politicians to distort their decisions? Public officials must be subject to greater scrutiny and be required to explain their actions much more than is currently the case. Insisting that conflict of interest situations must be avoided without exceptions may be one area to begin reform.[2] We may need to extend laws that give rights to citizens to sue their elected officials along the line of rights that shareholders have to sue their managers.

Finally, Cragg and Woof demonstrate quite clearly that a fight against corruption is unlikely to succeed if the objective of reducing corruption is allowed to become subordinated to other goals. While the Foreign Corrupt Practices Act may have been introduced with the best of intentions, it had little chance of success once foreign policy considerations were allowed to dominate the application of the law. The exigencies of politics led the political leadership to set aside society's values (at least as reflected in the laws) with impunity.

Recent experiences in France indicate that corruption can be fought. A political and administrative elite that manipulated the nation's economy according to its needs dominated the French system in the 1970s. Changes became necessary when political competition increased while resources were decreasing. Privatization and internationalization of the French economy put demands on the system that a close-knit political elite could not satisfy. With public support and disgust, the media become more involved in exposing corruption and a small number of judges became more active. While there is a lot to be done, "change is unstoppable" (Mény 2001).

The main objective of this volume has been to highlight the centrality of politics in combating corruption. The contributors have emphasized the importance of the design of the system, the motivations of voters, the importance of the history of the political system, and the ability of decision-makers to usurp public property for personal benefits. These "imperfections" are rational responses of actors to incentives they face. Reform of political systems – which is essential if we are to improve the quality of governance – must recognize that system designs cannot be based on the idealized assumptions that politicians, legislators, and administrators are driven by a desire to serve the public; they will do so only when the system knows how to look after its interests. The challenge of reformers is to incorporate changes that convey this message.

Notes

1 In August 2000, Canadian RCMP was threatening to fire Corporal Robert Reed who had provided information about illegal activities of RCMP officers in Hong Kong. His information had led to the reprimanding and disciplining of thirty officers. Corporal Reed was being charged with violating the oath of secrecy (*Globe and Mail* 2000a, August 29).

2 Another example from Canada may illustrate this point. In September 2000, Canada's minister of foreign affairs, Lloyd Axworthy announced that he was going to accept the position of the chairman of a newly formed center for international

relations at a university in Canada. This is the same center that had been started with seed funding from his department when he was the minister. Although it could be argued that he was very well qualified to take that position and that he did not influence (in any observable manner) the choice of the chairman for the center, the conflict of interest is obvious and creates a bad precedence for the future (*Globe and Mail* 2000b, September 23).

Bibliography

Ades, A. and Di Tella, R. (1997) "National Champions and Corruption: Some Unpleasant Interventionist Arithmetic," *Economic Journal* 107: 1023–42.

Elliott, K. A. (ed.) (1997) *Corruption and the Global Economy*, Washington, DC: Institute for International Economics.

Globe and Mail (2000a) August 29: A5.

—— (2000b) September 23: A4.

Jain, A. K. (ed.) (1998) *Economics of Corruption*, Boston, Mass.: Kluwer Academic.

—— (2001) "Corruption: A Review," *Journal of Economic Surveys*, special volume on Issues in New Political Economy (February): 71–121.

Johnson, S., Kaufmann, D., and Zoido-Lobatón, P. (1998) "Regulatory Discretion and the Unofficial Economy," *American Economic Review* 88: 387–92.

Kaufmann, D. (1998) "Research on corruption: critical empirical issues," in A. K. Jain (ed.), *Economics of Corruption*, Boston, Mass.: Kluwer Academic: 129–76.

La Porta, R., Lopez-Silanes, F., Shleifer, A., and Vishny, R. (1997) "Legal Determinants of External Finance," *Journal of Finance* 52(3): 1131–50.

Mauro, P. (1995) "Corruption and Growth," *Quarterly Journal of Economics* 110(3): 681–712.

—— (1997) "The Effects of Corruption on Growth, Investment, and Government Expenditure: A Cross–Country Analysis," in K. A. Elliott (ed.), *Corruption and the Global Economy*, Washington, DC: Institute for International Economics: 83–107.

Mény, Y. (2001) "Something rotten in the republic," *Financial Times*, January 29: 17.

Pritchett, L. and Kaufmann, D. (1998) "Civil Liberties, Democracy, and the Performance of Government Projects," *Finance and Development* 35(1): 26–9.

Rose-Ackerman, S. (1999) *Corruption and Government: Causes, Consequences, and Reform*, Cambridge, UK: Cambridge University Press.

Scharfstein, D. F. and Stein, J. C. (2000) "The Dark Side of Internal Capital Markets: Divisional Rent-Seeking and Inefficient Investments," *Journal of Finance* 55(6) (December): 2537–64.

Tanzi, V. and Davoodi, H. (1997) "Corruption, Public Investment, and Growth," IMF Working Paper WP/97/139, Washington, DC: International Monetary Fund.

Treisman, D. (2000) "The Causes of Corruption: A Cross-National Study," *Journal of Public Economics* 76 (June): 399–457.

Van Rijckeghem, C. and Weder, B. (1997) "Corruption and the Role of Temptation: Do Low Wages in Civil Service Cause Corruption?" IMF Working Paper WP/97/73, Washington, DC: International Monetary Fund.

Index